The Essential Guide to Computer Data Storage

From Floppy to DVD

D1406929

ISBN 0-13-092739-2

90000

9 780130 927392

Essential Guide Series

The Essential Guide to Computer Data Storage

From Floppy to DVD

ANDREI KHURSHUDOV

Prentice Hall PTR, Upper Saddle River, NJ 07458
www.phptr.com

Library of Congress Cataloging-in-Publication Data available

Editorial/Production Supervision: *MetroVoice Publishing Services*
Acquisitions Editor: *Mike Meehan*
Editorial Assistant: *Linda Ramagnano*
Buyer: *Maura Zaldivar*
Art Director: *Gail Cocker-Bogusz*
Interior Series Design: *Meg Van Arsdale*
Cover Design: *Bruce Kenselaar*
Cover Design Direction: *Jerry Votta*
Project Coordinator: *Anne Trowbridge*

© 2001 Prentice Hall PTR
Prentice-Hall, Inc.
Upper Saddle River, NJ 07458

Prentice Hall books are widely used by corporations and government agencies for training, marketing, and resale.

The publisher offers discounts on this book when ordered in bulk quantities.
For more information, contact Corporate Sales Department, phone: 800-382-3419;
fax: 201-236-7141; e-mail: corpsales@prenhall.com
Or write: Prentice Hall PTR
    Corporate Sales Department
    One Lake Street
    Upper Saddle River, NJ 07458

Printed in the United States of America
10   9   8   7   6   5   4   3   2   1

ISBN 0-13-092739-2

Prentice-Hall International (UK) Limited, *London*
Prentice-Hall of Australia Pty. Limited, *Sydney*
Prentice-Hall Canada Inc., *Toronto*
Prentice-Hall Hispanoamericana, S.A., *Mexico*
Prentice-Hall of India Private Limited, *New Delhi*
Prentice-Hall of Japan, Inc., *Tokyo*
Pearson Education Asia Pte. Ltd.

To my dear wife, Anjella; my little daughter, Anna; my parents, Eleonora and Georgii; and my sister, Irina

Contents

3   Magnetic Recording Storage Systems   71

Preface

A world without data storage is like a mankind without memory. Thanks to various information storage methods developed in the last 22,000 years, we are able to document our history, to learn from each other's experience, and, ultimately, to create the world as it is today.

The future of computing is dependent on how well the enormous amount of generated information will be managed. But which technology will be used in the future to store new knowledge and experiences? Will we use holographic storage? Or store data by moving single atoms? Or will data be stored via the Internet on huge storage servers 10,000 miles away from your home? Or will the more traditional magnetic and optical recording technologies survive for the next 10 to 50 years? It is hard to guess. The amount of data we have generated so far is small compared to what is coming tomorrow.

The purpose of this book is to provide a practical guide and an easy reference for the majority of computer users and technical professionals. Whether you are a beginner or an experienced PC user, you will find here some useful information on computer storage systems design, selection, and technology.

The focus of this book is on the various types of computer storage devices: hard disk drive, DVD, CD, removable media storage systems (such as Zip, Jaz, etc.), RAID, and others. The book also discusses interfacing storage with a computer via IDE, SCSI, USB, FireWire, and other interface protocols. A possible future of the Web storage will also be addressed as an alternative storage technology.

Special chapters will discuss selection of storage systems for your computer and will deal with accidental data loss. An extensive glossary of PC data storage terms will complete the book. At the very end, references for further learning and a deeper under-standing of the discussed subjects will be provided.

This book is not intended to be a "nuts-and-bolts" textbook. Also, by no means can it be a complete guide to a subject that is evolving continuously. Even now, as I write these words, new ideas are being born, new technologies are being invented, new companies are being started to surprise others with the newest, hottest storage product.

Instead, this book tries to serve as an essential guide to the computer storage tech-nology *of today*, and even sometimes makes a *short-term* prediction of the future.

The main reason for not making long-term predictions? Well, they are *hardly ever right*. Examples? Find below three particular favorites of mine and let's then proceed to the first chapter.

> *Where a calculator on the ENIAC is equipped with 18,000 vacuum tubes and weighs 30 tons, computers in the future may have only 1,000 vacuum tubes and perhaps weigh 1½ tons.*
>
> —*Popular Mechanics,* March 1949

> *There is no reason anyone would want a computer in their home.*
>
> —Ken Olson, President, Chairman, and Founder
> Digital Equipment Corp., 1977

> *I think there's a world market for about five computers.*
>
> —Thomas Watson
> Founder, IBM, 1943

Acknowledgments

I greatly appreciate the support of my wife, Anjella, whose sacrifices made this book possible.

My special thanks to Robert J. Waltman from IBM for his continuous help and support.

I would also like to acknowledge the following people, who invested a lot of their time and experience to make this book better (listed alphabetically): James Brannon, Kevin Coffey, Peter R. Ivett, Mohammad Mirzamaani, Adam Polcyn, Timothy M. Reith, and Richard L. White (all from IBM) and Vijay Prabhakaran (from ReadRite Corp.).

1 Introduction

In this chapter...

BRIEF HISTORY OF INFORMATION STORAGE
TECHNOLOGY . . . .

Early Storage Technologies

The first documented examples of mankind attempting to store and share information can be traced back to the earliest prehistoric cave paintings. Those paintings are approximately 22,000 years old and are found in northeastern Spain. This even can be called the first attempts of storing and communicating information *optically*. Naturally, the eyes were the devices of data retrieval and a stone was the recording medium for the next 20,000 years.

The very first optical recording technology that *encoded information* was called *writing*, dating back to 3500 BC, and attributed to the Sumerians of Mesopotamia. Their writing system was logographic, characterized by numerous signs called logograms, which represented complete words. This system of writing was ambiguous, yielding errors during data retrieval, or *reading*.

Optical recording technology with even more advanced information encoding was introduced about 5,000 years ago, when the Egyptians started using hieroglyphic and alphabetic writing systems (Figure 1–1). Their writing system allowed for storing, retrieval, and duplication of data *almost without errors* (except for misspellings and misunderstandings). Thanks to this, we were able to document our history, to learn from each other's experience, and, ultimately, to create the world as it is today.

In about 2500 BC, the Egyptians started using a much more advanced and mobile storage medium—the *papyrus*, which they were making from stems of reeds. Clay tablets were also used as an alternative medium for writing. All of this allowed for stor-

Figure 1–1
Example of Egyptian hieroglyphic writing (about 2500 BC).

ing of a significant amount of information, duplicating it, and passing it to the following generations. No surprise that information started accumulating exponentially.

In 540 BC probably the first public library was founded by Pisistratus (circa 600–527 BC) in Athens and about 200 years later the Greeks had adopted a 24-letter alphabet. During the zenith of the Alexandrian civilization (about 300 BC to 30 BC), the two royal libraries accumulated a respectable number of scrolls: about 490,000.

During the period from 200 to 150 BC, a new "advanced" recording medium—*Pergamum*—was developed by the Greeks from animal skins.

In about 100 BC, the final 23-word version of the Roman alphabet was adopted. At that time Romans already had a working network of publishers, and used copyrighting, censorship, copying, and commercial distribution of books (scrolls), storing them in the public libraries. The recording medium was changed again to parchment (untanned animal skins). Newer Chinese *paper*-making technologies became available in Asia in about 600 AD, and reached Europe in the 13th century.

The very first complete *printed book,* the "Diamond Sutra" (British Museum), manifested the beginning of a new era in information storage and exchange. Printing technology had practically no competition until relatively recently, when the newer methods of storing not only the text, but sound and picture, were invented. Even now, in the age of electronic communication and paperless storage, we still use paper extensively, and this very book is good proof of it.

The above story proves how critically important data storage is for all of us: born when the first human decided to pass his life story to the future generations, it ultimately allowed us to keep the experience of the past with us.

Storage of Sound

Storage and retrieval of audio data started in 1877, when American Thomas A. Edison invented his phonograph (Figure 1–2).

The phonograph had a rotating cylinder with a thin tin foil wrapped around it, a recording horn, a flexible membrane, and a stylus attached to the membrane. Vibrations

Figure 1–2
The phonograph by T.A. Edison (about 1877).

of the voice spoken into the horn caused the membrane to vibrate and the stylus to indent and cut grooves on the foil, thus storing the data. The second stylus and membrane were attached in order to play back the recording. The needle moved up and down following the grooves and produced vibrations that were then amplified by a horn. This method of recording was called the "hill-and-dale" process. The phonograph was initially meant by Edison to be a dictating machine only, but further improvement of its design turned it into an artistic medium.

The next level of improvement was introduced by German-born American Emile Berliner and came in the form of a *gramophone,* or a phonograph with a flat disk recording medium in 1887. The gramophone used similar principles for recording and playback, was powered by a spring motor spinning at 78 rpm (revolutions per minute), and always needed rewinding. The flat records were made of shellac, were brittle, and broke easily. The gramophone had incredible success in Europe and the United States and was primarily used for reproduction of music.

In the 1920s, electrical recording and reproduction was introduced when the vibrations of the needle started being amplified using an electromagnet instead of the conical horn. Later, the gramophone added an electric crystal pickup. In the 1930s, the popularity of the gramophone increased even more due to broadcast AM radio stations that made the standard playing (SP) 78 rpm records popular.

In 1948, CBS introduced the 33 ⅓ rpm long-playing (LP) record with two sides and about 50 minutes of total playing time. Next, the extended play (EP) 45 rpm records were introduced by RCA. At about the same time, several companies pioneered new lightweight pickup mechanism design.

In the early 1960s, two media types were used for sound recording and reproduction: record and tape. FM radio broadcasting started replacing AM with continuous improvement of sound quality. At that time, sound was stored, retrieved, and broadcast in an analog form.

In the early 1960s, *stereo* broadcasting was introduced. Stereo sound allowed a listener to experience what he could feel while being near the real sound source. Two separate channels would record somewhat different sound signals coming from the left and the right. For example, the records for the gramophone will have two separate grooves scanned simultaneously by two styluses. The tape will have two separate magnetic tracks—one for each of the channels. Introduction of stereo sound was one of the most important steps in the history of sound recording.

In 1967, the next major achievement came in the form of *digital audio* demonstrated by NHK (Nippon [Japan] Broadcasting Corporation). The medium used was a 1-inch tape for a helical-scan video tape recorder (VTR). The encoding used for recording was called PCM (pulse code modulation). This first digital sound system is a close relative of the modern computer magnetic tape, the floppy disk, and the hard disk drive. The advantages of the digital recording and disadvantages of analog recording will be discussed later in greater detail.

From this point in time, high-quality audio technology became *digital*. A mix of sound and picture eventually gave birth to a new nonmechanical (like the gramophone) and nonmagnetic (like the tape) technology—the *compact disc*, or CD.

In 1977, three Japanese companies—Sony, Mitsubishi, and Hitachi—demonstrated their *optical* digital audio disk (DAD) systems, which used a large disk about 30 cm in diameter (like the LP records). By 1978, Philips developed a much smaller version of DAD. It used disks with a diameter of only 11.5 cm. After some negotiations, a compromise was reached and the modern CD was born with a diameter of 12 cm and with 74 minutes of playback time. This is the approximate length of Beethoven's *Ninth Symphony*. Today, compact disc is the most popular media for high-quality digital audio playback.

The major limitation of the compact disc was that it could only be used for playback and no new information could be added or overwritten. To overcome this limitation, the recordable CD-R and, later, rewritable CD-RW were invented.

The last big hit to mention was the so-called MiniDisk (MD), developed by Sony. The MiniDisk uses a magneto-optical technology (not just magnetic or optical) and allows for easy rewriting of data while still offering both high-quality digital sound and random access to data. The disk capacity was matched to that of a CD, to 74 minutes.

Computer Data Storage

Before magnetic and optical recording became the major technologies of computer data storage, other, less sophisticated technologies were used.

In the 1940s, data was mostly stored on *punched cards* and *punched paper tape*. This storage was *nonvolatile*, meaning that it retained all the information after the system power shut down, was inexpensive, and was reasonably reliable. The downside of this technology was that it had very slow data access due to the serial nature of the tape and card storage. The punched cards and tapes, by the way, are the distant relatives of the modern CD and DVD disks, which use small, "punched" pits to store information.

Early computer designers already realized that a successful computer memory and storage device should have the following important properties:

- be erasable and rewritable
- be nonvolatile (keep data for a long period of time)
- be inexpensive
- be fast
- be large
- have high storage density (high capacity and small size)

Apparently, punched cards and tapes didn't meet some of the above requirements such as erasability, rewritability, high storage density, and so on. The need for better memory and data storage technology resulted in fabrication of various memory devices: thermal devices, mechanical devices, delay lines, electrostatic storage mechanisms, rotating magnetic memories, and stationary magnetic memories. Among the above-mentioned devices, those operating on magnetic principles better satisfied the basic requirements for memory and storage.

The first magnetic memory was introduced in the late 1940s in the form of an array of magnetic cores, with each core storing one "bit" of data (the smallest unit of data storage). The interconnections between the cores allowed for random access to the data during read and write operations. This memory was nonvolatile, reliable, and fast, but, unfortunately, the data was erased every time it was read, requiring an immediate rewrite. This technology later evolved into three-dimensional arrays of doughnut-shaped ferrite cores with "large" capacities of a few kilobits (kB).

The need for large and inexpensive nonvolatile storage culminated in 1951 in the UNIVAC 1 (universal automatic computer), the first computer to use *magnetic tape* for storage. It still used sequential files and batch data processing procedures inherited from the punched cards. However, it was rewritable, had higher storage density, and allowed for quicker data backup and recovery without any loss of data.

Magnetic tape remained the primary data storage medium from the 1950s until the mid-1970s, when large and reliable *hard disk drives* with direct data access became the computer storage of choice. Today, and in the foreseeable future, magnetic tape will remain the best solution for data backup and archiving.

In 1956 IBM introduced the RAMAC (random access method of accounting and control; see Figure 1–3)—the first commercial hard disk drive—thus giving birth to the storage technology that has ruled the computer industry for 45 years, and does not appear to be going away any time soon.

Figure 1–3
RAMAC (random access method of accounting and control) virtual array (about 1956) (courtesy of IBM).

In 1961, the first hard disk drive with the air-bearing slider was introduced by IBM, advancing hard disk drive technology toward much higher recording densities and reliability.

In 1962, the laser diode was invented (also at IBM) becoming the fundamental technology for read-write optical storage devices. And in 1963, IBM introduced the first storage unit with removable disks (IBM 1311), effectively ending the era of the punch cards.

In 1967, IBM decided to discontinue the development of magnetic core memory in favor of volatile *monolithic semiconductor memory chips* with much faster data access and lower cost. This completed a logical separation of computer memory and storage.

In 1970, portable storage was born with the invention of the *floppy disk*.

In 1978, the first patent for RAID (Redundant Arrays of Independent Disks) technology was filed. IBM subsequently cosponsored research by the University of California at Berkeley that led to the initial definition of RAID levels in 1987.

In 1981, IBM introduced its first personal computer, the IBM PC, which rapidly became a standard in microcomputing. Six years later, in 1987, a 1-gigabit-per-square-inch (1 Gb/inch^2) *magneto-optical* recording with a blue-wavelength gas laser was demonstrated. A few years later, in 1989, the same recording density barrier was broken for magnetic recording with the help of the first *magnetoresistive (MR) head*.

In 1998, the first DVD-ROM drives became available for computer users. In the same year, IBM demonstrated the ability to write 100 GB of data on a single LTO (linear tape open) cartridge, the highest tape cartridge capacity in the industry at the time.

In 2000, IBM introduced the 1 GB Microdrive, which was smaller than a matchbook and weighed only 16 grams.

BASIC CONCEPTS . . . .

The basic concepts of data storage are discussed below. A portion of this chapter also discusses subjects that, at first, seem somewhat unrelated to the main subject of the book. Nevertheless, to understand digital storage technology one needs to know what an analog signal is and its limitations, how the analog signal is converted into its digital equivalent, and the problems inherent in this process. Some understanding of a binary system of notations is also helpful and is discussed below.

The Modern Computer

From the application point of view, there are up to four large groups of computer systems available today that have different needs for processing power, memory, size and weight, network computing capabilities, and, what is most important for this book, the size and characteristics of storage.

Mobile computer systems (laptop, notebook, hand-held, etc.) are built for high mobility, word processing, multimedia applications, network computing, Internet access, and other forms of online communication. These computers require lightweight, large capacity, and power-efficient storage. Data access can be comparably slow than that for the *server* class (discussed later) since its primary applications are not as time-intensive. This storage has to be tolerant to frequent "on" and "off" operations. The devices working with mobile computers must support plug-and-play features and be as easy to use as possible.

Desktop computers for home and office are meant for network computing, Internet access, email, word processing, spreadsheets, finance software, graphics, and multimedia applications. The storage, therefore, has to be large, relatively fast, but, most importantly, inexpensive. The types of interfaces used most often are ATA/IDE (the dominant), ATAPI, parallel, serial, USB, and, more often today, IEEE 1394 FireWire.

High-end professional *workstations* are used for real-time digital signal and image processing, video production, heavy-duty computations, 3D graphics and special effects, animation, and so on. The type of storage needed here is based on such interfaces as Ultra SCSI, Ultra2 SCSI, Ultra160 SCSI, Ultra160+ SCSI, and Fibre Channel (FC). Apparently, price is not a major concern here. Performance is the main quality required.

Server computer systems are designed for multiuser multiapplication environments such as the Internet or Intranet. These computers deal with intensive data and image processing, video editing, data mining, online transaction processing (OLTP), large databases, and so on. Storage for server computers needs to have high capacity, fast performance, and great reliability. These systems are also quite expensive and rely on the same high-performance interface types as the workstations.

These four groups of computer systems are different in speed, memory, storage capacity, size, and so on, but inside, they all have the same structure and same key elements. Figure 1–4 shows a simplified schematic of a computer.

The main elements of a computer are:

- CPU (central processing unit), or just processor. In human terms this is the equivalent of the brain.
- Memory or RAM (random access memory) is the working area where programs are run and data is processed. Fast, expensive, and volatile equiva-

lent of human memory with the exception that when you wake up (computer power-on) after sleep (power-off), you still remember something from yesterday. Computer RAM doesn't.

- System bus (Memory bus, IDE bus, PCI bus, etc.). Performs a function similar to linking different organs in the human body. Works like the neurons and moves commands and information from one part of a PC to another. Works like the heart when it moves blood (power) to different devices.

- Storage. Can be compared to a long-term memory, which keeps information one doesn't use quite often and that requires effort and time to access.

- Output and input ports are equivalents of our ears, eyes, speech, writing, and other ways of communication and information exchange.

This book concentrates on *storage*, discusses the *interface*, and just touches on the subject of *memory*.

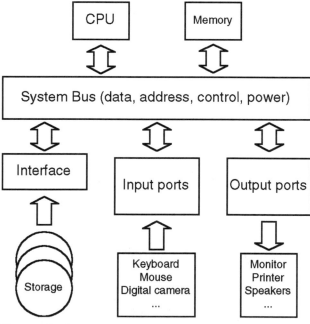

Figure 1–4
A simplified schematic of a computer.

Memory and Storage

First of all, we need to define the terms *memory* and *storage*, which will be used extensively in this book.

Computer memory is the place where a computer can store data and programs and execute them as needed.

PC memory (see the memory module in Figure 1–5) is random access memory (RAM), which enables the computer's CPU (central processing unit) to access required instructions and data at a high speed. The reason for the CPU to keep all important information in the memory is that this information can be accessed much faster than from computer storage, such as hard disk drive, CD-ROM, and so on.

Figure 1–6 shows a kind of hierarchy of computer memory and storage. Apparently, there is always a compromise between the capacity, data access rate, and

Figure 1–5
168-pin DIMM random access memory.

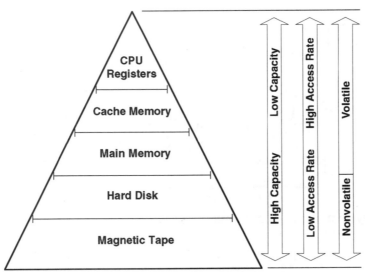

Figure 1–6
The hierarchy of computer memory and storage systems.

volatility. Also, cost is another important factor; the closer we come to "perfect" memory (large, fast, and nonvolatile), the higher the cost.

Semiconductor memory, for instance, is very fast (access time of 50 to 100 ns compared to 10 ms for hard disk drive) and can be made nonvolatile (i.e., Flash memory). But the cost of this memory is orders of magnitude higher (per unit storage) than that of hard disk or tape drive. This is why different types of memory and storage are used for different tasks.

People sometimes use the terms *storage* and *memory* concurrently, since both of them are used to store computer information. But they are quite different, since the hard disk drive or CD-ROM are not the place where a computer can store data and programs and execute them when necessary, as was defined above. Hard disk drive, CD-ROM, floppy drive, and so on, are the places where a computer can store data and programs *only*. When the program needs to be executed, it has to be transferred from the *storage* into the *memory*.

Storage is meant for less frequently used data or data that could be accessed at a relatively slow speed (still very fast). Memory is the place where the computer keeps its most needed and frequently used data, which can be accessed at much faster speeds. An analogy with the file cabinet (storage) and the work table (memory) is sometimes used to illustrate this difference. One keeps the materials he uses frequently right in front of him on the desk (memory), while all other materials are kept in the file cabinet (storage). Clearly, if one will keep too much data on the desk, it will become increasingly difficult to locate the needed item, and the access speed will suffer. Also, a very large desk will be too expensive. This is why computer memory is typically much smaller than computer storage.

Another critical difference between storage and memory is that storage is always *nonvolatile*, while memory is mostly *volatile* (see Flash memory for nonvolatile memory).

This means the following: when the power is turned off, the nonvolatile memory (hard disk drive, tapes, CD, etc.) retains all the information stored while the volatile memory (DRAM, SRAM, etc.) loses all the information stored.

This book concentrates on *nonvolatile data storage*, or just *storage*.

Binary System

This part of the introduction is needed for understanding how the data is represented in the computer when it is being manipulated and stored.

Everywhere, except for digital computer-related operations, the main system of mathematical notation today is the decimal system, which is a base-10 system. As in other number systems, the position of a symbol in a base-10 number denotes the value of that symbol in terms of exponential values of the base. That is, in the decimal system, the quantity represented by any of the 10 symbols used—0, 1, 2, 3, 4, 5, 6, 7, 8, and 9—depends on its position in the number. Unlike the decimal system, only two digits—0 and 1—suffice to represent a number in the binary system. The binary system plays a crucial role in computer science and technology.

The first 20 numbers in the binary notation are 1, 10, 11, 100, 101, 110, 111, 1000, 1001, 1010, 1011, 1100, 1101, 1110, 1111, 10000, 10001, 10010, 10011, 10100, the origin of which may be better understood if they are rewritten in the following way:

1:	00001	11:	01011
2:	00010	12:	01100
3:	00011	13:	01101
4:	00100	14:	01110
5:	00101	15:	01111
6:	00110	16:	10000
7:	00111	17:	10001
8:	01000	18:	10010
9:	01001	19:	10011
10:	01010	20:	10100

Any decimal number can be converted into the binary system by summing the appropriate multiples of the different powers of two. For example, starting from the right, 10101101 represents $(1 \times 2^0) + (0 \times 2^1) + (1 \times 2^2) + (1 \times 2^3) + (0 \times 2^4) + (1 \times 2^5) + (0 \times 2^6) + (1 \times 2^7) = 173$.

Let's now convert the binary number 10100 into its decimal equivalent: starting from the right, $10100 = (0 \times 2^0) + (0 \times 2^1) + (1 \times 2^2) + (0 \times 2^3) + (1 \times 2^4) = 4 + 16 = 20$. This example can be used for the conversion of binary numbers into decimal numbers.

For conversion of decimal numbers to binary numbers, the same principle can be used, but in the reversed manner. One first needs to find the highest power of two *that does not exceed the given number*, and then place a 1 in the corresponding position in the binary number. For example, the highest power of two in the decimal number 300 is $2^8 = 256$. Thus, a 1 can be inserted as the 9th (8th + 1) digit, counted from the right: 100000000. In the remainder, 300–256 = 44, the highest power of 2 is 32 = 5, so the sixth (5th + 1) zero from the right can be replaced by a 1: 100100000. The next remainder, 12, is $2^3 + 2^2 = 8 + 4$. Therefore, the fourth and third zeroes are replaced by a 1. The final binary equivalent of digital number 300 is 100101100.

Arithmetic operations in the binary system are simple. The basic rules are: 1 + 1 = 10, and $1 \times 1 = 1$. Zero plays its usual role: $1 \times 0 = 0$, and 1 + 0 = 1. Table 1–1 illustrates the binary addition and multiplication.

Table 1–1   Binary Addition and Multiplication

+	0	1	×	0	1
0	0	1	0	0	0
1	1	10	1	0	1

Addition, subtraction, and multiplication are done in a fashion similar to that of the decimal system:

```
  101101          1011010           1011
 +100111          -110101         x  101
 1010100           100101           1011
                                    0000
                                   1011
                                  110111
```

The simplicity of the binary operations is one of the reasons why the binary system is used in digital computers. Another reason is discussed next.

Bits, Bytes, and Beyond

Since only two digits, or states (on and off, 1 and 0) are involved, the binary system is used in computers, which are digital devices. The "on" position corresponds to a 1, and the "off" position to a 0 (in fact, this assignment can be opposite with the same result).

In magnetic storage devices (hard disk drives, floppy drives, tape drives, etc.), a magnetization of small areas of the media is used to represent binary information: a change in direction of magnetization between two of these areas stands for 1, and no change stands for 0. Flip-flops—electronic devices that can only carry two distinct voltages at their outputs and that can be switched from one state to the other state— can also be used to represent binary numbers; the two voltage levels correspond to the two digits. Optical and magneto-optical storage devices also use two distinct levels of light reflectance or polarization to represent 0 or 1.

Bit is an abbreviation for *binary digit*—the smallest unit of information in a digital world. A bit is represented by the numbers 1 and 0, which correspond to the states on and off, true and false, or yes and no. Bits are the building blocks for all information processing that goes on in digital electronics and computers. The term bit was introduced by John Tukey, an American statistician and early computer scientist. He first used the term in 1946, as a shortened form of the term binary digit. Bits are usually combined into larger units called *bytes*.

A byte, in computer science, is a unit of information built from bits. One byte equals 8 bits. The values that a byte can take on range between 00000000 (0 in decimal notation) and 11111111 (255 in decimal notation). This means that a byte can represent 2^8 or 256 possible states (0–255).

Bytes are combined into groups called *words*. The size of the words used by a computer's central processing unit (CPU) depends on the bit-processing ability of the CPU. A 32-bit processor, for example, can use words that are up to four bytes long (32 bits). The term byte was first used in 1956 by German-born American computer scientist Werner Buchholz to prevent confusion with the word *bit*. He described a byte as a group of bits used to encode a character. The eight-bit byte was created that year and was soon adopted by the computer industry as a standard.

Computers are often classified by the number of bits or bytes they can process at one time, as well as by the number of bits or bytes used to represent addresses in their main memory (RAM). A computer graphic is described by the number of bits used to represent *pixels* (short for picture elements), the smallest identifiable parts of an image.

In monochrome images, each pixel is made up of one bit. In 256-color and grayscale images, each pixel is made up of one byte (eight bits). In true color images, each pixel is made up of at least 24 bits. The particular sequence of bits in a byte encodes a unit of information such as a keyboard character. One byte typically represents a single character such as a number, letter, or symbol.

Regular users or professional programmers use computers and software to basically combine bytes in complex ways and create meaningful data in the form of text files or binary files (files that contain data to be processed and interpreted by a computer). Bits and bytes are the basis for representing all meaningful information and programs in computers.

The number of bits used by a computer's CPU for addressing information represents one measure of a computer's speed and power. Computers today often use 16, 32, or 64 bits.

Bytes are also the major unit for measuring quantities of data or data storage capacity. Data quantity is commonly measured in *kilobytes* (about 1,000 bytes), *megabytes* (about 1 million bytes), or *gigabytes* (about 1 billion bytes). A regular floppy disk normally holds 1.44 megabytes of data, which equates to approximately 1,440,000 keyboard characters. At this storage capacity, a single disk can hold a document approximately 700 pages long, with 2,000 characters per page.

Just a few years ago, megabytes represented the largest quantity of data available. Nowadays, gigabytes (GB) are already a common thing, and it is almost time to learn the next measure of data, such as the terabyte.

Table 1–2   Some Capacity Conversions from Binary to Decimal Values

Term	Abbreviation	Binary power	Binary value	Decimal value
Kilobyte	KB	2^{10}	1,024	1,000
Megabyte	MB	2^{20}	1,048,576	1,000,000
Gigabyte	GB	2^{30}	1,073,741,824	1,000,000,000
Terabyte	TB	2^{40}	1,099,511,627,776	1,000,000,000,000

Storage Capacity Definitions

We note that the terminology "1 KB" actually means 1,024 bytes (which is 2^{10}), not 1,000 bytes. The difference is actually quite small and, in most cases, unimportant. Table 1–2 summarizes some capacity conversions from binary to decimal values.

In a hard disk drive, real capacity can be calculated using the following formula (the terms used will be defined in Chapter 3):

```
Capacity = Heads × Sectors × Cylinders × 512 (bytes per sector)
```

Disk drive manufacturers use decimal values of capacity. For example, an 8.4 GB hard disk drive with 16,383 cylinders, 16 heads, and 63 sectors has a storage capacity equal to 8,455,200,768 bytes. Therefore, the drives we buy are slightly larger in capacity than is advertised.

DIGITAL AND ANALOG SIGNALS . . . .

Analog versus Digital

Most signals in nature are *analog* and their characteristics vary continuously with time. The sounds we hear, the light we see, the temperature we sense, all of them represent a continuous signal—a data stream with a specific value at any given instance of time. The movements of the trees in the forest or the waves in the ocean are registered by our sensors as a continuous analog signal.

Human vision, hearing, and speech are analog too. When we speak, for example, we generate continuous sound waves that travel in the air by creating pressure fluctuations. When these waves are received by the listener's ear, they cause the eardrum to vibrate and send appropriate signals to the brain, similar to the membrane in Edison's phonograph. A continuous sound wave carries continuous information.

Another type of signal we use is a *digital* signal, which represents an analog signal, encoded into a sequence of numbers. Modern computers and computer data storage systems all use digital signals. So, what is the reason for not going analog and choosing the more "natural" way of processing, storing, transmitting, and replicating data?

To better understand this, let's first look at signals 1 and 2, shown in Figures 1–7 and 1–8. They look quite similar, since the second signal is derived from the first one by picking only some of the points at fixed time intervals, which is called *sampling*.

Signal 2 looks like a good approximation of signal 1, but not its exact copy. The main difference between these signals is that the second signal is not continuous and

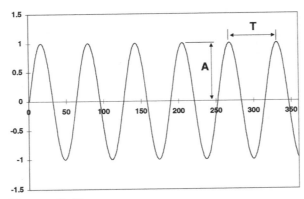

Figure 1–7
The analog signal 1.

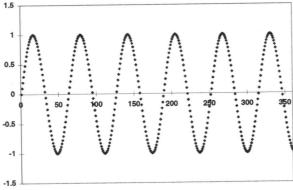

Figure 1–8
The sampled version of the analog signal 1.

its values exist only at *some* instances of time, while the first signal represents a continuous amplitude changing with time and its values exist at *any* instance of time. The first continuous signal is called an *analog signal*. The second signal represents a *sampled* version of signal 1—a step toward the *digital* signal.

The real analog signals we deal with typically represent a mixture of many different waves, and each of them can be characterized by the frequency f (or period T) and the amplitude A (see Figure 1–7). The frequency of a signal corresponds to the number of full oscillations—cycles—the wave completes per unit time, and can be calculated using the period T as `Frequency = 1/Period`.

The higher the frequency, the more cycles the wave completes in one second. The frequency f is measured in Hz, which is the number of cycles per second. When the signal combines many signals of different frequencies, the *frequency range* or the *bandwidth* is used to describe this signal. The signal bandwidth is the difference of the highest and the lowest frequencies contained in the signal. For example, if the signal covers the frequency range from 20 Hz to 20 kHz, its bandwidth is 19.980 kHz. The Appendix to this chapter contains a description of a complete electromagnetic spectrum.

Since an analog signal contains a complete set of data, it seems perfect for data transmission, storage, duplication, and so on. Unfortunately, it has some important shortcomings.

For example, both analog and digital signals suffer from different imperfections of the electronic systems: noise, nonlinearity, sudden current fluctuations, and so on. All of them change the signal *and change the information it carries*. However, the reconstruction of the original *analog* signal is complicated by the fact that the signal sent contains the infinite variations of some continuous parameter (i.e., light intensity, voltage, the strength of magnetic flux, etc.). Thus, there is no simple criteria in order to distinguish the real variations from the noise. Some effects like timing instability can never be separated from the real signal in an analog system.

The Figures 1–9 and 1–10 show how a random noise can alter a perfect sine wave of signal 1. The noise mixes with the real signal, resulting in a modified signal (Figure 1–10).

Of course, analog signal processing is a mature field, but still, the copying and subsequent transmission of the analog signal *always* causes signal quality degradation. The noise can be often filtered out, but *never completely*. Therefore, every time the signal is transmitted or duplicated, more imperfections are added to the original signal. In fact, the final degradation of the output analog signal is the sum of all the degradations introduced at each stage the signal passed.

When the music is being copied from one analog audio tape to another, the first copy already differs from the original because of media imperfections, electronic noise, tape speed nonlinearity, thermal drift, and so on, which are added to the original signal. After a number of copies, the quality will degrade noticeably since all signal imperfections are added to each copy, which then becomes the original for the next copy.

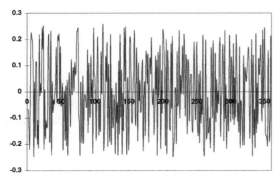

Figure 1–9
A random noise.

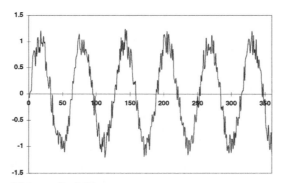

Figure 1–10
A random noise superimposed to the sine-wave signal.

Since the signals surrounding us are analog, the first electronic devices created were analog devices operating with analog signals: radio, telephone, TV, and so on. But with time, the need for better quality and higher density of the signal forced a switch to the use of a *digital* or *binary signal* consisting of the discrete elements of information.

In computing, *digital* is synonymous with *binary* because the computers we use today process and store information coded as combinations of binary digits (bits). One bit can represent at most two values, 2 bits = four values, 8 bits = 256 values, and so on. Values that fall between two numbers are represented as either the lower or the higher of the two. Since a digital form represents a value as a coded number, the range of values represented can be very wide with a number of possible values being limited by the number of bits used.

The digital signal is stored, reproduced, copied, and transmitted in a discrete, noncontinuous way. When necessary, it is converted back to the analog form. The signal on a compact disc sounds continuously to our ear. Still, it is essentially a discrete replica, sampled at a frequency of 44.1 kHz, of the original analog signal. By making time gaps between the discrete elements of the digital signal small enough, we preserve the entire content of the original analog signal.

Perhaps the main reason for going digital is its almost error-free transmission and replication process. By properly processing the signal, we can amplify it, reduce the noise, eliminate nonlinearity, separate different signals in the same data stream, compress the data, and do many other useful things. This part of science and technology is referred to as digital signal processing (DSP).

Like an analog signal, the digital signal is also subjected to noise and distortions during transmission, replication, and so on, but, since there are only two possible states of the signal—1 and 0—it can be reconstructed more easily. Figures 1–11 and 1–12

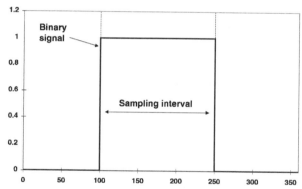

Figure 1–11
An example of the binary signal.

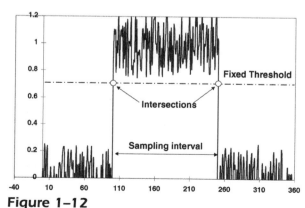

Figure 1–12
A random noise superimposed to the binary signal. The 'threshold' method allows for the reconstruction of the initial signal.

show a simplified example of how noise and other imperfections in a binary signal can be eliminated by using a "fixed threshold" method: all you need to know is the sampling interval and if there are intersections with the threshold at the points of sampling. Even the noisy signal will intersect that threshold, allowing for a complete reconstruction of the initial signal.

The main advantages of digital signal processing over the analog could be summarized as follows:

- Perfect signal reproduction: Copies are identical to an original. Digital signal can be copied or reproduced almost as many times as necessary without any quality degradation.
- Quality independence: If a digital system is properly designed, the quality of recording and transmission is independent on the media or channel. This means that all factors affecting the quality can be made as small as necessary by proper signal processing.
- No drift with temperature or age.
- Flexibility: Digital system can often be *reprogrammed* to perform different functions without modifications to the hardware part.
- Some tasks (linear phase response; adaptive filtering) can be achieved by using digital signal only.

While digital signals and digital signal processing have major advantages over analog signals, it would be wrong to forget some disadvantages of digital. They include:

- Cost could be very high for high-bandwidth applications.
- An added design complexity.
- A larger bandwidth than for analog system is required.
- The hardware with sampling needed for guaranteed accuracy may be too expensive.

While these disadvantages exist, they are still minor compared to the quality gained. Now, let's take a look at how an analog signal gets converted into its digital equivalent.

Analog-to-Digital Conversion

As mentioned above, most signals surrounding us are analog in nature and need to be converted into a digital form for further high-quality transmission, storage, duplication, and so on. This stage—a so-called analog-to-digital conversion (ADC)—is probably the most critical element for the quality of the signal.

A schematic of an analog-to-digital conversion system is shown in Figure 1–13.

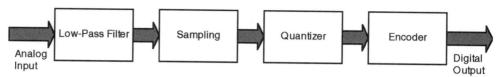

Figure 1–13

A schematic of an analog-to-digital conversion system.

- Filtering: It narrows the bandwidth of the analog signal. The low-pass filtering means that only the signal below a specified frequency, as determined by the filter, will pass. The low-pass filtering limits the signal to the highest needed frequency and cuts off unnecessary higher-frequency information.
- Sampling: By picking values at given time intervals, sampling converts an analog continuous-time signal (Figure 1–7) into a discrete-time signal (Figure 1–8).
- Quantization: It converts a continuous-value signal into a discrete-value signal with 2^{bit} levels.
- Encoding: It converts the discrete amplitudes into the binary words.

After the signal is digitized, we will deal with the numbers only. Therefore, it is critically important to digitize it correctly. The second step, data sampling, is perhaps the most important.

Data Sampling and Undersampling

The idea of sampling was already illustrated in Figures 1–7 and 1–8. Sampling occurs when a continuous (analog) signal is acquired at the fixed discrete time intervals. It seems at first that some loss of information occurs when signal 2 is used instead of signal 1. But, according to the theory, it is possible to sample a continuous signal and not lose any of its relevant content. This theory is based on the so-called Nyquist theorem.

According to this theorem, *one needs to sample the signal at the sampling rate equal to or exceeding the doubled maximum frequency contained in the signal.* If this condition is met, the entire information content of the signal will be acquired without any losses.

If the maximum frequency f_{max} of the signal is known, then the sampling rate N_s should follow the following relationship: $N_s \geq 2\ f_{max}$.

The frequency f_{max} (equal to one-half of the sampling frequency) is called the Nyquist frequency. Let's assume that we want to digitize an audio signal, which has a typical frequency range from 20 Hz to 20 kHz (this is the range audible to the human

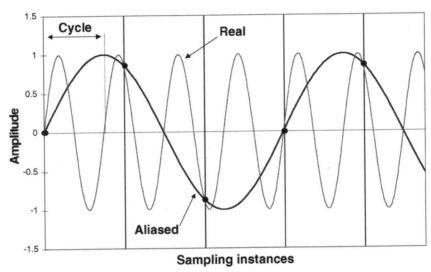

Figure 1–14
An example of "aliasing," which causes a false translation of an analog signal into its binary equivalent.

ear). According to the Nyquist theorem, the sampling frequency of the ADC has to be
equal to 40 kHz.

If the sampling rate is less than specified by the Nyquist theorem, a so-called
aliasing will occur. The aliasing causes false translation of an analog signal into its
binary equivalent, which is illustrated in Figure 1–14.

For the original sine wave (real signal), the critical sampling rate is two points per
cycle. When this condition isn't met, a new "aliased" signal of lower frequency is
acquired.

To prevent aliasing, one needs to know precisely the frequency range of the continuous signal or enforce a known limit by low-pass filtering and then use sampling
according to the Nyquist theorem.

Anti-Aliasing Filter Design

Before the sampling is started, filtering of the input signal is needed to limit the bandwidth and to cut off all the unnecessary information present in the signal at higher frequencies. Since the sampling frequency is selected on the basis of the maximum
frequency in the signal f_{max}, the filter cut-off at f_{max} should be as sharp as possible.
Since "perfect" filters are not practically available, filter imperfection must be com-
pensated for in order to avoid aliasing. Figure 1–15 compares the frequency responses

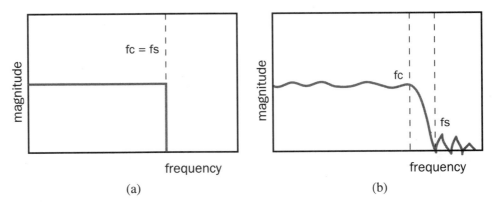

Figure 1–15
Frequency responses of an ideal (a) and realistic (b) filter.

of an ideal (a) and a realistic (b) filter. In this figure, f_c represents the desired cut-off frequency equal to the f_{max} of the signal to be acquired, and f_s is a real stopband frequency, determined by the filter characteristics.

Clearly, if the sampling (with the realistic filter) will be done assuming f_c to be the Nyquist frequency, some extra signal from the region f_s-f_c will be acquired undersampled (Figure 1–15 [b]), falsely translated, and added to the original signal. To avoid this, the sampling frequency N_s can be increased to account for the filter roll-off of the high frequency and the effective Nyquist frequency f_{max} used should be equal to f_s.

This is addressed, for example, in the CD-ROM electronics by slightly increasing the sampling frequency. The CD-ROM uses the sampling rate of 44.1 kHz instead of just 40 kHz needed to completely sample the audible range. This is done to compensate for the filter imperfection.

Data Quantization and Encoding

When the signal reaches the quantization stage of the ADC process, it is discrete in time (sampled) and continuous in amplitude. At this stage, the infinite number of voltages is replaced by a finite number of corresponding values. The signal becomes amplitude-discrete by assigning one of 2^n values to each of its sampled points, where n is the number of bits used by the ADC. This number of bits used by the ADC is called the *resolution*.

The quantization principle is illustrated in Figure 1–16 using a 3-bit resolution with 8 (or 2^3) levels of quantization.

The quantizer rounds up whatever voltage of the input signal to the closest number of the interval it falls into. Therefore, quantization introduces some error to the signal. This error is typically limited to $\pm Q/2$. Apparently, the *error* introduced during

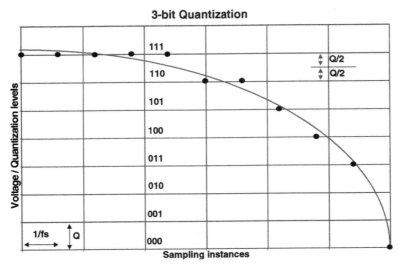

Figure 1–16
Quantization using a 3-bit resolution and 8 levels.

quantization is also a function of the number of bits; the more bits, the more quantization levels used, the lower the error. For example, if the range of an analog signal is 0 to 5 V, then, for a 3-bit quantization we will have $2^3 = 8$ quantization levels, with each step equal to 5/8 = 0.625 V. The quantization error equals half, or 0.3125 V.

If the same signal is quantized using 16 bits, the levels equal 5/256 = 0.0195 V, and the quantization error is 0.0098 V. Clearly, more bits is better. In practice, the cost, speed, and the noise of the input analog signal are the main limiting factors for increasing the number of bits used. Most DSP applications require no more than 12 to 16 bits for the desired high quality.

After the quantization is complete, the above signal is encoded into a set of 3-bit words that looks like this:

111, 111, 111, 111, 111, 110, 110, 101, 100, 011, 000.

This binary data is now ready to be stored, duplicated, and transmitted.

Data Transmission

There are two major ways to transmit the binary signal: in series or in parallel.

In the serial mode, the bits of data are transmitted sequentially, one after another. In the parallel mode, the bits are transmitted simultaneously over several wires (four in Figure 1–17). The parallel transmission is faster but serial is cheaper and more suitable for use over larger distances. To function properly, all bits on parallel wires should arrive to the receiving device almost simultaneously, which is more difficult to achieve over longer distances.

Also, there are three main modes of data transfer used in data transmission: *asynchronous*, *synchronous*, and *isochronous*.

The *asynchronous* mode provides for communication with no time restrictions and allows packets of data to be transferred after having a response from the receiving device. The retries are mandated if errors occur. This method sacrifices transfer speed for reliability and is used in electronic mail, over the Internet, and on Ethernet protocols, and so on.

In the *synchronous* transmission mode, data are sent with the clock pulse defining the intervals between bits, as opposed to asynchronous data transfer. This mode defines the maximum end-to-end delay for each packet of data and this upper bound is never violated. Thus, the information moves faster with reliability being somewhat sacrificed.

The *isochronous* mode implies the most uniform in time data transfer and provides the guaranteed bandwidth by transferring the same amount of data every second. This method is used, for example, in video cameras, where if the error has occurred, it's too late to resend the data again. This means that the delay of each data packet is bounded on both ends with minimum and maximum end-to-end delays being defined and enforced. The isochronous mode allows for very high-bandwidth capabilities.

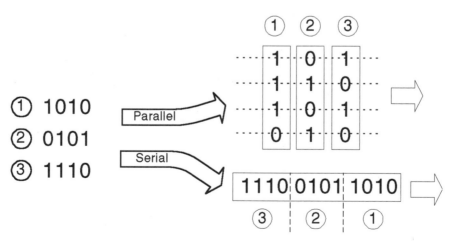

Figure 1–17
Parallel and serial ways of transmitting four bits of data.

Error Detection and Correction

In spite of the fact that the digital data recording, transmission, duplication, and so on, are much more tolerant to noise, dropouts, and so forth, when compared to an analog data, errors in data may still occur. Luckily, error detection and correction is much simpler for the binary data since there are always only two possible values for every bit: 1 and 0.

For example, if the following sequence of bit is sent:

1,1,0,1

and the following sequence of bit is received:

1,1,0,0,

then how can the receiving device know that there was an error during transmission? To address this, special error-detection algorithms are used.

The simplest of them is called the bit parity check. In this method, an extra bit is added to a group of bits before the transmission. It is also agreed that if the number of 1s in the group of bits (word) is *odd*, then the extra bit, called the *parity bit*, will be 0. This is called *odd parity*, and illustrated below:

1,1,1,0   ➤ 0
1,0,1,0   ➤ 1.

If it is agreed that the parity bit will be equal to 0 if the number of 1s is *even*, then this is called *even parity*:

1,1,1,0   ➤ 1
1,0,1,0   ➤ 0.

This method is very effective for detecting errors. For example, if we use the *odd* parity, and the received word and a parity bit looked like this:

1,0,1,0   ➤ 0

it is easy to conclude that there was an error during data transmission.

Unfortunately, this simple method of error detection has some significant limitations. First, it is impossible to say which bit in the above example is faulty. All we know is that there was an error.

Second, what if instead of the 1,1,1,0 ➤ 0 sequence we receive 1,0,1,1 ➤ 0? There are two bits that changed their value, but the parity check will *detect no error* since the number of bits is still odd! Of course, the probability of this event to occur is much lower than that for one bit only, but it is still possible. To deal with this, some more complex error-detection schemes are used.

One of them is called the Hamming code, and uses more then one parity bit per word. In fact, k parity bits are added to an n-bit long word, forming a new word of $n+k$ bits. For example, for the 8-bit word, there will be 4 extra bits forming the following 12-bit composite word:

Bit position:	1	2	3	4	5	6	7	8	9	10	11	12
Bit values:	P_1	P_1	1	P_4	1	1	1	P_8	0	0	1	1

where P is the parity bit. According to this algorithm, each parity bit will calculate the parity of 5 other data bits, forming different combinations for different parity bits. Then, every P in this sequence will be substituted with its value (0 or 1), and the whole composite 12-bit word will be transmitted. When the data are received, a parity check will be done again, but now, instead of 5 data bits to check, 6 bits (5 data and one P) will be checked for parity. It was shown theoretically, that this algorithm allows for detecting *both the error and the position* of the faulty bit! Still, the Hamming code can detect and correct only a single-bit error.

More efficient error-detection code is called the *cyclic redundancy check* (CRC) code. This code has relatively complex logic and its explanation is beyond the scope of this book. But, CRC checking is very effective in transmission error detection. For example, for a 16-bit CRC code, the error detection probability is 99.9985%.

The main task of the successful error detection code is to detect the error and its place in the data stream. Then, the error can be corrected.

In the modern digital storage systems, the error detection codes are often added to the data before it is recorded, allowing for error detection and correction, which is performed by the error correction channel (ECC) electronics. This increases the size of the data to be stored, but also increases the reliability of the storage system.

APPENDIX . . . .

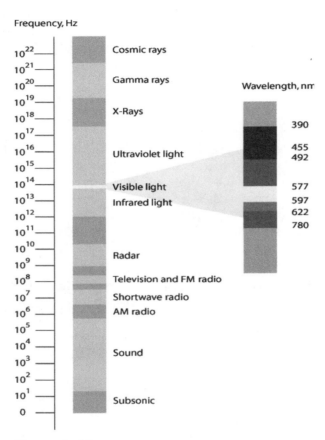

Figure 1–18
A complete electromagnetic spectrum.

2 Computer Interfaces

In this chapter...

INTRODUCTION . . . .

This chapter provides an overview of computer interfaces, which is needed for understanding the material in the following chapters. Here, I discuss those PC interfaces used to connect different storage devices to the PC.

Peripheral devices are connected to a computer by means of the *interface*.

In its basic definition, an *interface* is a hardware and/or software data transmission regulator that controls data exchange between the PC and other devices, including such data storage devices as hard disk drives, floppy disk drives, tape drives, CD drives, DVD drives, and so on. The interface is supported by the electronics of the data transfer controller and the drive electronics. There are standards adopted for the interface protocols, allowing connection of any standard peripheral device.

There are *special-purpose*, *multi-purpose*, and *general-purpose* interfaces.

The keyboard, sound card, mouse, and connectors, for example, represent special-purpose interfaces. They cannot be used for any other device.

The parallel port (printer port), serial port, universal serial bus (USB), integrated device electronics (IDE), PC Card, IEEE 1394 FireWire, and SCSI represent multipurpose interfaces since they can be used for various peripheral devices, including data storage devices. These kinds of interfaces will be the subject of this chapter.

The slots on the motherboard, such as PCI (Peripheral Component Interconnect) and ISA (Industry Standard Architecture) slots, can be used to connect various devices (via the plug-in cards) and represent truly general-purpose interfaces.

Let's take a closer look at the computer motherboard. Figure 2–1 shows a typical modern motherboard that supports Intel Pentium II/III slot1 processors up to 1 GHz and has most of the interface connectors needed to attach the storage devices.

This motherboard supports the latest Ultra ATA-100 (and older) interfaces with connectors integrated into the motherboard. Next to the ATA connectors, there is a traditional floppy drive connector. Six PCI slots on the motherboard can be used for connecting SCSI, IEEE 1394 FireWire, and other interface adapter cards, when necessary.

The lower part of the picture shows two USB connectors, the parallel port connector, and one serial port connector (COM1).

The interface by itself consists of four basic parts:

- Physical: cables, connectors, etc.
- Transport protocol: rules for data and command exchange
- Electrical: voltage levels, signals
- Commands: defined set of commands

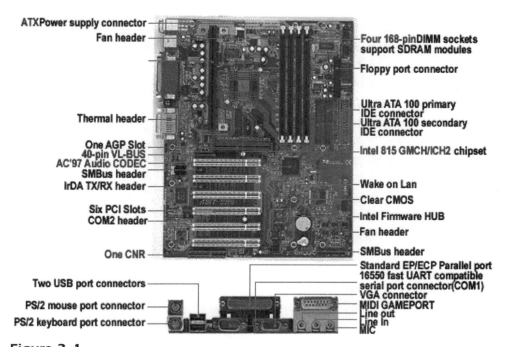

Figure 2–1
Modern PC motherboard with support for Intel Pentium II/III slot1 processors up to 1 GHz and various interface connectors (courtesy of Abit Computer Co.).

Interface Speed Summary

The interface speed (or throughput or data rate) is typically measured in MB/sec and corresponds to the *maximum* (burst) rate at the best conditions, and not the *sustained* rate, which is lower. The sustained rate is the rate that the interface can support consistently.

Figure 2–2 summarizes the speed performance of the most popular interfaces.

The SCSI has been a clear winner in the race for speed for many years, with FC-AL being used for high-end applications only (RAID, SAN). Recently, the faster ATA interfaces were introduced with a maximum data transfer rate in the range of 66 MB/sec to 100 MB/sec, becoming a good choice for many PC users.

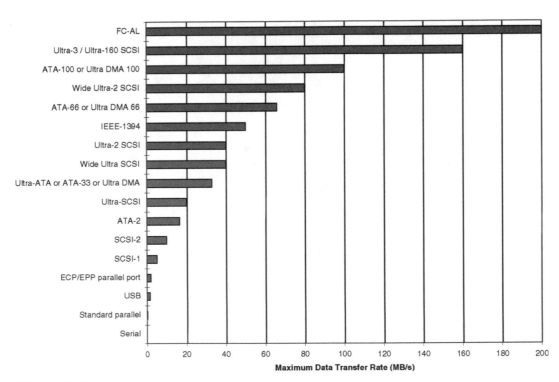

Figure 2–2
Interface speed performance summary.

Data Transmission: Serial versus Parallel

All interfaces can be divided into two categories: *serial* and *parallel.*

The bits of data are transmitted over the interface in two ways: one by one in a serial interface and simultaneously over the parallel lines in the case of a parallel interface.

During a serial data transmission, data travel between devices one after another over the same data line. This is the slower way of the two but is often used where the ultimate speed is not critically important or a sufficient speed can be achieved with the serial scheme. Some slower devices inside the computer, such as a modem, keyboard and mouse, speakers, and so on, exchange data in a serial way.

The faster way is to transmit many bits (or even bytes) simultaneously over many lines. Most high-performance devices, such as the CPU, video, memory, internal storage devices, and so on, are connected in the parallel way. However, a parallel transmission may not be the best method over longer distances. First, using many cables instead of one over the miles is more expensive. Second, the parallel data transmission of 8 bits is like a race of 8 cars that starts at the same time and are supposed to arrive to the finish line also at the same time. If this doesn't happen, it may create some problems, cause delays, and lower the effective data transfer rate.

Now, let's discuss the most popular interfaces.

SERIAL INTERFACE . . . .

If you send bits one at a time, you are using serial communication. If you send one extra bit for each 8 bits to make sure your data got there intact, it is called a parity bit (see Chapter 1). Bit parity can be odd or even. It is even if you assign 0 to the parity bit when the sum of 8 bits is an even number. You assign 1 to the parity bit when the sum is an odd number. The parity is called odd if the logic is reversed. After the byte has arrived, the system will sum 8 bits and check if the result matches the even-or-odd-ness predicted by the parity bit.

Two common connector types used for serial communication are the 9-pin connector DB9 and (less often) 25-pin DB25 connector, which are essentially the same. Figure 2–3 represents a serial port female connector.

The heart of the serial communication technology is the UART (Universal Asynchronous Receiver/Transmitter), which converts parallel streams of data into a single sequence. As soon as the CPU sends the bits to the UART, it will convert the data into a single sequence of bits and send the bits one at a time over the serial cable using the internal clock to define the time interval for the next bit to be sent. The UART will also send the start bit, the stop bit, and the parity bit (if necessary).

Modern PCs can exchange data over the serial port at rates up to 115 Kb/s, but this will translate into a maximum data rate of about only 11.5 Kb/s without parity and 10.5 Kb/s with parity due to the serial communication protocol overhead.

Figure 2–3
Serial interface connector (female).

PARALLEL INTERFACE ····················

The parallel port was originally created for communication with a printer and thus is called a printer port. A PC may have at most 3 parallel ports, which are named LPT1, LPT2, and LPT3. A printer port female connector has 25 pins and is shown in Figure 2–4.

At least 8 wires are needed for parallel transfer of 8 bits, but the standard IBM-type printer port uses 17 wires for data transfer plus some more to ground the system. These extra wires are used in an intense hand-shaking process between a PC and a printer.

The computer puts 8 data bits on the 8 data lines and sends (on a separate line) a so-called strobe signal to the printer to inform it that 8 bits are ready to be transmitted. The printer reads the strobe signal, then 8 bits, and then sends an acknowledgment signal on another wire back to the computer. In this way, the PC printer port does not send data to the printer faster than the printer can accept it. This data is not in any way synchronized by the clock signal and goes as fast as it can. There are five status wires that allow the printer to let the computer know when it is busy processing the data, when it is out of paper, or when it experiences a paper jam, for example. Four control wires allow the computer to command the printer to reset itself, to skip the page, and so on. This standard parallel port interface can sustain data rates up to 0.15 MB/sec, which is faster than the serial port can reliably operate. To connect a parallel port to the printer, one has to use special 25-pin to 36-pin cable since the parallel cable connector (female) on the printer side typically has 36 pins (Figure 2–5).

Figure 2–4
Parallel interface connector (female).

Figure 2–5
The 36-pin printer side parallel cable connector (female).

This standard parallel port is currently described in the IEEE (Institute of Electrical and Electronic Engineers) 1284 standard as a "compatibility mode." There are *four* more newly created modes, which enhances parallel port performance.

One of the new modes is called a *nibble-mode reverse operation*, and another is the *byte-reverse operation*. Both of them represent modifications toward the bidirectional parallel port. The two other modes—the newest—are the EPP (*Enhanced Parallel Port*) and ECP (*Extended Capability Port*), which allow for much faster data transfer rates and are widely used in parallel port storage devices such as Zip drives, hard drives, CD-ROM drives, and so on.

In the EPP design, five more CPU addresses were added to the initial three addresses to allow the CPU to transfer data in just one command rather than being involved in various steps of the PC, which is called printer handshaking. This, along with multiple bytes transfer (available for some EPP hardware designs), improved data transfer rates up to almost 2 MB/sec—about 10 times faster than the standard compatibility mode. EPP design also allowed block transfer of data and intermixing data directions (from and to the computer) with no additional delays, which made it suitable for such peripherals as a Zip drive.

The ECP interface was meant for even higher data transfer rates than EPP. It utilizes data compression using the RLE (Run Length Encoding) protocol, which is most useful for compressing long sequences of repeated numbers. For example, if the sequence includes 105 zeros, it will be compressed by transmitting the following statement: "here is 105 zeros" or "105×0" instead of sending them all one by one.

A relatively loose handshaking protocol, along with direct memory access (DMA), made possible even higher data transfer rates in one direction. But, to reverse the direction of data transfer, ECP needs several time-consuming steps. This makes the ECP interface less suitable for the external storage devices that constantly intermix directions of data transfer (read and write operations).

IDE, EIDE, UDMA OR ATA, AND ATAPI . . . .

The IDE interface is closely related to the ISA interface—one of the general-purpose interfaces that can be found on the PC's motherboard along with the PCI interface slots. In fact, IDE is the part of ISA needed to support various internal devices, such as disk drives, CD-ROMs, internal Zip drives, and so on, that was redirected and turned into the different connector to save on the use of larger ISA slots. The only way to connect an external device to IDE is via the PC Card (former PCMCIA card) connector or using special docking devices (see Chapter 3).

ATA was the standard bus interface on the original IBM AT (Advanced Technology) computer and is also called IDE, for *Integrated Drive Electronics*, and Ultra DMA, for Ultra *Direct Memory Access*. ATA is the official ANSI (American National Standards Institute) standard term that defines the physical, electrical, transport, and command protocols for the internal attachment of storage devices. Nowadays, ATA interface is the dominant interface for storage systems on personal computers and is used in over 90% of all PCs. Most motherboards include two ATA 40-pin connectors each capable of supporting two devices (one master and one slave). Typically, the master should be at the end of the 40-pin ribbon cable, and the drives, which are similar in speed, should be attached to the same IDE connector. Newer ATA-66 and ATA-100 require 40-pin 80-conductor cable to perform at maximum speed.

Being the least expensive hard drive interface, ATA is, in general, slower than SCSI interface, and is used for single-user PCs and low-end RAID systems.

There are two ways IDE devices get connected to the PC (see Figure 2–6.): using an integrated into the motherboard IDE connectors (a) and using an IDE adapter interface card connected to the slower ISA or faster PCI bus (b).

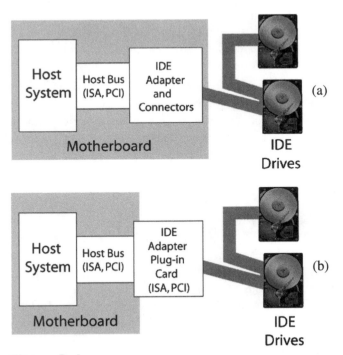

Figure 2–6
Two ways of connecting IDE devices to the PC: using an integrated into the motherboard IDE connectors (a) and using an IDE adapter interface card connected to the slower ISA or faster PCI bus (b).

The history of the IDE interface started in 1984 at Compaq with an idea to embed the hard disk drive controller into a drive. Compaq, together with Western Digital Corporation, produced the ST506 controller that could be mounted on a hard disk drive and connected to a PC using a 40-pin cable. Later, in 1985, a company called Imprimis built the first IDE drive by integrating an ST506 controller in a hard disk drive. Eventually, the IDE standard was approved by ANSI under the name ANSI X3.221-1994. In this standard, IDE interface got a new name—ATA (Advanced Technology Attachment). The interface compliant with this standard is also called ATA-1 or IDE.

With time, ATA evolved, and the new features and new standards were introduced. The main reason was that the drive rotational speed was increasing constantly (up to 10,000 rpm in the newest high-end drives), thus increasing the internal data transfer rate (between the media and the drive's memory buffer). In order to prevent potential bottlenecks, the interface has to provide even faster data transfer between the drive's buffer and the host system.

ATA-2 (or Fast ATA or EIDE [Enhanced IDE])

The interface that complies with the ANSI X3.279-1996 standard and is the AT Attachment Interface with Extensions, which offers higher DTR and some new commands.

Apple-ATA

The interface that complies with the ANSI X3T9.2/90-143 Revision 3.1 standard is Apple's implementation of the ATA interface. It offers higher DTR and some new commands and requires the IDE drive to support LBA (logical block address) mode.

ATA-3 (or Fast ATA or EIDE [Enhanced IDE])

The interface that complies with the ANSI X3.279-1996 standard and is the AT Attachment-3 Interface. ATA-3 doesn't offer higher speed but adds new commands and more precisely defined procedures.

ATAPI

AT Attachment Packet Interface is an extension to the ATA protocol and is used for connecting such devices as CD-ROM and tape drive to the same IDE interface. ATAPI commands are a subset of ATA commands.

ATAPI standard is designed in such a way that:

- the ATAPI device (CD-ROM, etc.) doesn't affect other IDE devices, such as hard disk drives.
- the computer doesn't confuse the ATAPI device for the hard disk drive.
- both ATAPI and IDE devices share the same cable and connector and support the same master/slave protocol.

ATA/ATAPI-4 (Ultra ATA, UDMA, or ATA-33)

The interface that complies with the ANSI NCITS 317-1998 is the AT Attachment Interface with Packet Interface Extension. It supports the maximum DTR of 33 MB/sec (in burst mode), and provides for enhanced reliability and data integrity through the use of double-edge clocking and Cyclical Redundancy Checking (CRC).

ATA/ATAPI-5 (or ATA-66, Ultra ATA-66, or Ultra DMA-66)

The interface that complies with the ANSI NCITS 340-2000 is the AT Attachment Interface with Packet Interface-5. It is one of the newest and fastest IDE interfaces that double the maximum DTR of ATA-33 to 66 MB/sec (in burst mode). It provides enhanced reliability and integrity through CRC and the use of newer 40-pin 80-conductor cable instead of the 40-pin 40-conductor cable. The 80-conductor cable reduces the cross talk and improves data integrity by using 40 additional ground lines. Still, the connector is completely compatible with the existing IDE connectors. The ATA-5 drives are completely backward compatible with the previous ATA drives and host systems.

ATA/ATAPI-6 (or ATA-100 or Ultra ATA-100)

This is the newest and the fastest IDE interface. It supports the maximum DTR of 100 MB/sec (in burst mode) and provides enhanced reliability and integrity through CRC. It uses a new 40-pin 80-conductor cable instead of the 40-pin 40-connector cable. The first ATA-100 hard disk drive was announced in June 2000 by Quantum Corporation, which also previously pioneered the 33 MB/sec and 66 MB/sec drives. The new connector is completely compatible with the existing IDE connectors and the ATA-6 drives are completely backward compatible with the previous ATA drives and host systems.

Table 2–1 summarizes the main performance characteristics of different ATA generations.

Table 2–1   Main Performance Characteristics of Different ATA Generations

Interface Name	ATA-2	ATA-3	ATA-4	ATA-5	ATA-6
Maximum data transfer rate (MB/sec)	16.6	16.6	33	66	100
Maximum number of supported devices (per channel)	2	2	2	2	2
Maximum bus width (bits)	16	16	16	16	16

The newest ATA-66 and ATA-100 drives rival (as ATA-33 did before) the SCSI drives while being much cheaper and simpler to install and use. Older computers, to benefit from high performance of ATA-33, 66, and 100, require a special PCI adapter card. Newer computers come equipped with motherboards with integrated Ultra ATA controllers (as the motherboard shown earlier).

Data transfer over the IDE interface can be done in two ways: using programmed I/O (PIO) or using direct memory access (DMA).

When a non-DMA peripheral (i.e., an older HDD) performs a data transfer, it generates an interrupt signal to the CPU. Then, the CPU interrupts its current task, saves its state information, and calls an interrupt handler routine. The interrupt handler directs the CPU to transfer data from the peripheral into a CPU internal register. The CPU then transfers the data from the internal register to some location in memory. Finally, the CPU restores the state information it had before the interrupt and then continues its previous task.

Summary

The transfer occurs in two steps: first, from the peripheral device to the CPU; second, from the CPU to the memory.

A DMA data transfer doesn't involve the CPU and is performed by generating a sort of DMA request signal to a DMA controller in the system. Then, the DMA controller uses the system bus to transfer data from the DMA peripheral to the memory. No CPU is involved in this process.

There are several PIO and DMA modes with higher numbers, meaning faster data transfer. For example, PIO 1 is faster than PIO 0. The modes that are faster than the ISA bus (8.3 MB/sec) require a faster bus to work with, such as a PCI bus (Table 2–2).

The PIO method uses the CPU to transfer data from the ATA device. DMA allows the drive to bypass the CPU and directly exchange data with the host memory. The main reason for the ATA device to support all slower modes instead of only the fastest mode is the need for its backward compatibility.

Table 2–2   Data Transfer Rates

Mode	PIO DTR (MB/sec)	Single word DMA DTR (MB/sec)	Multiword DMA DTR (MB/sec)	UDMA DTR (MB/sec)
0	**3.3**	**2.0**	**4.2**	16.7
1	**5.2**	**4.1**	13.3	25.0
2	**8.3**	**8.3**	16.7	33.3
3	11.1			44.4
4	16.7			66.7
5				100.0

Note: The data rates in bold were already defined in the ATA-1 standard.

What follows are the system requirements for Ultra ATA-33/66/100:

- Ultra ATA-compatible chipset on the motherboard or compatible PCI host adapter card
- Ultra ATA-compatible BIOS
- Ultra ATA device drivers for the OS
- Ultra ATA-compatible drive (hard disk drive, CD-ROM, etc.)
- 40-pin 80-conductor cable (needed for UDMA modes 3,4,5). The cable length is limited to 18 inches. Requires the master drive at the end of the cable and the slave in the middle (blue cable connector is for the host, black is for the master, and gray is for the slave).

The ATA/IDE connectors are shown in Figure 2–7.

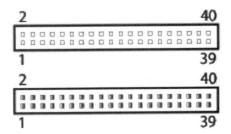

Figure 2–7
Cable connector (upper image) and adapter connector (lower image).

The Future of ATA

The future of ATA may be connected to a *serial* rather than *parallel* data transfer. Serial ATA 1x is the new standard, which can increase the DTR up to 150 MB/sec over the narrow 4-wire cable. The main advantages of the Serial ATA are the small cables and connectors that save lots of room and do not disrupt the airflow inside the PC (which is critical for good cooling).

While being a serial interface, the Serial ATA will maintain backward compatibility with the parallel ATA devices. Most of the storage industry companies are participating in the Serial ATA Working Group (*www.serialata.org*) in order to develop a specification. In the future, the Serial ATA has the potential of increasing the DTR to 500 MB/sec and beyond.

PC CARD INTERFACE (FORMER PCMCIA) . . . .

PC Card interface is an important element of the modern computing systems such as notebooks and subnotebooks, handheld PCs, digital cameras, mobile audio recorders and MP3 players, portable GPS systems, and so on. In the early 1990s, a need for smaller, lighter, and more portable tools for information processing resulted in the birth of the PC card technology.

At first, this interface was called PCMCIA for PC Memory Card International Association. The first standard release (1.0/JEIDA 4.0-1990) defined the 68-pin interface and the Type I and Type II PC Card form factors. The size of the PCMCIA card was defined to be 85 × 54 mm with three different thicknesses of 3.3, 5.0, and 10.5 millimeters for Type I, Type II, and Type III cards, respectively.

Following updates to the standard (Releases 2.0, 2.01, and 2.1 [1991–1994]) defined an I/O interface for the same 68-pin interface, made clarifications to the first release, added support for dual-voltage memory cards, and so on. Release 2.01 added the PC Card ATA specification, the Type III card type, and the Auto-Indexing Mass Storage (AIMS) specification, which targeted digital imaging. In 1995, improved compatibility and added support for features such as 3.3 volt operation, DMA support, and 32-bit card bus mastering were added.

The PC Card interface was, initially, a 16-bit interface. With time, it was updated to 32-bit allowing for faster data transfer. This extension to the PC Card interface, called *Card Bus*, is a PCI-like bus. Among other things, Card Bus supports DMA (direct memory access) and plug-and-play features.

PC Card interface is used in the modern Flash memory cards and, basically, is an ATA interface (see earlier in the chapter), and the PC Cards emulate ATA disk drive operation and do not allow the host CPU to access the Flash memory directly. The two types of ATA Flash cards—PC cards and Compact Flash™ cards—are also similar conceptually.

Nowadays, Type I PC Cards can be found in PC memory devices such as RAM, Flash, OTP, and SRAM cards. Type II PC Cards are typically used for I/O devices such as data/fax modems, LANs, and mass storage devices. Type III PC Cards are used for thicker devices.

UNIVERSAL SERIAL BUS (USB) . . . .

The USB interface is a revolutionary multidevice interface designed for easy, hassle-free, and relatively inexpensive low- and medium-speed applications. USB is a peripheral bus specification developed by PC and telecom companies including Compaq, DEC, IBM, Intel, Microsoft, NEC, and Northern Telecom. At the low end, USB can sustain a rate of less then 0.2 MB/sec; in its fastest mode USB is capable of about 1.5 MB/sec.

A growing variety of devices with USB support (USB 1.1 standard) is currently available: printers, scanners, modems, digital cameras and camcorders, keyboards, mice, joysticks, audio speakers, and so on. The main reason for this popularity is the set of attractive features the USB possesses (Table 2–3).

Table 2–3   Universal Serial Bus Features

Feature	Description
Low cost	USB has a great balance of low cost and good performance with DTR up to 1.5 MB/sec.
Hot pluggable/swappable	Automatic detection and configuration of the USB device by the PC. Devices can be also attached and removed without restarting the computer.
Single type device-side connector	Unlike, for example, SCSI, USB uses one connector type for any USB device.
Multiple devices	Supports up to 127 devices per channel.
Reasonable performance	In its slowest mode USB is capable of about 0.2 MB/sec; in its fastest mode USB is capable of about 1.5 MB/sec.
Integrated power cable	Allows to power low-power peripheral devices directly with one USB cable.
Automatic power saving	USB devices automatically switch to power-saving mode 3 ms after pause in bus activity.
Error detection and correction	Included error detection and correction mechanism.

One of the best USB features is the so-called "hot-swapping": there is no need in shutting down and restarting the PC in order to attach or remove a peripheral. The device you plug in is automatically recognized and configured by the USB. This can be especially useful for notebook computer USB peripherals that are frequently connected and disconnected.

On the newer computers, the USB host controller with two hubs resides on the PCI bus and is integrated into the motherboard. Figure 2–8 shows how the USB devices are connected to the PC.

USB makes adding peripheral devices very easy and is quickly replacing different kinds of serial and parallel port connectors with one standardized plug and port combination. The main hardware used in USB includes:

- USB Host Controller (Root Hub)
- USB Hubs (for multiple USB connections)
- USB devices

The USB Host Controller is the central connection point between the bus and the devices. The USB Host Controller includes the so-called Root Hub—the attachment ports for USB devices on the bus. All communication on the USB is originated at the host. The host controller writes to the target device, reads from the device, performs parallel-to-serial conversions, and so on. The root hub controls power to the USB devices, enables and disables ports, recognizes devices on the bus, and sets and reports status events.

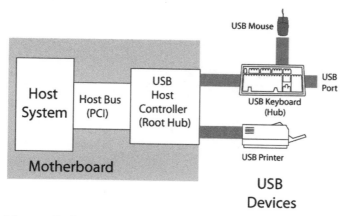

Figure 2–8
Connection of USB devices to the PC.

USB Hubs

In theory, a USB channel can support up to 127 individual USB peripherals at a time. The practical maximum number of devices is less since some of them reserve USB bandwidth. An additional PCI-based USB card provides an independent USB channel so that even more peripheral devices can be connected. For practical connection of multiple devices to the host (root), special hubs are required. Hubs notify the host when nodes (devices) attach or detach from the hub to provide the real-time reconfiguration of the system and device identification. Hubs can have up to seven connectors to nodes or other hubs. They could be self-powered or powered by the host. Figure 2–9 shows the topology of USB where hubs are the attachment points for the USB devices.

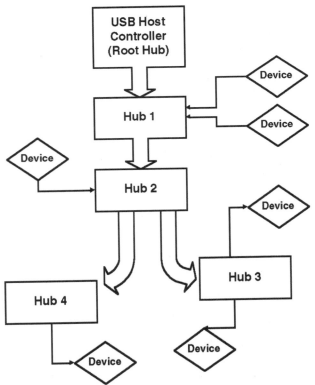

Figure 2–9
Topology of USB where hubs are the attachment points for the USB devices.

Connectors and Cables

USB connectors are designed for connection of any USB device to the hub port. Some of the USB devices have their cable permanently integrated (like the mouse), and the other devices have USB ports for the detachable cables.

USB systems use two types of connectors: one for the hub, another for the device. The hub port connectors are called *Series A connectors* (Figure 2–10a), and the device connectors are called *Series B connectors* (Figure 2–10b). Each connector has four contacts: two for power (longer connector pins) and two for differential data signal.

USB cables must meet the following requirements:

- Be no longer than 5 meters for high-speed (and higher quality) cables and 3 meters for low-speed cables
- Provide for 500 mA current (otherwise, may overheat)
- Have one Series A and one Series B connector
- Be properly shielded

For low-speed USB devices, a cheaper low-speed cable can be used (Figure 2–11a). This cable has a differential signal pair that can be nontwisted 28 AWG stranded conductors. Also, cable shielding is not required. The low-speed cables allow for DTR of 0.2 MB/sec and are up to 3 m long.

High-speed cable requires shielding of both the cable and twisted differential data lines (Figure 2–11b). These cables allow for DTR of up to 1.5 MB/sec and are up to 5 m long.

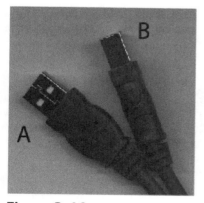

Figure 2–10
The hub port USB connectors are called Series A connectors, and the device connectors are called Series B connectors.

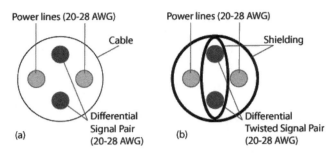

Figure 2–11
USB cables schematics: low-speed (a) and high-speed (b) cables.

Five-meter-long cables allow (with the maximum of 5 hubs connected) for the device to be as far as 30 m away from the computer. With a low-speed device, you will be able to get a range up to 27 m.

USB OS Support

Windows 98 supports USB and there was a limited support for USB in Windows 95. Windows 2000 does have USB support. Windows NT 3.5 and 4.0 (including service pack 4) do not support USB.

An installation of the USB device on the USB-capable computers requires only two steps:

- Run any installation software necessary for your device.
- Plug in your device.

USB 2.0

The future version of much faster USB may be realized in USB 2.0.

The USB 2.0 specification has a design data rate of 60 MB/sec, with final specification being released recently. This will become a new step for this interface that was initially designed to be a low-cost, easy-to-use interface with up to 1.5 MB/sec maximum performance.

A 40-times increase in bandwidth for USB 2.0 shouldn't make it less simple. It still uses small connectors, only one cable type, and supports plug-and-play. USB 2.0 is fully backward- and forward-compatible with USB 1.1. Existing USB peripherals should continue to work with USB 2.0 computers. Also, most USB 2.0 peripherals should work with a USB 1.1-based PC under USB 1.1 operating conditions. In either case, the system continues working flawlessly, and runs at the fastest common speed. USB 2.0 uses the same cables as USB 1.1 with the same shapes of connectors. Even the topology of USB 2.0 is the same. In practice this means that the user may not even know which USB version his is using.

USB versus Serial and Parallel Interface

There is no question here—in the near future USB will replace all other interface types, including serial and parallel, in the low- and medium-speed devices, such as printers, scanners, joysticks, and so on. USB has too much to offer when compared with serial and parallel interfaces (plug-in-play connectivity, faster DTR, 127 devices, hot-swappability, etc.).

For the peripherals requiring higher DTR, such as data storage devices, USB 2.0 can be used.

IEEE 1394 FIREWIRE . . . .

The IEEE 1394 standard for the High Performance Serial Bus, also called FireWire, is a *serial* data transfer protocol and interconnection system. The main feature of the FireWire that assures its adoption for the digital audio and video (A/V) consumer application is its relatively low cost. A FireWire interface is capable of supporting various high-end digital A/V applications, such as consumer A/V device control and signal routing, digital video (DV) editing, home networking, and more than 32 channels of digital mixing. FireWire allows for video capture from both newer DV camcorders with FireWire ports and older analog equipment using A/V to FireWire converters.

The first commercial products implementing FireWire technology were Sony's DCR-VX700 and DCR-VX1000 digital video camcorders, introduced in 1995. Nowadays, a growing variety of electronic products rely on the FireWire technology. Also, FireWire allows for easy data exchange between such devices as computers, camcorders, TV sets, speakers, and other consumer electronic devices.

The advantages of the FireWire interface are summed up in Table 2–4.

Table 2–4   Advantages of the FireWire Interface

Feature	Description
Very fast	DTR up to 50 MB/sec (400 Mb/sec), which is about 30 times faster than USB.
Hot pluggable/swappable	Automatic detection and configuration of the FireWire device by the PC. Devices can also be attached and removed without restarting the computer.
Multiple devices	Supports up to 63 devices (16 daisy chained) with cable length up to about 4.5 m (14 feet).
Easy connection	FireWire cables are very easy to connect (like USB).
Supports fair arbitration	The *isochronous* applications are guaranteed a constant bandwidth, and *asynchronous* applications are permitted access to the bus on base of a fairness algorithm.
Peer-to-peer transfer	Devices on the bus can perform transactions between themselves without the intervention of a CPU.
Integrated power cable	Allows to power low-power peripheral devices directly with one cable.
Automatic power saving	FireWire devices automatically switch to power-saving mode after pause in bus activity.
Error detection and correction	Includes error detection and correction mechanism.

FireWire was originally developed to replace fast but complex SCSI and offers both *isochronous* and *asynchronous* data transfer modes. Like USB, FireWire provides plug-and-play and hot plug-in capabilities, which allows to connect or disconnect devices without powering down and restarting the system. The list of devices supporting IEEE 1394 standard is growing since it also enables transmitting audio, video, and control signals via the same cable. Since the power line is a part of the cable, power can be supplied directly to the low-power devices.

Even on the newer computers, the FireWire adapter is rarely integrated into the motherboard and needs to be installed as a plug-in card. Figure 2–12 shows how the FireWire devices are connected to the PC.

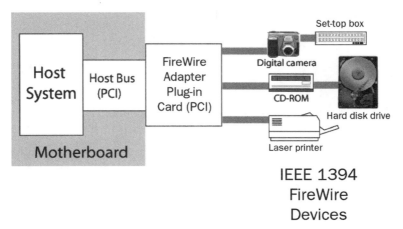

Figure 2–12
FireWire device connection to the PC.

Basic Architecture

The following terminology is needed to describe the physical and logical organization of the FireWire system:

- Unit—smallest element of the node, which operates independently within a node and identifies processing, memory, and I/O functionality. Processor, hard disk drive, I/O devices, and physical interface (PHY) are the examples of the units.
- Node—A larger element that may include one or many units. A node is a logical element within a module. Each 1394 node usually has up to three ports.
- Module—a physical device on the bus, which may include one or more nodes.

First, the FireWire is a *peer-to-peer protocol* with point-to-point signaling. Each port on a node works as a repeater and retransmits signals received by other ports within the node. Because of this, any specific host isn't required for the FireWire bus. Thus, a digital camera can easily communicate directly with the digital DVD or VCR without assistance from other devices on the bus.

The FireWire bus is a noncyclic network with finite branches, consisting of bus bridges and cable devices (nodes). Noncyclic means that one *can't plug devices together to create a loop*. Finite branches refer to up to 16 cable hops allowed between *nodes*. 16-bit addressing allows up to 63 nodes to be connected to a single bus bridge. Thus, 63 connected devices is a limit for a conventional IEEE 1394 card in a PC.

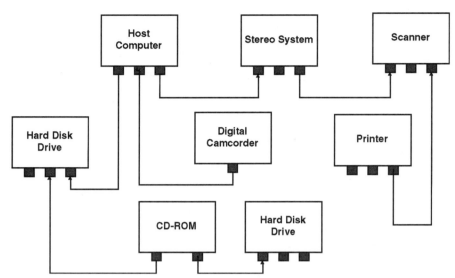

Figure 2–13
An example of the FireWire system topology.

Each 1394 node usually has up to *three connectors*, and *up to 16 nodes* can be connected in a daisy chain through the connectors with standard cables up to 4.5 m long for a total of 72 m. Special high-quality fatter cables allow for even longer interconnections. Additional devices can be added in a leaf-node configuration (see Figure 2–13). Physical addresses are automatically assigned to the devices on bridge power up (bus reset) and when a new node is added or removed from the system. Hot plugging of the devices is fully supported. No device ID switches are required. Figure 2–13 shows an example of the FireWire topology.

Basic Design

FireWire serial interface uses a simple cable with two types of small and inexpensive connectors: 6-pin (Figure 2–14) and 4-pin (Figure 2–15) connectors, to carry multiple channels of digital video data and control information plus the power.

The original 1394-1995 specification defined a single 6-pin connector type. The cable connectors are identical on both ends. The 1394a specification defined an additional *less expensive* 4-pin connector and cable without power pins. The cable for a 4-pin connector may have a 6-pin connector on one side and a 4-pin connector on the other side, or 4-pin connectors on both sides.

Table 2–5 specifies signal assignment for the 4-pin and 6-pin connectors.

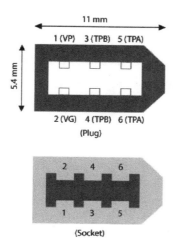

Figure 2–14
6-pin FireWire connectors.

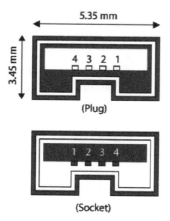

Figure 2–15
4-pin FireWire connectors.

Table 2–5   Signal Assignment for the 4- and 6-pin Connectors

Contact Number	Description
1	Power (8–40 V dc)
2	Ground
3–4	Twisted pair B—differential data and differential strobe
5–6	Twisted pair A—differential data and differential strobe

Two categories of devices may benefit from a 4-pin connector:

- Battery-operated devices with less expensive cable and connectors
- Handheld devices with smaller connectors (digital cameras, camcorders, etc.)

Figure 2–16 shows schematics of two FireWire cable types used. The electrical characteristics for 4-pin and 6-pin cables are the same. The suggested maximum length for these cables is 4.5 m.

During data transfer over the shielded double twisted pair cable, a clock signal is automatically generated from the data signal and the strobe signal. This eliminates the need for the high-speed phase lock loop (PLL) circuits used by other interfaces at both ends of the communication channel. As a result, IEEE 1394 is much less expensive.

The FireWire interface is implemented in three layers: the Transaction layer, the Link layer, and the Physical layer (see Figure 2–17).

The Transaction layer supports asynchronous data transfer only. It includes read, write, and lock operations. Each asynchronous transaction includes a request and a response.

The Link layer supplies acknowledgments to the Transaction layer and handles all packet transmission and reception, and provides cycle control for the isochronous channel. The CRC (cyclic redundancy check) validates data. The Link layer chip both transmits and receives 1394-formatted data packets and supports asynchronous or isochronous data transfer modes. Isochronous capabilities allow PCs to handle high-bandwidth data, typical in multimedia applications, more efficiently. Isochronous data handling is especially important for consumer audio/video products where data is stored on the PC hard disk drive.

The Physical layer provides the actual interface to the serial bus. It includes the logic needed to perform arbitration and bus initialization functions. It does all needed

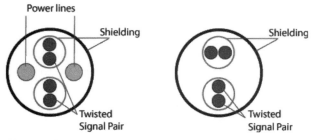

Figure 2–16
Schematics of two FireWire cable types used. The electrical characteristics for 4-pin and 6-pin cables are the same.

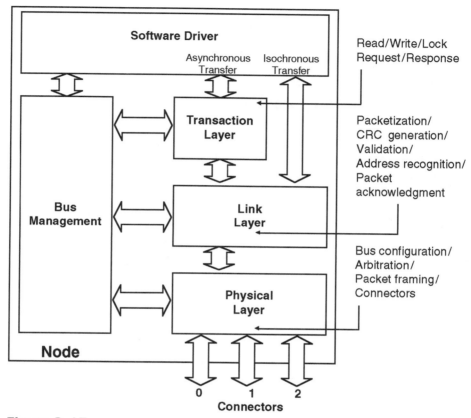

Figure 2–17
The FireWire interface implementation in the three layers: The Transaction
layer, the Link layer, and the Physical layer.

initialization and arbitration to assure that only one node at a time is sending data. It also
translates the serial bus data stream and signal levels to those required by the Link layer.

Bus management supports bus configuration and the application of power for
each node. All nodes include support for automatic bus configuration.

USB 1.1 versus IEEE 1394 FireWire

They are both serial type interfaces and transmit data one bit at a time. They are also
meant to be used with various peripherals ranging from a mouse to the speakers, DVD
players, or even a hard disk drive. Both interfaces are capable of supporting multiple
devices and enable communication between different peripherals. Also, both USB and

IEEE 1394 cables contain power wires as well, which is enough to power up such devices as a mouse or a keyboard.

On the other hand, these two interfaces were designed for different data transfer rates and cost ranges. The FireWire IEEE 1394 interface is meant for high bandwidth and can be more then 30 times faster than USB. In the near future, FireWire may become even faster. At the same time, IEEE 1394 interface is considerably more expensive than USB.

USB and 1394 technologies are easy to use and complement each other in terms of performance and cost and give a choice between high performance and high cost. The comparison of USB with FireWire is shown in Table 2–6.

Table 2–6   Comparison of FireWire and USB

	IEEE 1394 FireWire	USB 1.1
Maximum number of connected devices	63	127
Hot-swap?	Yes	Yes
Plug-and-play?	Yes	Yes
Cable length between devices	4.5 m	5 m
Data transfer rate (MB/s)	12.5/25/50	1.5
PC/Mac	Yes/Yes	Yes/iMac only
Embedded power line	Yes	Yes
Peripheral devices	D-Camcorders D-Cameras Set-Top Boxes HDTV DVD-ROM, RAM Hard Disk drives Printers Scanners Keyboards Mice PC Monitors Joysticks Low-resolution D-Cameras Low-speed CD-ROM, RW Modems	Keyboards Mice PC Monitors Joysticks DVD-ROM, RAM Low-resolution D-Cameras Low-speed CD-ROM, RW Modems Printers Scanners
Relative cost	Higher	Lower

SMALL COMPUTER SYSTEMS INTERFACE (SCSI) . . . .

SCSI (pronounced "scuzzy") is the acronym for Small Computer System Interface, a high performance parallel peripheral interface that can independently distribute data among peripherals attached to the PC. Unlike ATA, SCSI incorporates those instructions needed for communication with the host PC. Freeing the host computer from this job makes it more efficient in performing its user-oriented activities. SCSI is a specification for a peripheral bus and command set defined in an ANSI standard X3.131-1986.

SCSI drives are usually more suitable for high-end computer systems, which require maximum possible performance. SCSI provides for higher data transfer rates and less CPU load than ATA but also has higher cost and complexity in the setup. Also, SCSI supports more devices than ATA.

There are various flavors of SCSI—different in width (8-bit versus 16-bit) and speed (standard versus fast). Most SCSI products are backward-compatible. A faster, newer drive can still work with the older and slower controller, but will, of course, lose in performance.

SCSI is a device-independent I/O system that allows for a wide variety of devices to be linked to a computer. Device-independence means that no knowledge about a device and device-specific details is needed in order to connect a device. SCSI will take care of this part by querying the device.

Initiator and Target

The main element of the SCSI is the SCSI bus that can be shared by multiple devices as both a physical (interface consists of the cables, connectors, etc.) and logical (communication protocol, commands, etc.) interface.

All devices connected to the SCSI bus are either *initiators* or *targets*.

An initiator is a device that requests another device on the bus to perform some operation. A target is the device that is an object of this request. Some devices can perform as both a target and initiator, but most devices are either one or another. A SCSI host adapter is an initiator, while the hard disk drive is a target.

The main way of connecting the SCSI devices to the PC (see Figure 2–18) is by using a plug-in SCSI host interface adapter card connected to the fast PCI base. Unlike the IDE interface, where the devices and host adapter are directly connected to the devices, the SCSI host adapter is connected to the device controllers, which are typically integrated into the device.

SCSI technology evolved with time by adding width and improving the data transfer protocol. Fast SCSI doubles the data transfer rate over the same 50-pin cable by

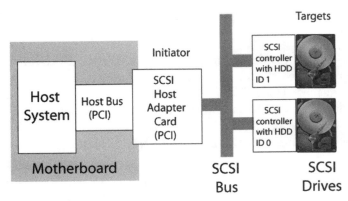

Figure 2–18
The main way of connecting the SCSI devices to the PC.

using synchronous (versus asynchronous) data transfer. Wide SCSI uses "wider" 68-pin cable to allow 16-bit data stream versus 8-bit for a 50-pin connector. A combination of both wide and fast technologies provides for greater than 80 MB/sec data transfer rates.

The history of SCSI goes back to 1981, when Shugart Associates (presently Seagate Technology Corporation) joined NCR Corporation in their efforts to develop an intelligent interface for hard disk drives. This new interface was called Shugart Associates Systems Interface, or SASI Interface. In 1982, SCSI was born on the base of SASI. In 1986, ANSI accepted SCSI-1 as an ANSI standard. Nowadays, the SCSI standard can be divided into SCSI (SCSI-1), SCSI-2 (SCSI wide and SCSI wide and fast), and newer SCSI-3.

SCSI-1

The original SCSI-1 interface used a 50-pin connector with 8 conductors allocated for data. Thus, it became known as an "8-bit wide SCSI" or "narrow SCSI." This interface allowed for DTR of up to 5 MB/sec. The problem with this standard was in some weakly defined definitions resulting in different implementations of SCSI-1 devices, leading to their incompatibility. For example, format parameters were not standardized for hard disk drives. Both single-ended (SE, see details below) and differential versions (known today as high voltage differential, or HVD) were available.

SCSI-2

In 1994, SCSI-2 became an ANSI standard X3.131-1994. By incorporating *synchronous* data transfer mode, SCSI-2 increased DTR to 10 MB/sec. Nowadays, SCSI-2 is, perhaps, the most popular version of the SCSI and is used for hard disk drives, CD-ROM players, tapes, scanners, and so on.

SCSI-3

SCSI-3 standard is a collection of many smaller documents, each addressing a layer of the interface. SCSI-3 led to Fast Wide SCSI with 8 more data bits, increased maximum DTR of 20 MB/sec, 16 supported devices, and a wider 68-pin connector.

In the next Ultra-2 SCSI, a new signaling method called LVD (low voltage differential) was used to allow for long connecting cables and faster data transfer, which reached 80 MB/s in the "wide" version of Ultra-2 SCSI.

Next was the Ultra-3 SCSI with multiple additional features (double transition clocking, cyclic redundancy check [CRC], etc.) allowing to again double the data rate to 160 MB/s with the wide bus.

The evolution of SCSI standard continues with newer SCSI-320 and SCSI 640 becoming a reality. The main characteristics of different SCSI standards are summarized in Table 2–7.

Table 2–7   Main Characteristics of SCSI Standards

Interface Name	SCSI-1	SCSI-2/ Fast SCSI	SCSI-3/ Fast Wide SCSI	Ultra SCSI/ Fast-20	Wide Ultra SCSI	Ultra-2 SCSI	Wide Ultra-2 SCSI	Ultra-3/ Ultra-160 SCSI
Maximum (burst) data transfer rates (MB/sec)	5	10	20	20	40	40	80	160
Maximum number of supported devices	8	8	16	4–8	4–8	8	16	16
Maximum bus width (bits)	8	8	16	8	16	8	16	16
Maximum cable length (m)	6	3	3	1.5–3	1.5–3	12	12	12
Connector type	50-pin	50-pin	68-pin	50-pin	68-pin	50-pin	68-pin	68-pin

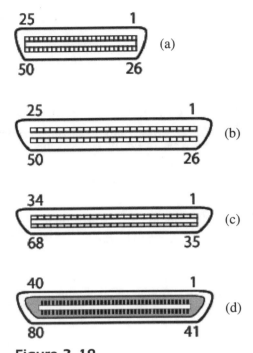

Figure 2–19
SCSI female connector: (a) SCSI-1 (5 MB/s) Centronics 50-pin (8-bit) connector; (b) Fast SCSI (10 MB/sec) 50-pin (8-bit) high-density connector; (c) Wide SCSI 50-pin (16-bit) high-density connector; (d) New SCA (single connector attachment) 80-pin connector (for wide SCSI bus versions).

Figure 2–19 shows SCSI female connectors.

Single-Ended and Differential SCSI

There are two electrically incompatible variations of the parallel SCSI interface: the single-ended and the differential, which cannot be used on the same SCSI bus.

The most popular SCSI is the single-ended, which is too short and is interference-prone, but provides satisfactory quality at short distances (typically, 1.5–3 m, 6 m for "slow" SCSI-1). Short cables may be adequate for use inside a PC, but may create problems when used in the server environment where a large number of different devices is being connected to the same cable. The alternative solution is to use longer cables but to use differential SCSI devices with much better noise immunity.

A differential SCSI supports a maximum cable length of 25 meters. In a differential SCSI, two wires are used to carry each signal. One wire carries a signal, and another its logical inversion. The differential signal measured on the receiving side is stronger and, thus, less affected by the noise.

Differential SCSI devices are more expensive, and are typically used for high-end applications.

The low-voltage differential (LVD) SCSI is a cheaper interface with considerably reduced power consumption, which is a problem for differential design. The low voltage of LVD allows the differential systems to be integrated into the drive's on-board SCSI controller, eliminating the need for separate and costly external high voltage differential components.

Termination

In order to function properly, SCSI bus requires correct electrical termination using appropriate resistors at both ends of the bus. This is needed to prevent signal reflections at the ends of the cable, which may increase noise and cause problems like "ghosted" SCSI devices, data errors, and other anomalies. Termination is used to prevent reflection and instead "absorb" the signals. Termination must be done at the beginning and at the end of the bus, and must occur within 4 inches of the physical ends of the SCSI bus. The first and the last SCSI devices, connected in the daisy chain, should be properly terminated. The first device is the SCSI controller itself. The devices in between should not be terminated.

Both active and passive termination is used, with active termination being more common and the better way to go. In case of passive termination, resistor networks is driven directly by the term power on the bus. In case of active termination, resistor networks is driven by voltage regulators inside the terminator. All LVD terminators are assumed to be active.

SCSI versus IDE/ATA

SCSI is designed for high-performance systems with multiple devices of different types and extended cable length. IDE/ATA devices are more suitable for home users and computer systems with a limited number of peripheral devices. Main features of SCSI and IDE are summarized and compared next.

IDE/ATA:

- Less expensive
- Fast: up to 100 MB/sec (ATA-6 or ATA-100)

- Easy to install/integrated host adapters
- Less overhead per command
- Two devices per channel with (typically) two channels per motherboard only
- Limited types of devices: hard disk drives, CD-ROM, Zip, tape, etc.

SCSI:

- More expensive
- Extremely fast (up to 160–320 MB/sec)
- Somewhat harder to install, needs plug-in card, and requires termination
- Supports more devices (up to 7 or 15 devices)
- Supports various peripheral devices (hard disk drive, JAZ, tape, CD-ROM, scanners, etc.).

SCSI versus USB and IEEE 1394 FireWire

In spite of the high convenience of USB and FireWire interfaces, the SCSI will most likely remain the interface for high-performance systems with multiple devices. USB, with its plug-and-play multidevice features, is still much slower than SCSI and is designed as a low-cost interface. The much faster FireWire can compete with SCSI in many areas, and the outcome will depend on the new speed records set by these interface types in the future.

Future of SCSI

The SCSI Trade Association (STA) has unanimously adopted the Ultra160, Ultra320, and Ultra640 SCSI naming conventions. Here are the mandatory and optional features for each format (*see www.quantum.com*):

Mandatory features for Ultra160 SCSI include:

- 160-megabyte per second data transfer rate using DT data transfers
- 32-bit CRC
- Simple domain validation
- Backward compatibility

Optional features for Ultra160 SCSI include:

- Information unit transfers
- QAS
- Fairness
- AIP

Mandatory features for Ultra320 SCSI as currently defined include:

- 320-megabyte per second transfer rate using DT data transfers
- 32-bit CRC
- Simple domain validation
- Backward compatibility
- Packetized transfers only
- A free-running clock
- Skew compensation
- A training pattern
- Transmitter precompensation with cutback

Optional features for Ultra320 SCSI currently include:

- AAF
- QAS
- Fairness
- AIP

Mandatory features for Ultra640 SCSI are currently defined to include:

- All of the mandatory features of Ultra320 SCSI
- 640-megabyte per second transfer rate using DT data transfers

Potential features for Ultra640 SCSI include:

- It is most probable that some sort of receiver improvement (like AAF) will be mandatory for Ultra640
- All other features are "to be discussed"

FIBRE CHANNEL-ARBITRATED LOOP (FC-AL) . . . . .

Fibre Channel-Arbitrated Loop (FC-AL) is a *serial interface* designed for high-bandwidth high-end systems. Its development started in 1988 in an attempt to enhance the Intelligent Peripheral Interface (IPI). Eventually, fibre channel became, perhaps, the most significant advance in the field of data communication and interfacing. The first fibre channel standard, x3230-1994, was approved by ANSI in 1994.

FC-AL uses fiber optic cabling and copper wires to produce a maximum (burst) data transfer rate of more than 100 MB/sec. FC-AL is capable of supporting up to 127 devices as far as 10 kilometers away, thus opening a new perspective for remote data storage (*web storage* and *storage networking*). FC-AL allows "hot-swapping" of the connected drives without interfering with the work of the entire system. Also, FC-AL devices can be designed with two ports to double the data transfer rates.

There are two very different ways to transfer data between computers or between computers and peripheral devices: via I/O channels and via networks.

An approach based on channels provides for a direct or switched point-to-point connection between the devices. This method is designed to be hardware-intensive and transports data at the high speed with low overhead. A SCSI interface is a good example of the fast and effective channel. SCSI transfers data in *parallel* over some relatively short distances using a number of lines (for example, 16 for 16-bit SCSI). Channels emphasize high performance and the hardware is optimized to meet that need. Channels tend to use more simple protocols and to minimize software involvement in data transfer operations. Also, channels provide highly reliable data transmission.

Another approach, networks, is based on connecting distributed elements (nodes) like workstations, file servers, and peripherals using network *serial* protocol that supports interaction among the nodes. Networks are software-intensive (high overhead), and tend to be slower than channels. On the other hand, networks have simpler cabling, connectors, and work over much greater distances (worldwide, if necessary). They can also handle a wider range of tasks than channels, and emphasize connectivity and protocol flexibility (e.g., IP [Intelligent Peripheral Interface]). In the case of networks, transmission of data isn't as reliable.

Fibre Channel is an attempt to combine *the best of these two methods of communication* and to create a new superior I/O interface with the following features:

- Serial data transfer (for greater distances and simplicity)
- Compatibility with various already existing protocols
- High data transfer rate
- Reliable data transfer

- Packetizing data (called frames in FC-AL world)
- Support for a large number of devices
- Routing information using switches

Therefore, the Fibre Channel isn't a channel nor a network, but allows for an active intelligent interconnection scheme, called a fabric, to connect heterogeneous computer systems and peripherals with all the benefits of the above two methods. In fact, Fibre channel supports its own protocol plus some other higher level protocols such as the SCSI, HIPPI (High Performance Parallel Interface Framing Protocol), and IPI (Intelligent Peripheral Interface). Peripherals can include storage devices such as disks or tape arrays.

Basic Terms

First of all, the very term *fibre* may refer to an optical cable or a copper cable.

Second, the Fibre Channel is similar to other interfaces and unique at the same time.

For example, SCSI has targets and initiators, and Fibre Channel has responders and originators. SCSI has packets; FC-AL has frames. FireWire has nodes, and Fibre Channel also has nodes. Any FC devices with at least one port is called a *node*. A *port* interfaces the FC cable and the device. The cable is also called a *link*. Fibre Channel connection is based on two cables: one to transmit and another to receive data.

Topology: Point-to-Point Connection

The simplest FC topology type is the so-called point-to-point topology, when two nodes (e.g., a computer and a hard disk drive) are connected directly. Apparently, this type of connection quarantines the fastest possible access with no interference from other devices.

Two computers can share an access to the above disk drive if it has two ports, creating two point-to-point connections (see Figure 2–20), or a two-node loop.

Arbitrated Loop

A Fibre Channel loop can have up to 127 ports connected in a series from the originator and back. An example is shown in Figure 2–21.

When devices form a Fibre Channel Arbitrated Loop, the transmitters are connected to a receiver for all nodes involved. When a node port wins arbitration, it establishes a point-to-point connection with another node. All other ports act as repeaters passing a

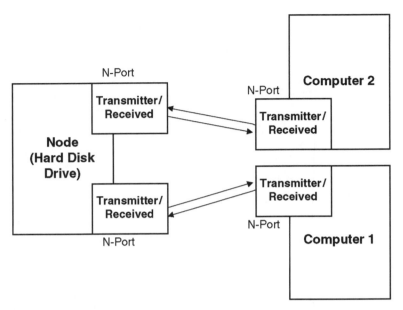

Figure 2–20
The simplest FC topology—the so-called point-to-point topology, when two nodes (e.g., a computer and a hard disk drive) are connected directly.

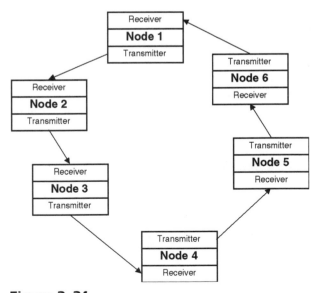

Figure 2–21
A Fibre channel loop topology (can have up to 127 ports connected in a series from the originator and back).

signal to the right node. Therefore, only two nodes connected in the arbitrated loop ports can communicate directly at a time. When their communication ends, new connections can be established. "Fairness" during arbitration provides equal access to all ports.

Fabric

Fabric is the web of connections using the switches or routers. In fact, an FC switch itself is called a fabric. Any device connected to a fabric can establish communication with any other connected device. Any node port (N_port) can access any other port attached to a fabric (see Figure 2–22).

Using this method, some very complex Fibre Channel structures can be designed with dozens of computer systems in different buildings connected with each other and with the mass storage devices. With present technology, the distance between the buildings can be up to 10 km when a single-mode optical fibre is used. While point-to-point topology is limited to just two ports, the fabric topology allows for up to 2^{24} ports (more than 16 million) to be interconnected.

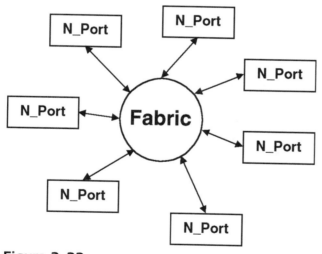

Figure 2–22
Any device connected to a fabric can establish communication with any other connected device.

FC Architecture

Fibre Channel has a multilayered architecture with layers numbered from FC-0 to FC-4, with layers FC-0 to FC-2 implemented at the port level and layers FC-3 and FC-4 implemented at the node level (see Figure 2–23).

The lowest layer, FC-0, represents the physical link in the system and includes fibers, connectors, receivers/transmitters, encoders/decoders, and serializers/deserializers.

FC-1 defines the transmission protocol, including the encode/decode scheme, synchronization, and character-level error control. The 8B/10B encoding scheme encodes 8-bit bytes into 10-bit byte transmission characters. This technique (developed at IBM) was found to be the best in terms of error rate.

The FC-2 level deals with optimizing the data flow control and breaks data sequences into individual *frames* (discussed below), which are the basic carriers of information and basic building blocks of FC data transfer. Other building blocks provided by the FC-2 layer are *sequences* (groups of frames), *exchanges* (sets of sequences), and *packets* (groups of exchanges).

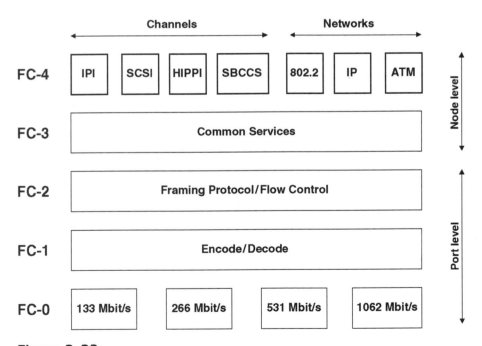

Figure 2–23
A multi-layered architecture of Fibre Channel with layers numbered from FC-0 to FC-4. Layers FC-0 to FC-2 implemented at the port level and layers FC-3 and FC-4 implemented at the node level.

The FC-3 layer contains services that are available to all ports on a node and includes *striping* (transmits information across multiple links to increase bandwidth), *hunt groups* (allows for all ports on a node to respond to the same alias address, which decreases business of ports), and *multicast* (delivers single transmissions to multiple ports).

FC-4 does the *mapping,* which allows to move information between the upper level protocols and defines the application interfaces that can be executed over the Fibre Channel. Some of the protocols currently supported by the FC-4 layer are listed below:

- SCSI
- IPI (Intelligent Peripheral Interface)
- HIPPI (High Performance Parallel Interface Framing Protocol)
- IP (Internet Protocol)
- FC-LE (Fibre Channel-Link Encapsulation)
- IEEE 802.2
- FC-SBCCS (Single Byte Command Code Set Mapping)

Frames

To move data from one FC device to another, the data is organized into discrete packets, called *frames* (see Figure 2–24). Frames are similar to packets in the world of networks. The "payload" is the term used for the transmitted data.

All information transferred in FC is packaged in frames. In fact, the frame can be imagined as an envelope, which provides a structure to carry *any* information inside.

Start of Frame (4 bytes)	Frame Header (24 bytes)	Optional Headers (64 bytes) + Payload (2048 bytes)	CRC (4 bytes)	End of Frame (4 bytes)

Figure 2–24
A structure of the FC frame. The payload is the term used for the transmitted data.

Cables and Connectors

To be as flexible as possible, FC has four types of connectors: the *single mode* and *multimode* SC, the *coax*, and the *STP 9-pin* connectors for copper cable.

Fibre channel uses standard SC type optical connector for both single mode and multimode optical cables. Single mode optical cable is thinner and has less bandwidth than the multimode cable, but provides for longer distances (up to 10 km versus 500 m).

The connectors look similar (see Figure 2–25) but have different guides to prevent them from being used concurrently.

The optical cable consists of the optical fiber (core and cladding), which is coated with silicon and inserted into the protective buffer jacket, wrapped with a strengthening material, and inserted again inside the outer polyurethane jacket.

The optical core and cladding are typically made of silica and are responsible for guiding the light through the optical fiber. The optical fibers can be classified by the number of mode supports. A multimode fiber (Figure 2–26a) has either 50-micron or 62.5-micron diameter core with a 125-micron in diameter cladding. The cladding surround the core and, with its different optical properties, reflects the light back into the core, thus keeping it from leaving the fiber. The multimode optical fiber allows for many rays of light to travel inside simultaneously by bouncing back from the cladding layer. During this bouncing, some light intensity is lost, which reduces the total distance this method can be used over.

A single-mode fiber (Figure 2–26b) is made much thinner (9-micron core and 125-micron cladding) with much less light dispersion. This allows for a gigabit optical data transfer using the single-mode cables over distances up to 10 km.

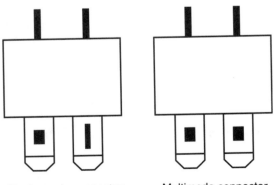

Single mode connector   Multimode connector

Figure 2–25
FC *single mode* and *multimode* connectors. The connectors look similar but have different guides to prevent them from being used concurrently.

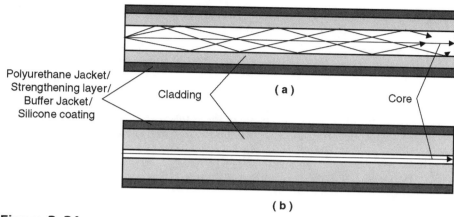

Polyurethane Jacket/
Strengthening layer/
Buffer Jacket/
Silicone coating

Cladding

(a)

Core

(b)

Figure 2–26
The optical fibers: (a) multimode and (b) single mode.

The bending of the optical cables must be limited to the bend radius of about 3 cm due to possible signal loss and data corruption, due to the effect bending has on the light path inside the cable. Also, the optical components of the cable may crack if bent too much.

FC Summary

In conclusion, it can be stated again that the Fibre Channel isn't meant to be *a channel nor a network*, but is designed for fast, reliable, and flexible interfacing of heterogeneous computer systems and peripherals with all the benefits of the above two methods using a so-called fabric.

Nowadays, Fibre Channel is the almost mandatory interface for high-end mass storage products, such as disk or tape drive arrays.

SSA (SERIAL STORAGE ARCHITECTURE) . . . .

SSA is another high-performance interface that provides high throughput (160 MB/sec) and has other useful features. SSA was introduced by IBM in 1991 as an alternative to the parallel SCSI-3 interface. SSA objectives were somewhat similar to those of FC-AL.

For example, SSA supports up to 128 total devices at distances up to 10 km with a fiber optic extender. SSA throughput is also impressive with up to 160 MB/sec maximum. It may sustain data rates as high as 90 MB/sec per adapter in non-RAID mode and 85 MB/sec in RAID mode. And in 8-way clusters, up to 600 MB/sec and 60,000 I/Os per second are possible. Like FC-AL, it maps the SCSI command set, making it possible for existing applications to migrate to Serial Storage Architecture-based subsystems.

Nevertheless, for one or another reason, the SSA technology didn't "take off" and the industry seems to be more interested in a similar Fibre Channel interface technology. I will not make predictions about the future of the SSA versus FC-AL battle. For example, IBM is still supporting this technology in its newest products. At the moment, Fibre Channel architecture looks like the high-end interface for enterprise environment in the near future.

INTERFACE SUMMARY . . . .

The following interface comparison summarizes the chapter.

- Serial: Set up is easy; external; slowest
- Parallel: Set up is easy; external; slow
- IDE. Set up is moderately difficult. For internal devices and short cables. Requires opening your PC and connecting some cables inside. Performance is much better than parallel or serial interface, or USB-devices and FireWire devices. Supports two devices per channel only.
- PC Card: Set up is easy. Good performance. Typically used for laptop computers and other mobile information devices.
- USB: Set up is very easy. Good performer. Hot-swappable. Requires Windows 98 and higher. Multiple devices (up to 127).
- IEEE 1394 FireWire: Set up is easy. Excellent performer. Costly. Requires Windows 98 and higher. For external devices mostly. Multiple devices (up to 63).
- SCSI: Set up is even more difficult than for IDE. Best performer. Best when multiple devices are used. Generally needs a separate SCSI card. Multiple devices (up to 15).
- FC-AL: High-end interface for enterprise environment. Setup is difficult. Expensive. Best performer over long distances (up to 10 km). Multiple devices (up to 127).

3

Magnetic Recording Storage Systems

In this chapter...

INTRODUCTION . . . .

Progress in magnetic recording technology in the last 40 years has been amazingly fast, with the density of recording for hard disk drives doubling every two years in the last decade. Newer technology typically translates into more data written on a smaller area (higher recording density), faster data transfer rates (higher performance), better reliability (lower cost of ownership), smaller size (mobility), lower cost, and so on.

Nowadays, magnetic storage devices range from old and proven floppy disk drives to the newest removable storage systems, like IBM 1 GB Microdrive or Iomega's 40 MB Clik! drive. These devices target different applications, have different designs, performance characteristics, and price tags. However, data storage and retrieval are all executed based upon the same underlying principles.

Magnetic storage devices such as the hard disk drive and tape drive, as well as the various removable storage devices (Zip, Jaz, Orb, Clik!, external hard disk drives, etc.) are discussed in this chapter from the viewpoint of their design, performance characteristics, cost, and target applications.

Hard disk drives are the fundamental elements of the modern computer systems that manage to combine the steady increase in storage density and capacity with the concomitant decrease in the cost per megabyte.

Tape drives, being even cheaper per megabyte stored than any other storage technology, continue to remain the best choice for data backup and for applications where access time is not critical.

Removable media storage devices have also evolved significantly from the small, slow floppy disk drive toward the much faster and higher storage capacity Zip, Jaz, and so on.

Table 3–1 illustrates the pace of this progress using two important parameters: areal density and slider/disk distance. Areal density is a storage capacity per unit area.

Table 3–1   Pace of Progress in Areal Density and Slider/Disk Distance

Year	Areal density (Mb/in²)	Slider/disk distance (nm)
1957	0.002	20,000
1980	1.25	320
1987	36	215
1990	100	150
1994	500	100
1997	1,000	30–60
2000	>10,000	10–20

The slider/disk distance, called a flying height, is the minimum distance between a flying slider and spinning disk. The data in the table are taken for the hard disk drives that always represent a combination of all the best this field has to offer.

In the first 35 years or so, the industry's high growth rate was attributed to the following factors:

- Fast computerization and increased demand for personal computers
- Migration from large mainframe computers with centralized storage toward small personal computers with individual storage units
- New families of computers: mobile computers
- Introduction of redundant array of independent drives (RAID), which consisted of more than one drive
- Greatly increased size of software products (operating systems [OS], graphic files, multimedia files, video, etc.). For example, the older DOS operating system required only one 1.44 MB floppy disk while the modern Windows 2000 OS occupies 10s of megabytes and comes on a compact disc (CD).

As often happens, this dynamic and profitable industry attracted new players and expanded to the point of complete market saturation when supply started exceeding the demand. The result was that the price of a megabyte of storage dropped dramatically in recent years (below $5 per GB), leaving most of the drive manufacturers with a much smaller profit margin or even "in the red." At the same time, the need for market domination forced the same companies to keep improving the technology even faster than before, rendering the hard disk drives into real high-tech bargains.

Nowadays, there is new hope for this industry. Currently, there are new driving forces:

- The Internet, as an information superhighway, will require massive storage capacities, meaning many hundreds and thousands of terabytes of data storage (terabyte = 1000 gigabytes).
- SANs (storage area networks), a corporate storage solution that, in most cases, uses RAID technology with multiple drives.
- Data backup requires large storage capacities and becomes mandatory since it is too expensive to lose data.
- New applications: that is, TiVo, digital cameras, PDA, and so on. Personal video recorders with internal storage based upon the hard disk drive. Digital cameras (Figure 3–1) and camcorders with data storage on a high-density floppy or on a small hard disk drive are another example.

Figure 3–1
A digital camera which uses the IBM Microdrive to store the images
(courtesy of IBM).

Despite the continuing development of the competing optics-based storage technologies, which will be discussed in future chapters, magnetic storage devices are still
better suited for the above-mentioned applications because, for example, of a better
combination of high performance, low cost per megabyte, and rewritability. Thus, new
changes bring new hope for even better and cheaper magnetic storage products.

This chapter reviews the fundamentals of magnetic storage technology and discusses the main storage systems that are based upon the principles of magnetics to
store the data.

BASIC PRINCIPLES OF MAGNETIC RECORDING . . . .

Magnetic Materials and Hysteresis Loop

A long time ago mankind discovered some natural materials, called the *lodestones*, that
could attract another lodestone or small pieces of iron. If a piece of this material is sus-
pended in the air, it aligns itself to follow the north-south direction. These materials are
called *natural magnets*.

A magnet has two poles: north (positive) and south (negative). But if the magnet
is cut into two parts, each of them will again have two opposite poles. Thus, the magnet

may have more than two poles but always an equal number of north and south poles. Also, *it is impossible* to make a magnet with only one pole. Magnetic poles produce the magnetic field, as shown in Figure 3–2 (only the field outside the magnet is shown).

When a magnetic field is first applied and then removed, some materials become magnetized permanently. This type of material is called *ferromagnetic*. Thus, a permanent magnet is composed of ferromagnetic material. The property of staying magnetized after the external magnetic field is gone can be illustrated using the so-called *hysteresis loop*, shown in Figure 3–3.

In Figure 3–3, **M** represents the magnetization, and **H** is the applied magnetic field. **Mr** is the residual, or *remnant magnetization*, left after the field **H** is removed. **Hc** is the reverse magnetic field needed to reduce the magnetization to zero, called the *coercivity*. The parameter **MrHc** measures the strength of the magnet.

The hysteresis loop is different for different materials. Some of them (iron, for example) are called "soft magnetic materials" and have low coercivity **Hc** and become

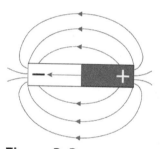

Figure 3–2
The magnetic poles produce the magnetic fields (only the field outside the magnet is shown).

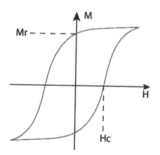

Figure 3–3
The property of a material to stay magnetized after the external magnetic field is gone can be illustrated using the so-called *hysteresis loop*.

magnetized and demagnetized relatively easily. Those materials aren't good for magnetic data storage since they can be accidentally demagnetized by relatively weak external magnetic fields and thereby lose the stored information. Other materials (ferroplatinum alloy, for example) have high **Hc** and are much harder to magnetize and demagnetize.

When a piece of magnetic material is brought close to a magnet, it also becomes a magnet, as shown in Figure 3–4. In this case, the direction of magnetization will become opposite to the one of the magnet, and the magnetization will depend on the properties of the material (**Hc**) and the field of the magnet (**M**).

Since the direction of magnetization of material 2 can be controlled by the direction of magnetization of magnet 1, and since there are only two possible directions (south and north), this can be used to store binary information. It can be agreed, for example, that the direction from "+" to "–" (or from "north" to "south") corresponds to a binary "1," and the opposite direction corresponds to a binary "0." In this case, the information can be stored magnetically in binary form (see Figure 3–5).

Let's assume we have a surface with a track formed on it of many similarly shaped magnets with different directions of magnetization. Then, the whole byte, for example, 11000101, can be written and stored magnetically (see Figure 3–6), where each rectangular magnetic area represents *one bit* of information.

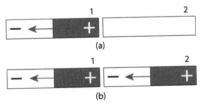

Figure 3–4
When a piece of magnetic material is brought close to a magnet (a), it also becomes a magnet (b).

Figure 3–5
It can be agreed, that the direction from "+" to "–" corresponds to a binary "1", and the opposite direction corresponds to a binary "0".

Figure 3–6
With a track formed out of many similar magnets with different directions of magnetization, the whole byte, for example, 11000101, can be written and stored magnetically.

Next, I discuss the main definitions of recording density and ways to increase the density of magnetic recording.

Density of Recording

Figure 3–7 shows how the data is organized physically on the recording medium. The bits of data are typically organized in concentric circles, forming a large number of so-called *data tracks*, or just *tracks*.

The following terms are used to describe the density of recording:

- Track density is defined as the number of tracks per unit length and is measured in tracks per inch, or tpi.
- Linear density (a bit density) is the number of bits per unit length and is measured in bits per inch, or bpi.
- Areal density equals the number of bits per unit area and is measured in bits per inch^2, or b/in^2. In today's systems having high recording density, it is more practical to specify areal density in Gb/in^2 ($10^9 \times$ b/in^2). Areal density can also be calculated by multiplying track density by bit density: b/in^2 = bpi $\times$ tpi.

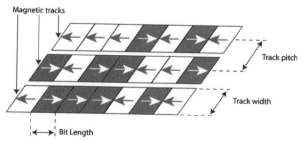

Figure 3–7
The bits of data are typically organized in concentric circles forming the so-called *data tracks*.

Since areal density is the product of bpi and tpi, higher areal density can be achieved by increasing one or both of them. Among the magnetic recording storage technologies (tape, Zip, floppy, etc.), hard disk drives have the highest density of magnetic recording.

Reading Data with Inductive Heads

A device that reads and writes data on magnetic media is called a "magnetic head." The initial design of both read and write magnetic heads was based upon Faraday's law and the principles of magnetic induction (in fact, the same head was used for reading and writing). Faraday's law states that if a conducting loop of **n** turns is subject to a transient magnetic flux ϕ, then the *electromotive force* **V**, or *emf*, is induced in this loop and is proportional to the rate of change of this flux ϕ: $\mathbf{V} = -\mathbf{n}\, d\phi/d\mathbf{t}$, where **t** is the time. The unit of electromotive force is the *volt*, the unit of time is the *second*, and the unit of magnetic flux is *weber*.

Figure 3–8 shows the basic design of an *inductive read head* moving over the magnetic track with every bit behaving as a magnet with one of two possible directions of magnetization.

The head's magnetic yoke "senses" the fields in the bits while passing over them. The field inside the yoke is changing continuously at a rate that is dependent on the relative speed of the head (or medium), and this generates an *emf* in the coils.

More then one coil is typically used to increase the head's sensitivity (output voltage). The field in the yoke and the current in the coils change direction when the bit

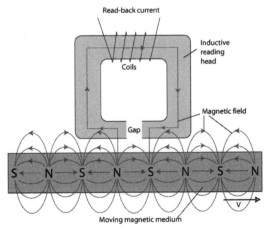

Figure 3–8
The basic design of an *inductive read head* moving over the magnetic track.

magnetization changes direction. When the head passes the junction of two bits with the opposite magnetization, the following output voltage is measured (see Figure 3–9).

Figure 3–10 shows how a real track looks when measured with magnetic force microscopy (MFM), a technique that images the magnetic field in a medium. Light areas correspond to positive (see Figure 3–9) and dark to negative transitions. Figure 3–10 also specifies the dimensions of the track and a bit of data. The data encoded into this track is just a sequence of ones: 1,1,1,1,1,1,1,…

In real recording systems, the information is encoded not inside the bits, but in the bit transitions where the magnetization changes (or not) its direction. If two adjacent bits have the same magnetization, then they look like one larger area with the same direction of magnetization, and the head doesn't detect any transition. This is considered to be a "0." If the direction of magnetization changes between two bits, it creates a magnetic flux "irregularity," which is sensed by the head and interpreted as a "1."

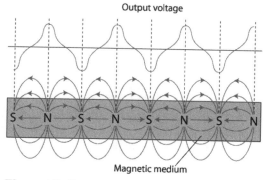

Figure 3–9
When the head passes the junction of two bits with the opposite magnetization, the following output voltage is measured.

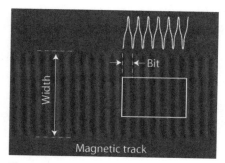

Figure 3–10
The way a real track looks when measured with the magnetic force microscopy (MFM)—a technique that images the magnetic field in a medium.

Summary

The reading process includes excitation of the current in the head coil when the head "senses" changes in the magnetic flux. The read voltage, which pulses at the flux transitions, is then translated into sequences of bits equal to 0s and 1s.

The so-called Wallace's spacing loss factor postulates that *the loss of magnetic signal power is proportional to the media—magnetic head separation.* This requires magnetic heads to move as close to the disk surface as possible, which forces modern heads in the hard disk drives to fly at only a few nanometers above the disk surface (compare this to 20,000 nanometers back in 1957!). Some head designs—in the floppy disk drive, for example—utilize a contact recording scheme when the head, in order to minimize the magnetic spacing, continuously slides over the medium.

Data Reading: Magnetoresistive (MR) Heads

The need for higher density of magnetic recording eventually forced a switch from the inductive heads to a different type of read head: MR or magnetoresistive head.

This new type of read head was introduced in 1971 on the basis of the magnetoresistive effect observed in some materials such as Ni-Fe, Ni-Co, and Co-Fe as a *change in the material's electrical resistance in the presence of an external magnetic field.* Today's magnetic read heads for high-density systems (HDD, Jaz, ORB, high-density tapes) are typically the MR (magnetoresistive) or GMR (giant MR) heads, which is the evolution of the MR heads having much higher sensitivity. A basic simplified design of the magnetoresistive head is shown in Figure 3–11.

As mentioned above, the MR head design is based on the ability of magnetoresistive materials to change resistively in the presence of a magnetic field. This effect

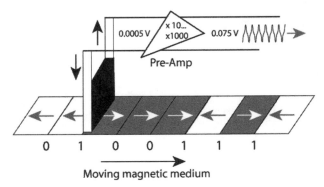

Figure 3–11
A simplified design of the magnetoresistive head.

was first discovered in 1857. The MR read element basically consists of a narrow stripe made of material with relatively high magnetoresistance, which has electrical contacts on both sides. The alloy of Ni and Fe (81% and 19%) is widely used in MR heads and is called *Permalloy*. MR heads are suitable for extremely high bit density and have superior signal-to-noise ratio when compared to the inductive read heads.

A signal from the MR head can be increased by increasing the current passing through it, which is not possible for an inductive head.

One more advantage of the MR head compared to the inductive read head is the following: unlike the inductive head, MR head isn't too sensitive to the medium velocity. The inductive head reads a stronger signal when the flux changes at a higher rate. Practically speaking, all the drives using magnetic recording principles have their disks spinning at high constant angular velocities. This means that the read head moves over magnetic media at different relative velocities at different radii and, therefore, the strength of the read-back signal becomes location-dependent for the inductive head. In the case of the MR head, its sensitivity is speed and it is location independent.

Also, the use of separate read (MR) and write (inductive) heads allows for a completely independent optimization of each head and improves the overall performance of the magnetic recording system.

Recording or Writing Data

In order to write the data on a magnetic medium, the basic design of the magnetic inductive head, illustrated in Figure 3–12, is used.

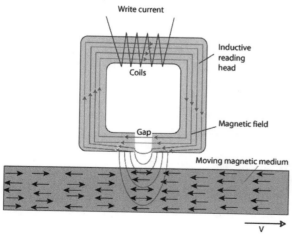

Figure 3–12
Data writing with the magnetic inductive head.

The magnetic flux in the write inductive head is delivered to the writing poles by a magnetic yoke. The flux is generated in the yoke when the current representing the signal to be recorded is fed to the writing coil around the yoke. The gap in the pole pieces of a recording head is designed to produce a field amplitude capable of recording the storage medium to a sufficient depth. The width of the gap affects the length of the written bit. The width of the inductive head defines the width of the bit.

When the magnetic field is applied to a medium having longitudinal anisotropy (the most commonly used type today, which "prefers" to be magnetized in the longitudinal direction), a predominantly longitudinal magnetization of the affected area occurs. When the applied magnetic field is strong enough, magnetic domains in the medium acquire the same direction of magnetization as the magnetic flux.

Figure 3–12 shows that instance when the head is positioned above the next bit of data to be written, when the magnetic field is generated and subsequently penetrates the surface where the magnetization hasn't yet changed.

In summary, the process of data recording occurs in the following sequence:

- The write channel receives binary data to be stored and generates a corresponding current.
- The writing current is sent to the head coil.
- The current in the coil causes magnetization of the head yoke, and the field in the gap spreads out and reaches the medium.
- The medium magnetization in one of two possible directions occurs.

Figure 3–13 illustrates the above writing sequence.

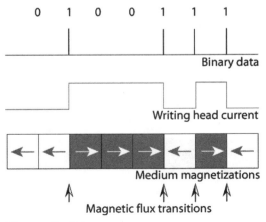

Figure 3–13
An illustration of the writing sequence.

The drive channel electronically receives the data in a binary form from the computer and converts it into the head coil current. The current in the coils reverses at each 1 and remains the same at each 0. This current interacts with the media and results in magnetization of the media, with the direction of magnetization dependent on the direction of the current in the coils.

Also, before the data is written, it has to be properly encoded, which is discussed next.

Data Encoding

Coding is the process of transforming data using a definite set of rules. The binary data can be recorded in the storage media *directly*, or in a somewhat changed form after *frequency modulation*. Modern recording systems use different frequency modulation techniques to address several issues such as:

- Signal timing loss
- DC (direct current) content elimination
- Signal dropouts

Before it is stored in the recording medium, a binary stream of 0s and 1s should be encoded in the most efficient way to maximize the recording density and to provide satisfactory reliability. This procedure is often called *channel coding*. Later, during reading, the signal is converted back into its original binary form by the read channel element, called the *decoder*.

Amplitude instabilities observed in a signal are called *dropouts* and come from defective areas of the recording media, from magnetic spacing fluctuations, and so on. The dropout causes not only a decrease in the signal, but the timing error in signal.

Since the signal detection mechanism operates on an external oscillator, which needs to be resynchronized as often as possible, the data stream without embedded timing marks may confuse the detection mechanism and cause timing errors. For example, variations in the recording media speed can be one reason for a timing error. Timing loss occurs also when the data is represented as a long sequence of, for example, 0s, which is not *a self-clocking sequence*. Properly selected *self-clocking* channel code can eliminate or minimize these effects.

There are several major encoding schemes used in a digital magnetic recording and these are discussed next.

Non-Return to Zero Code: NRZ-L

The logic of this code (see Figure 3–14) is that we record '1' as a positive medium magnetization and '0' as a negative magnetization. Unfortunately, this simple code is not self-clocking since it doesn't have a built-in mechanism for making sure that synchronization will occur often enough since the *maximum time between two transitions* could be infinitely long, causing timing errors (if the data contains a "loooooooong" sequence of 0s, for example).

Also, if a noise spike occurs in the middle of this long string of 0s (or 1s), then the entire string following the spike will be recorded as 1s (or 0s). This is called *error propagation* and must not be allowed.

Non-Return to Zero Code: NRZ-M

This is one of the oldest codes with the following logic: every '1' has a transition (negative or positive, whichever turn it is) and all zeros are just ignored (see Figure 3–15). This prevents the *propagation* of a possible error. But this method isn't self-clocking either (since the maximum time between two transitions could still be infinitely long), and also cannot distinguish between '0' and a possible amplitude dropout.

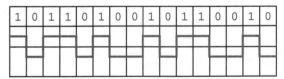

Figure 3–14
Non-Return to Zero -L (NRZ-L) code.

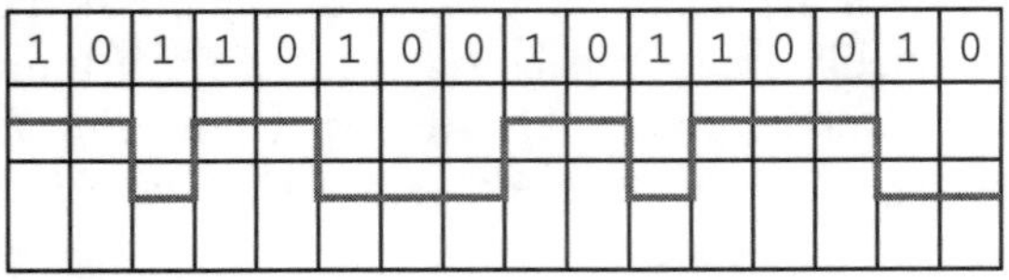

Figure 3–15
Non-Return to Zero -M (NRZ-M) code.

Bi-Phase (Manchester, or FM) Code

This code is known as a frequency doubling code, and was designed to address the self-clocking issue (see Figure 3–16). The basis of this code is in adding an extra transition at the beginning of each bit: the DC content is then eliminated and a signal synchronization becomes possible by synchronizing on the extra transitions. This code is used in some magnetic tapes, low density floppy disks, card readers, airspace recorders, and so on. The FM code requires the bandwidth twice that of the data, but the maximum time between two transitions is only 1 bit.

MFM (Miller) Code

This coding technique (see Figure 3–17) was widely used before in hard disk drives, floppy disk drives, and high-density digital tape drives. MFM code doesn't use excessive (clocking) transitions except for those separating the sequences of 0s. The code was patented by Miller (from Ampex) in 1963 and eliminated potential problems with long strings of 0s while losing self-locking for each bit (it now occurs at intervals no longer than 2 bits). Nevertheless, this code packs twice as much data as the FM code.

RLL (Run Length Limited)

This is a modern encoding technique used in hard disk drives to increase the amount of useful information in the coded data. This code has more complex logic and pro-

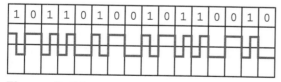
Figure 3–16
Bi-Phase (Manchester, or FM) code.

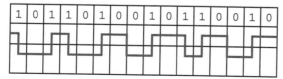
Figure 3–17
MFM (Miller) code.

vides for higher density of useful data. RLL transforms data bit into bytes. For example, RLL (1,7) transforms each two bits of user data into three channel bits using a specially provided look-up table, and has the maximum distance between two transitions equal to 7 bits. The *run-length* in RLL refers to the number of consecutive 0s before the appearance of a 1. This code and its advanced derivatives are now used for high-density storage.

Read Channel

Now that we understand how the data is physically encoded, written, and read, let's look at a bigger picture of the read and write channels (Figure 3–18).

Before the user's data is written on the disk, and even before it is encoded, it passes an ECC (Error Correction Code) encoder, where some extra information is added to it. This extra information allows for error detection and correction later, when the data is retrieved. After the data is encoded using the RLL (for modern hard disk drives) encoding scheme, it is written on the disk. The read channel then takes care of reading, conditioning, decoding, and correcting the data.

First, the amplified analog read-back signal goes through a low-pass filter, which limits the signal's bandwidth and noise entering the detection process (see Chapter 1 for ADC). The noise is proportional to the total bandwidth of the signal, and its high-frequency cutoff deals with high-frequency noise. Clearly, the filter should allow for only the useful signal to pass. After the low-pass filter, the signal is being equalized.

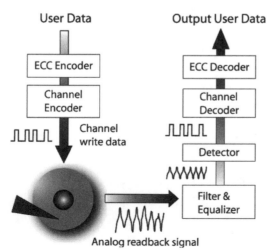

Figure 3–18
Read and write channels and data processing sequence.

Equalization, or the amplitude equalization process, compensates the signal for high- and low-frequency losses in order to restore the signal to as close as possible to the original. This compensation is made by the amplifier that boosts the low and high frequencies. After that, the signal is ready to enter the signal detector.

The older signal detector process is called *peak detection*. The way this method works is shown in Figure 3–19.

To recognize real data from noise and disturbances in the signal, the peak detector focuses on the peaks of the readback voltage (zero crossing for the differentiated signal). If the signal exceeds the clip level and fits into the clock window, it is considered to be a "1," otherwise, it's a "0."

When recording density is low, then magnetic transitions are relatively isolated, and the peak detection method is well-suited for the purpose. As the bit density increases, the possibility of *inter-symbol interference* (ISI) and signal overlap increases too, making it difficult to separate signals by "simple" peak detection. This is when the newer signal detection technology, PRML, becomes a necessity.

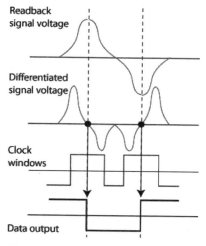

Figure 3–19
The procedure used in *peak detection* process.

PRML (Partial Response Maximum Likelihood)

PRML first digitizes the analog signal, and then works with the digital signal in order to detect the peaks. PRML employs digital signal processing (DSP) and maximum likelihood detection to find the data that was *most likely stored on the disk.*

PRML is based on two major assumptions:

- The shape of the read-back signal for an isolated transition is known exactly
- The superposition of the signals occurs linearly.

PRML can be considered to be a two-stage process. First, *partial response* (PR) results in a sampled signal. This sampling occurs fast enough to have more than one point per recorded bit. Second, the *maximum likelihood* (ML) detector addresses the entire waveform (a group of datapoints) and determines the most probable binary sequence for a given waveform. The ML detector continuously queries the most probable outcome for the particular sequence detected. Eventually, it determines the most probable outcome.

With the help of PRML, the effect of inter-symbol interference (ISI) is greatly reduced and the density of recording can be increased dramatically by placing bits closer to each other.

Limits of Magnetic Recording: Superparamagnetism

A current rate of areal density growth, which is about 60% a year, pushes magnetic recording systems toward the so-called *superparamagnetic limit.* With the present (end of 2000) demonstrated recording areal density equal to 54 GB/in² (Hitachi), it will take just a few years to reach this limit, which is predicted to be around 100 GB/in². This is the major concern in the field of magnetic recording (especially among the manufacturers of the high-density hard disk drives) and has prompted considerable research directed toward overcoming this major limitation.

First, what is this limit?

Every bit of data consists of hundreds of smaller magnetized areas, called *magnetic grains*, that are all magnetized in mostly the same direction and form the bit's magnetic field. In the current hard disk drives, magnetic grains are as small as ~10 nm in diameter. A boundary of two adjacent bits is shown in Figure 3–20.

Increasing recording density is equivalent to decreasing the bit size (and the track pitch), which translates into smaller grain size. Unfortunately, the smaller the grain (and its volume), the faster it loses its remnant magnetization. If the grain size becomes

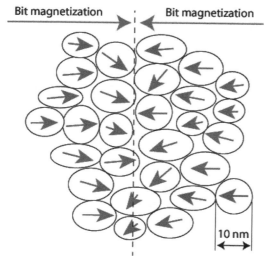

Figure 3–20
A boundary of two adjacent magnetic bits.

too small, the grain becomes demagnetized so fast that it cannot be used as a storage medium any longer. This phenomenon is called *superparamagnetism*. The basic concept of this phenomenon was introduced by Néel in 1949 and further developed by Brown in 1963.

Fortunately, there are some ways to circumvent this phenomenon. Some of the most promising techniques are listed below:

- *Perpendicular magnetic recording*. If the bits have a vertical magnetic orientation (not horizontal or longitudinal, as in most current systems), the bit volume can be increased by making it longer (deeper), thus moving away from the critical dimensions. The areal density can also be increased by packing those smaller bits more densely.

- *Anti-ferromagnetic coupled (AFC) media*. The magnetic layer is made of two separated parallel layers, which have opposite magnetization. The read-write head sees the upper layer only, while the effective storing "volume" of the bit is made of the volume of two layers and is consequently much larger.

- *Patterned magnetic media*. Instead of a matrix of nonuniform in size and magnetization magnetic grains, this method suggests an array of bits that are uniformly distributed and similar in size and magnetic properties. These bits are long, perpendicularly oriented, and well separated, which helps them to preserve their magnetization at a very small bit size. In fact, with this technique, a bit can be made of a single grain, as it is shown in Figure 3–21.

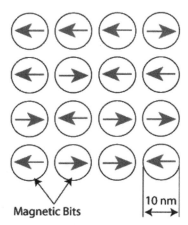

Magnetic Bits

10 nm

Figure 3–21
Design of the patterned magnetic media.

Unfortunately, there are still many problems that need to be overcome with the approaches outlined above. With continued research, these newer technologies should allow for magnetic recording density to successfully exceed 100 Gb/in^2.

HARD DISK DRIVE ....

Introduction

Introduced in 1957, the IBM-made random access method of accounting and control (RAMAC) was the first disk drive. It consisted of 50 magnetic disks of 24-inch diameter rotating at 1,200 RPM (rotations per minute).

Two air-bearing supported magnetic heads accessed all 50 disks. The total storage capacity of this system was 5 MB, with a data rate of 12.5 KB/s. The system was typically rented off to the end user for about $130 a month. The system used aluminum sliders, Mu-metal heads, had densities of 20 tpi and 0.002 Mb/in^2, and the slider/disk spacing was about 20 micrometers (or 20,000 nm).

This disk drive can be contrasted to its evolutionary disk drive achieved some 40 years later, the IBM Microdrive. The Microdrive drive has thin-film 1-inch disks and 2 ceramic sliders with GMR heads flying over the disk surface at only about a few tens nm. The track density is 16,000 tpi (track per inch) and the areal density is 4.1 GB/in^2. The drive's 33.3 MB/sec data transfer rate benefits from the Ultra DMA interface technology (see Chapter 2). This drive is so small that it finds its way into such applications as PDA, digital cameras, and handheld computers (see Figure 3–22).

Figure 3–22
Handheld computer with the IBM Microdrive storage.

A computer needs a hard disk drive (HDD) to store the operating system (OS), application programs, and the user's data. Fierce competition between the drive manufacturers has pushed the cost of a GB of data to a very small number of less than $3 to $5 per GB, rendering an HDD of several GB in capacity is relatively inexpensive and easily affordable by almost anyone. The HDD is one of the most important components of the modern PC: no application will run reasonably without the hard drive.

The HDD is based upon magnetic recording technology, the principles of which were discussed earlier in this chapter. The HDD combines the most recent achievements in the science and technology of magnetic recording, materials science and technology, and digital signal processing (DSP, see Chapter 1).

Drive Manufacturers

Unlike many other computer products, HDD manufacturing is limited to a relatively small group of furiously competing companies. All of them are publicly traded companies, except for Seagate Technology (since recently). A list of HDD manufacturers is compiled below. Their corresponding URL addresses (for HDD products) are provided as well.

IBM Corporation (*www.storage.ibm.com*)

Seagate Technology (*www.seagate.com*)

Quantum Corporation (*www.quantum.com*)

Maxtor Corporation (*www.maxtor.com*) (was recently acquired by Quantum)

Hitachi, Ltd. (*www.hitachi.com/products/information/storage2/index.html*, or go to *www.hitachi.com* and navigate to Storage Devices)

Toshiba Corporation (*www.toshiba.com/taecdpd/*)

Fujitsu, Ltd. (*www.fujitsu.com/products/prod_bus_it_storage.html*)

Samsung Electronics (*www.samsungcanada.com/products/infosys/isintro.htm*)

HDD Technology

Read/write elements and magnetic media are important components of the HDD.

The magnetic read head of a modern HDD is typically an MR (magnetoresistive) or GMR (giant MR) head (see earlier in the chapter). The write head is a thin-film inductive head. The basic design of the HDD's magnetic heads is shown in Figure 3–23.

Continuous improvement in the head design allowed for extremely high densities of magnetic recording, with magnetic bits getting smaller and smaller. However, the head is only one component of the magnetic recording system, with magnetic media being extremely important as well. The first magnetic media was called a "particulate media" because it included particles of iron oxide (as the magnetic medium) and aluminum oxide (for abrasive resistance). Modern magnetic media is called "thin-film media" and consists of very thin layers with a total thickness of about 500 to 1,000 angstroms or 50 to 100 nm. Figure 3–24 presents a schematic of a thin-film magnetic hard disk.

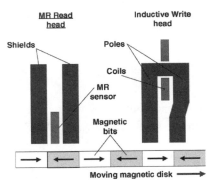

Figure 3–23
Basic design of the HDD's magnetic head.

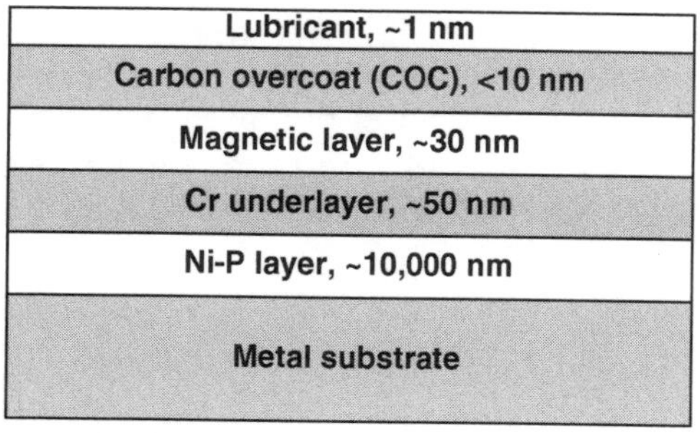

Lubricant, ~1 nm
Carbon overcoat (COC), <10 nm
Magnetic layer, ~30 nm
Cr underlayer, ~50 nm
Ni-P layer, ~10,000 nm
Metal substrate

Figure 3–24
Basic design of the thin-film magnetic rigid disk (out of scale).

The layering is achieved by the sequential physical vapor deposition on the metal or glass disk (when the atoms of different materials are deposited on the surface with a minimum of chemical reaction involved). Since the magnetic layer stores all of the data, it represents the most valuable asset in the structure. This layer is typically about a few hundreds Angstrom thick. However, this layer must be protected from the intermittent contact with the head and requires both a hard carbon overcoat and a thin film of lubricant. As they reduce the "wear" of the disk surface, the topmost two layers are relevant for the tribological durability of the disk structure.

The reasons for having a thin carbon layer are simple: it increases the mechanical durability of the disk and mitigates corrosion of the magnetic layer. This carbon is sometimes called a "diamond-like carbon (DLC)" since it has structural components similar to a diamond, in addition to amorphous and graphitic carbon. Table 3–2 compares hardness values for a few well-known materials and demonstrates how hard the DLC is.

Table 3–2   Hardness Values

Material	Hardness (Vickers, GPa)
Diamond	70–100
DLC (diamond-like carbon)	10–50
Silicon	10–12
Glass	12
Aluminum	0.25
Gold	0.66

A thin layer of lubricant on the top is used to minimize wear of a carbon layer. Quite amazingly, the thickness of the lubricant has decreased to the nano-scale levels over many years to allow the magnetic head to fly lower for higher recording density. The thickness of today's lubricant is in the tens of Angstrom regime. The science required to formulate these robust lubricants can be quite astonishing!

Basic Drive Design

Nowadays, hard disk drives come in different sizes or form-factors: 3.5-inch, 2.5-inch, 2-inch, 1-inch, and others.

Every hard drive has one or more disks, or platters (which store magnetic data), typically twice as many sliders with magnetic heads (to read and write data), an actuator arm (to hold the suspension with the slider at the end), and a voice-coil actuator (VCA) (to move the actuator when the head is accessing data) (see Figure 3–25). The drive is connected to the computer via an interface connector.

The disk drive manufacturers always present their drives to the potential buyers with the cover removed (see Figure 3–26). Since, the basic design of all drives is quite similar, the only important difference in the picture of the opened drive is the location of the parked head.

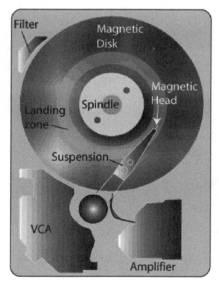

Figure 3–25
A schematic of the CSS drive.

The head can be parked closer to the center of the disk (on the disk surface, Figure 3–26) or on the outer diameter of the disk (on a special ramp, see Figure 3–27).

This difference represents a major difference in drive design, ideology, and technology: the difference between contact start-stop drives (CSS) and load-unload (L/U) drives.

The idea behind CSS is that when the drive is turned off and the slider is not flying, it is parked (landed) on a specially made landing zone. This landing zone consists

Figure 3–26
Modern CSS hard disk drive (IBM Deskstar family, courtesy of IBM).

Figure 3–27
Modern load-unload hard disk drive (IBM Ultrastar family, courtesy of IBM).

of tiny bumps (made by a short laser burst) that protrude from the disk surface. The slider rests on them until the next power-on cycle.

The reason for using these bumps is the following: the disk surface is so smooth that the slider, if allowed to land on it, will stick to the surface, thereby preventing the disk from spinning during the next power-on cycle, possibly damaging the head suspension. To prevent this, the disk surface is artificially roughened, locally forming a narrow circular landing zone closer to the center of the disk.

A durability of CSS drives is usually measured in CSS cycles (landing–take-off cycles). A typically advertised number of power-on/off cycles is about 40,000 to 50,000. Nowadays, the CSS design can be found in drives for most desktop computers, many mobile drives, and many of the drives for high-end servers.

The newest mobile and some of the high-end server drives use a different technology called Load-Unload (L/U), where the slider is parked on a special ramp when the drive is turned off (see Figures 3–27 and 3–28).

The main advantages of L/U systems are summarized below:

- Improved nonoperational shock resistance for greater disk durability and longevity
- Reduced power consumption for cost savings
- Potentially higher durability and life of the drive

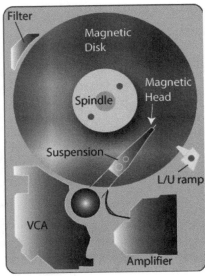

Figure 3–28
A schematic of the load-unload drive.

Improved shock resistance comes from the fact that the suspension together with the sliders rests (when the drive is off) on a specially designed ramp and not on the disk itself, as in the case of a CSS drive. When the drive experiences a shock, the slider and disk in the CSS drive are in direct contact and could be damaged. In an L/UL system, the slider on the ramp will be much less affected, and the media will not be affected at all. This feature is especially important for those drives used in mobile computers, handheld devices, digital cameras, and so on—in all devices exposed to impacts and vibrations.

A reduced power consumption in the L/UL design is attributed to the fact that the slider and disk are not in contact at rest. This is to be contrasted with the CSS drives, where, upon power-on, the slider is dragged on the disk surface before it can attain its nominal flying velocity (and spacing). The friction associated with the slider/disk contact causes extra energy to be drained from the drive's battery. Again, reduced power consumption is mostly valuable for the mobile computers that are frequently turned on and off.

A potentially higher durability of the L/UL system is directly attributed to the lack of slider/disk contact, where media damage and data loss is considerably reduced.

The main elements of the L/U drive are shown in Figure 3–28. L/U design is relatively new, and most companies still use a more traditional CSS technology.

Referring to Figure 3–28, a recirculation filter in the upper-left corner of the drive serves to remove particulate contaminants within the drive enclosure. Since the gap between the flying slider and rapidly spinning disk is small, large particles can cause considerable damage to the disk media, possibly making the drive crash.

The filter may additionally act as a desiccant to reduce the humidity inside the drive. High humidity enhances adhesion (stiction) between the sliders and the platters. Sometimes the stiction becomes so high that the drive spindle is unable to rotate the disk without causing mechanical damage to the suspension/slider system, resulting in data loss. Another reason why lower humidity inside the drive enclosure is desirable is to reduce corrosion of the metal surfaces inside the drive.

Now let's take a look at the slider/disk interface of the modern hard disk drive.

In order to keep the magnetic head as close to the disk surface as possible, a self-pressurized air-bearing design is used for the sliders (see Figure 3–29). Nowadays, the minimum gap between the slider and the disks is on the order of a few nanometers.

To get a feeling for what a "few nanometers" is, let's recall that a human hair is about 30 microns in diameter (1 micron = 1,000 nm) and an average bacteria is typically a few hundred nanometers in size. Using some imagination, the following example could be also used as an illustration.

If the slider/disk interface of the modern magnetic hard disk drive is scaled up to the extent that the slider becomes as long as a Boeing 747 jumbo-jet, then the following will emerge (see Figure 3–30).

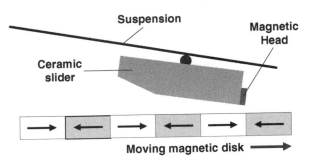

Figure 3–29
Slider/disk interface of the modern hard disk drive.

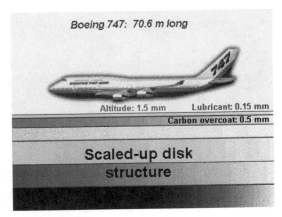

Figure 3–30
When the modern magnetic hard drive is scaled up to the extent that the slider becomes as long as a Boeing 747 jumbo-jet.

The slider-airplane will be flying at the altitude of a few mm only at the speed of approximately 65 mph periodically landing on its belly and taking off again for about 50,000 times. And yet the surface, our "airport," which consists of a few mm-thick layers, will stay intact for years. Plus, both the airplane and the airport will never be serviced or repaired.

In conclusion, all this incredible nano-scale technology does not cost millions, but just a few hundred dollars!

Physical Drive Dimensions and Performance

Today's drives come in several different sizes or so-called form factors. Each form factor is defined by an external dimension (width) and is traditionally measured in inches. Industry-standard form factors are typically 1.8", 2.5", 3.0", 3.5", and 5.25". Some other form factors can be found in newer products.

The largest available hard disk drives now are 3.5" drives, which are used in high-end servers, workstations, and desktop computers along with 3" and 2.5" disks. The drives used in servers are optimized for speed and have low error rates to deliver the highest possible data transfer rates at higher costs. In contrast, the desktop drives are optimized for low cost and usually have average performance except for the more expensive models.

1.8" and 2.5" drives are most suitable for mobile devices, like laptop computers. Their design is optimized for higher recording density and higher storage capacity at the expense of performance and cost.

Some new form factors, such as the 1" IBM Microdrive (see Figure 3–31), have emerged to meet an increasing demand for smaller drives with large capacity and fast data access. At present, the IBM Microdrive provides up to 1 GB of storage capacity. This type of drive targets video camcorders, personal digital assistants (PDA), smart cell-phones, and so on.

Figure 3–31
IBM Microdrive next to a quarter (courtesy of IBM).

Basic Drive Concepts

MTBF (Mean Time Before Failure)

MTBF is typically obtained by dividing the total number of operation hours observed by the total number of failures. Therefore, MTBF is measured in hours.

Today's drives are highly reliable with high MTBF on the order of 300,000 hours, which translates into 34 years of continuous operation, that is, for 24 hours a day, 365 days a year. Still, hard disk drives occasionally fail.

There are two kinds of failures, *predictable* and *unpredictable*, and they may occur gradually or quickly. The drive may fail unpredictably due to a design flow or some rare manufacturing defect. The drive's electronics, for example, may fail unexpectedly during a power surge. If the reason for this failure affects a large population of drives, it would most likely be detected before the drive becomes commercially available.

MTBF is a good measure of drive reliability, although it doesn't help the selection of the drive as most drive manufacturers report about the same MTBF numbers or, instead, just a number of cycles to failure.

Another kind of failure, predictable failure, is associated with a slow degradation of mechanical and electronic components of the drive. This type of failure can be predicted to some extent and will be discussed below in reference to a **S.M.A.R.T** system.

Data Transfer Rate (DTR)

The speed at which bits of data are sent is called data transfer rate, or DTR. For example, this could describe the speed at which the bits of information are read from the disk and sent to the drive's controller (*internal data rate*), or characterize the data exchange between the controller and PC's CPU (*external data rate*).

Rotational Latency

The average time it takes for a bit of data on the disk to rotate under the read element after the later was positioned over the needed track.

Seek Time

The average time required for a magnetic head to move to a new required track.

Track

A concentric set of magnetic bits on the disk is called a track. Each track is (usually) divided into 512-byte sectors (see Figure 3–32).

Sector

A part of each track defined with magnetic marking and an ID number. Sectors have a sector header and an error correction code (ECC). In modern drives, sectors are numbered sequentially (see Figure 3–32).

Cylinder

A group of tracks with the same radius is called a cylinder (see Figure 3–32).

Data Addressing

There are two methods for a drive's data addressing: CHS (cylinder-head-sector) and LBA (logical block address). CHS is used in most IDE drives, while LBA is used in SCSI and enhanced IDE drives (see Figure 3–32).

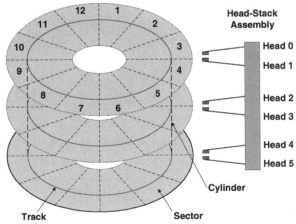

Figure 3–32
Logical design of the hard disk drive.

CHS locates data by simply specifying the cylinder (radius), head (platter and its side), and sector (angular position). LBA assigns each sector of the drive a sequential number, which is simpler.

If you look into your BIOS, you will find listed the number of cylinders, heads, and sectors for each drive you have. The BIOS makes it possible for a computer to boot itself. On PCs, the BIOS contains all the code required to control the disk drives, keyboard, display, serial communications, and some other functions. The BIOS is typically found on a ROM (read-only memory) chip, which comes with the computer.

Modern operating systems access data using LBA directly without the help of the BIOS. This helps to reduce incompatibilities.

Cache or Buffer

To improve performance and increase data rates, HDD utilizes a small amount of fast solid-state memory to store the most frequently used data. This memory is called cache, or buffer. It bridges data from the disk to the interface, since they operate at different data transfer rates. Retrieving data from the cache is much faster than from the disk (microseconds compared to milliseconds). In modern drives, cache memory often exceeds 1 MB.

For example, when a PC sends a read command to a drive, it first checks for requested data in the cache. If the data is in the cache, it can be accessed quickly and sent to the PC. If it isn't in the cache, the drive will find and read the data from the disk and transfer them to the cache. In fact, the drive will read more data than is requested, thus trying to guess the next possible PC request. This guess is typically quite good, since most applications process data sequentially and it is likely that the next request will be made for the data that follow the last request. This type of cache is referred to as *read cache* or *look-ahead cache*.

When the data is written on the disk, a similar approach can be used to speed up system performance. When the PC sends some data to the drive, it then waits for a confirmation that the task is completed. Since the data writing may take some time for a large block of data, this may slow the PC down significantly. Instead, the drive will place those data in the cache (which is done very quickly) and immediately respond to the PC that the task is completed, even if the data isn't stored on the disk yet! Then, a PC can forget about this task and proceed to other tasks. Thus, a large cache is clearly beneficial for the drive and PC performance, and is a good investment.

Formatting

Low-Level Formatting

Formatting is the first step in making the drive ready for data storage and retrieval. At this stage, the drive is being physically divided into tracks and sectors.

Low-level formatting stays unchanged for the entire life of the drive unless the drive is reformatted. Nowadays, drives are usually sold with low-level formatting already done.

Partitioning

Partitioning divides the drive into logical drives (C:, D:, E:, etc.). Every drive has at least one "primary partition" (C:) and may have many extended partitions. The primary partition contains drive-booting information in the Master Boot Record (MBR) and also keeps a record of all other partitions. A partition is usually made using the FDISK.exe program. The following procedure is typically used to partition the drive on a PC:

1. Remind yourself that all information present on the drive will be destroyed if you **complete step 2**!
2. Type "fdisk" command in a DOS window and press Enter.
3. Select "Create DOS partition or logical DOS drive" by pressing 1. Then press Enter.
4. Select "Create Primary DOS partition" by pressing 1. Create your first drive partition. To make this partition bootable, specify the partition as *active*.
5. Verify that all drive space was partitioned. If needed, create an extended partition with extra logical drives.

If the FDISK program doesn't work with the drive, type "fdisk/status" to check if your drive is present.

High-Level Formatting

High-level formatting prepares drive partitions for the operating system by creating a root directory, from which all other subdirectories can be created, and creating a File Allocation Table (FAT), which keeps track of all information on the disks and all the relationships between different pieces of information. A loss of the FAT is equivalent to loss of data, since the system will not be able to attribute data to the specific files even if the data themselves are intact. This operation is usually done using the FOR-MAT.exe program. The following procedure is typically used to format a drive on a PC:

1. Remind yourself that all information present on the drive will be destroyed if you complete step 2 below using the **wrong drive letter**!
2. In the DOS window, type "format x:/s," where x: is the letter of your first partition. Repeat the formatting process for all new partitions.

File System

The file system is a high-level environment allowing the user to interact with the data stored in files on various storage systems. It allows the user to actually address data as files by keeping track of the file location, name, length, and so on.

There are three primary file systems on today's IBM-based PC:

- FAT16 (DOS and Windows 3.x)
- FAT32 (Windows 95 and higher)
- NTFS (Windows NT)

The main problem with FAT16 is that it is unable to address more than 2.1 GB of data on each logical drive of the hard disk—a small number by today's standards. This means that if you use a FAT16 file system with a larger drive, you will be forced to partition it with the FDISK program to logical disks no larger than 2 GB. Otherwise, you will lose some of the drive's capacity. This is getting harder to do with modern disk drives of 20 GB in capacity and more. Another problem is with the way FAT16 divides sectors into clusters: the cluster size is only 2 KB for logical disks less than 128 MB and 32 KB when the disk size exceeds 1 GB. This means that the system will allocate 32 KB for even the smallest files of 1 KB.

There is no problem with addressing data with FAT32 and NTSF systems. At least, problems won't appear until about 4 TB (terabytes) of storage capacity. The minimum cluster size for FAT32 is reduced to 16 KB. The main problem here is that the FAT32 and NTFS systems cannot read each other's disk partitions, which requires reformatting (FDISK and FORMAT) the drive when the system is changed.

Note:

> Windows 98 allows for changing an older, FAT16 file system to a newer 32-bit FAT32 using a built-in program Drive Converter (FAT32), which can be found in START → PROGRAMS → ACCESSORIES → SYSTEM TOOLS → Drive Converter (FAT32).

Drive Interface

As was discussed in Chapter 2, the interface is a hardware and/or software system that controls data exchange between the PC and disk drive. The interface is provided by the electronics of the data transfer controller and the drive electronics.

The hard disk drives are available with all available types of the interface: ATA/IDE, SCSI, PC Card (former PCMCIA), FC-AL, USB, FireWire, and so on. The definition and performance of these interface types was already discussed in Chapter 2.

The majority of drives sold are ATA/IDE drives, which remain, probably, the best choice for the general user. The "newest" ATA-66 and ATA-100 formats rival SCSI performance with their lightening-fast DTR of 66 MB/s and 100 MB/s.

SCSI is the right choice for multimedia professionals, graphic designers, network administrators, software developers, or for those who want to get maximum performance out of multiple hard drives. USB is the best simple choice for the external hard disk drive when the data rate is not an issue. FireWire is the best choice for the external hard drive when the data rate is a big issue and money is not.

Drive Capacity Choice

Storage capacity requirements depend upon the type of applications and intensity of usage. Methodologies used to estimate required capacities are available for desktop, workstations, server, or mobile computer. For example, the drive capacity calculator, which can be found on the IBM Storage web site (*www.storage.ibm.com/hard soft/diskdrdl/dadvsr/desktop.htm*), is suitable for this job.

I have done some estimates using this calculator and they look quite reasonable and just a little bit on the larger side. This estimate was done for the home desktop computer with the following set of applications:

- calendars and scheduling—minimum
- contacts management (names, addresses, phones)—minimum
- Finance software—minimum
- Games and hobbies—average
- Office suite (a complete version including word processor, spreadsheet, presentation graphics, etc.)—average

Total estimated required capacity was 5 to 7 GB. If the digital audio recording (average intensity) is added, the required capacity increases to 9–13 GB. Add high-end graphic design (average intensity), and 12 to 17 GB is recommended.

Since some of the applications are computer type-specific (say, no heavy graphic design is expected to be done on laptops), the recommendation varies with the computer type.

Drive's RPM: The Need for Speed

When asked about required drive characteristics, average users often suggest the following ranking:

- Reliability (and, therefore, lower cost of ownership)
- Speed
- Quietness (if the PC is in, say, your bedroom)

Speed of the hard disk drive is a function of more than the drive's RPM, but also of the type of interface, the amount of on-board cache, the PC's CPU clock-speed, PC memory size, and so on. But, the drive's RPM is perhaps one of the most important mechanical characteristics of the drive. Increasing RPM is, perhaps, the easiest way to improve the drive's rotational *latency*, *internal data transfer rates*, and overall performance.

Table 3–3 summarizes an effect of the drive's RPM on performance using IBM's Ultrastar high-end drive family (source: *www.storage.ibm.com*):

Table 3–3   Effect of RPM on Drive Performance

Performance parameter	Ultrastar 9LP	Ultrastar 9ZX	Ultrastar 18XP	Ultrastar 18ZX
Drive model	DGHS-39110	DGVS-39110	DGHS-30110	DRVS-09V
RPM	7,200	10,000	7,200	10,000
Maximum internal data rate (MB/s)	22.4	25.6	22.4	30.5
Average access time (ms)	6.5	6.3	6.5	5.3
Latency (ms)	4.17	2.99	4.17	2.99

The drive's characteristics, such as internal data rate, access time, and latency, improve significantly with RPM. This is why the high-end drives are continuously increasing their rotational velocity. For example, the Seagate Cheetah X15 (with capacity of 18 GB) became the first hard drive to feature 15,000 RPM with an average seek time of 3.9 ms, the fastest seek rate yet.

But, there are some drawbacks associated with the higher rotational velocity. Higher speed increases vibrations of the drive and makes faster drives acoustically louder than the low-speed ones. Power usage also increases dramatically (see Table 3–4. Source: *www.storage.ibm.com*) due to a rapidly increasing air drag between the surfaces of rotating disks and air. This causes heat dissipation, making drives much hotter and, therefore, requiring forced cooling.

Table 3–4   Effect of RPM on Power Usage

Performance parameter	Ultrastar 18XP	Ultrastar 18ZX
RPM	7,200	10,000
Number of disks	5	5
Average idle power (W)	9.2	11.2
Power during read/write operation (W)	11.6	13.2

Energy loss becomes even more noticeable with increasing number of disks (increasing drive capacity). For some applications, such as TV set-top boxes (TiVo, ReplayTV, etc.) the acoustic noise and high heat dissipation are not acceptable at all. The noise will affect the quality of TV sound. The same can be said of heat: in order to keep the system as quiet as possible, TiVo avoids using forced cooling (fans). If the drive dissipates too much heat without cooling, it may damage itself and the surrounding electronic parts.

In the case of mobile devices—laptops, handheld PCs, PDA, and camcorders—energy conservation is a major issue. Therefore, high-RPM drives cannot be used there. This is why the drive's rotational velocity is application-dependent.

Nowadays, for products requiring low power consumption and low acoustic noise, much lower velocity drives—approximately 4,000 to 5,400 RPM—are most appropriate. For data-intensive applications and when performance is first at any cost, the high-end drives with 10,000 and 15,000 RPM rotational velocity are the drives of choice.

How S.M.A.R.T. are Drives?

Fortunately, today's hard disk drives are smart enough thanks to S.M.A.R.T.—Self-Monitoring, Analysis, and Reporting Technology.

Some time ago, drive designers realized that some of the drive performance parameters (head flying height, data transfer rate, seek error rate, etc.) they typically use in research, development, and testing could be hard-wired into the drive to monitor its own performance. If the drive could detect any problem before it became catastrophic, it could alarm the user to take action.

Nowadays, most ATA and SCSI drives use S.M.A.R.T. to predict failure and protect data. Predicting mechanical failures of the drive, for example, prevents about 60% of drive failures. Not all failure (even the gradual ones) can be predicted, but S.M.A.R.T. keeps evolving and has reached its third generation already. S.M.A.R.T.-III not only monitors the drive activity (for failure prediction) but adds failure prevention by attempting to detect and repair sector errors.

There are four major areas S.M.A.R.T. keeps an eye on:

- Heads: contamination build-up, cracking, bad connection, handling damage
- Media: scratches, defects, bad servo, ECC corrections, handling damage
- Electronics: failures, bad connection to drive or bus, handling damage
- Motor and bearing: failure, wear, excessive runout, handling damage

For example, for predicting head failure, S.M.A.R.T. may use the read error rate and servo error rate.

Below is a list of some major attributes that are monitored by S.M.A.R.T. to predict failure:

- Head flying height
- Spin-up time
- Data transfer rates
- Re-allocated sector count
- Seek error rate
- Seek time
- Spin retry count
- Drive calibration retry count
- Drive temperature

These attributes are typical reliability indicators and are customized by manufacturers for every specific type of drive.

Drive Installation

Drive installation is a relatively easy process in today's computers: most newer ATA drives, for example, are plug-and-play drives. This means that one just needs to connect the drive to the PC and restart it: a computer will take care of the rest. If some BIOS configuration is needed, follow your manual closely.

Installation of a SCSI drive or configuring the RAID environment can be trickier and require a close following of the installation instructions. Try to use the software often provided with the drive for its *partitioning* and *formatting*.

Here are some tips to remember when installing the drive:

ATA/IDE Drive

1. ATA/IDE systems allow for no more than two devices per cable and no more than four devices total (including HDD, CD-ROM, Zip, etc). Additional ATA/IDE device(s) can be added by installing an additional ATA/IDE adapter (card).

2. If this is the drive to boot from, make sure the jumpers are set to "Master." If it is a secondary drive, set jumpers to "Slave."

3. If the cable has a red stripe on one side, this side should be closer to the power connector.

4. The faster device should be at the end of the cable. Also, try to group devices by their speed on the same cable.

5. Remember, your system will work as fast as its slowest element. For example, an ATA/66 drive on an Ultra ATA/33 adapter will perform similar to an ATA/33 drive.

6. When attaching an ATA/100 or ATA/66 drive to an Ultra ATA/33 adapter, you may need to upgrade your BIOS. Anyway, your devices will not work faster than your adapter will (33 MB/sec tops).

7. For Ultra ATA/66 drives and adapters, you have to use an Ultra ATA/66 adapter's 80-conductor cable. Your computer must run Windows 98 and higher and support UDMA modes 3 and 4. Also, the devices should be correctly attached:
   - Controller ➤ Blue
   - Master device (HD0 or ID0) ➤ Black
   - Slave (HD1 or ID1) ➤ Gray

If there are problems with drive installation (doesn't spin or work), check the following first:

1. If there is no sound from the drive when the PC is turned on, check the power cable.

2. Check that there are no damaged/bent connectors on the drive. If not, try replacing the cable.

3. Check if the cable is too long (should be less than 18 inches long).

4. For drives with capacities larger than 8.4 GB, you may need to upgrade your BIOS. Go to the web page of your BIOS manufacturer to download the software.

SCSI Drive

1. The SCSI interface supports 7 to 15 devices, depending on the type of SCSI (see Chapter 2). Each device has a unique ID, with the boot device being 0.

2. HVD (High Voltage Differential) SCSI devices are incompatible with SE (Single Ended) or LVD (Low Voltage Differential) devices.

3. The SCSI system must be terminated on both ends of the cable with the controller being on one side and the drive on the other side.

4. Any device that is not at the end of the cable must have internal termination. Use the same terminator type as the drive's type: an SE terminator for an SE drive, for example.

5. A 68–50 pin cable converter may cause problems by leaving 68–50 = 18 pins without termination.

6. If there are problems, first check the cable (for damage, right orientation, and length), pins (for damage), and power cable.

If you still have problems and are going to call for technical assistance, be prepared to provide the following typical information:

1. When and where your PC was purchased

2. PC, motherboard, and chipset manufacturers

3. BIOS information

4. List of adapter cards

5. List of other devices attached

6. Cabling of the drive (location on the cable, pin orientation, how good is the cable)

7. OS

8. Major applications used

9. Drive model/number

10. Installation error codes (if any)

Understanding the HDD Specification

Finally, let's take a look at the drive specifications (from *www.cnet.com*) and try to interpret them.

Table 3–5 describes drives for servers and high-end workstations. Server drives have the highest performance and highest cost and use the fastest and most advanced interfaces such as SCSI and FC-AL.

Table 3–5   Drive Description for Servers and High-End Workstations

IBM Ultrastar 36LZX 18.4GB (80-pin)		
Characteristic	**Comments**	
Platform(s)	PC	Meant for PC only
Internal or external	internal	Mounted inside the PC
Storage capacity	18.4GB	Formatted capacity
Rotational speed	10,000 rpm	High RPM means high performance and is used in high-end drives where performance is critical
Avg. seek time	4.9ms	Characterizes speed of access to randomized data 4.9 ms is a very good number for high-end drives
Avg. sustained transfer rate	29MB/sec.	The DTR the drive can sustain over a substantial period of time
Max. internal transfer rate	452MB/sec.	The DTR between the media and the data buffer: is a measure of how fast the drive is (excluding the drive-PC link)
Buffer	4MB	Larger buffer (cache) memory is always better
Interface(s)	SCSI	Doesn't tell much about the type of SCSI
SCSI type	Ultra/160	Means 160 MB/s burst DTR, 16 devices on a bus, 12 m of cable (see Chapter 2)
Number of heads	6	This number is twice that of the disks
Number of platters	3	Platters = disks
Chassis and Power Supply Dimensions (W × H × D)	1" × 4" × 5.78"	Typical size for a 3.5" drive
Base warranty	1 yr.	The warranty for high-end drives is shorter than that for the lower-end drives (which is, typically, 3 years)

Desktop drives have a mediocre performance and are low in cost, and typically use EIDE interfaces of different flavors (see Table 3–6).

Table 3–6   Drive Description for Desktop Computers

Maxtor DiamondMax Plus 45 20.5GB

Characteristic	Comments	
Platform(s)	PC, Mac	Meant for PC and Mac
Internal or external	internal	Mounted inside the PC
Internal drive	size 3.5 in.	The disk form-factor
Storage capacity	20.5GB	Formatted capacity
Rotational speed	7200 rpm	High RPM means high performance; 7200 RPM is a typical value for the desktop drives.
Avg. seek time	8.7ms	Characterizes speed of access to randomized data. Avg. seek time is, in general, longer for the desktop drives than for the server drives. 8.7 ms is a good number for desktop drive
Buffer	2MB	Larger buffer (cache) memory is better.
Interface(s)	EIDE	Or UDMA. Four drives can be connected directly to the motherboard connectors.
IDE/EIDE type	Ultra ATA/100	Allows for up to 100 MB/s burst DTR. May need a plug-in PCI card for older computers.
Number of heads	3	Apparently, one side of one disk isn't in use.
Number of platters	2	Platters = disks
Chassis and Power Supply Dimensions (W × H × D)	4" × 1" × 5.78"	Typical size for the 3.5" drive
Weight	1.00	Weight is hardly important for the desktop drive.
Base warranty	3 yr.	If you experience problems—don't open the drive or your warranty will be waved!

Mobile drives have the slowest performance, and are high in cost, but also have high capacity in a small size. Low weight and low power consumption (not mentioned in the table from CNET.com) are very important for mobile drives (see Table 3–7).

Table 3–7   Drive Description for Mobile Computers

IBM Travelstar 10GT 10GB EIDE Hard Disk		
Characteristic	**Comments**	
Internal or external	internal	Mounted inside the laptop computer. Check for compatibility with the computer you have.
Internal drive size	2.5 in. slim	The drive form-factor
Storage capacity	10GB	Formatted capacity
Rotational speed	4200 rpm	Slow. Used for mobile drives where performance is less of an issue compared to storage capacity.
Avg. seek time	12ms	Characterizes speed of access to randomized data. Avg. seek time is, in general, the longest for the mobile drives. 12 ms is an average number for the mobile drive
Max. internal transfer rate	118 Mbps	Burst DTR of 118/8 = 14.7 MB/s
Buffer	512K	Larger buffer (cache) memory is better
Interface(s)	EIDE	Or UDMA
IDE/EIDE type	ATA-4	Or ATA-33 with the maximum DTR of 33 MB/s (see Chapter 2)
UDMA? (Ultra Direct Memory Access)	yes	See above
Number of heads	6	This number is twice that of the disks
Number of platters	3	Platters = disks
Chassis and Power Supply Weight	1.00	Weight is very important for the mobile drive.
Warranty	3 yr.	If you experience problems—don't open the drive or your warranty will be waved!

REMOVABLE MAGNETIC STORAGE . . . .

Floppy Disk 1.44 MB

The history of floppy drives started with the first 8-inch (~203 mm) floppy drive, introduced in 1970. It was replaced by the 5.25-inch (133 mm) drive in 1976 and by the 3.5-inch (89 mm) "micro-floppy" in 1980. Initially, the floppy drive was single-headed (one-sided) and had a storage capacity of 322 KB. The disk was protected by a hard plastic jacket, which increased its durability and made handling easier. Gradually, the drive became dual-headed (double-sided) and eventually reached today's 1.44 MB capacity (2 MB unformatted). The drive's height also decreased from an initial 51 mm to 25 mm. Table 3–8 summarizes typical characteristics of a 1.44 MB micro-floppy disk drive.

Table 3–8   Typical Characteristics of a 1.44 MB Micro-Floppy Disk Drive

Parameter name	Value
Rotational velocity, RPM	300
Average seek time, ms	~100
Data transfer rate (DTR), MB/s	0.06
Track density, tpi	135
Bit density, bpi	17.4
Areal density, GB/in^2	0.02
Recording type	Contact
Magnetic head type	Inductive
Magnetic media	$Co-\gamma-Fe_2O_3$
MTBF, hours	> 30,000

Error rate
    Soft read error:
    Hard read error:
    Seek error:
	
	$<10^{-9}$
	$<10^{-12}$
	$<10^{-6}$

The floppy drive is a story of a product whose technological development is limited by the need to stay compatible with its previous generations. When compared to the modern hard disk drive (HDD), the floppy drive doesn't compare favorably (see Figure 3–33). It can be made much better, as has been done in some newer high-density products (discussed later), however, this creates a compatibility problem that limits market share of the product and, correspondingly, the financial success of the product.

Figure 3–33
Hard disk drive surrounded by floppy disks of equivalent total capacity (courtesy of IBM).

The capacity and data transfer rates of the floppy drives saturated a long time ago at a low level by today's standards levels. These parameters could be improved dramatically with today's technology, but do not expect changes. There are millions upon millions of floppy drives and disks out there and it is *too late* to change the standards.

Today, the only two functions left for floppy disks are serving as boot disks in case of system problems on your PC and serving as removable storage for those who still live in the sub-two-megabytes-of-storage universe. The main advantage of floppy drives is still its simplicity, low cost, and almost universal compatibility.

In its design, the floppy disk drive is somewhat similar to a hard disk drive; it operates on principles of magnetic recording and uses magnetic heads for data storage and retrieval from the rotating magnetic media. The main drawbacks of the floppy drive are the lower quality of the media leading to poorer magnetic performance, and lower rotational speed of the disk—about 300 rotations per minute, resulting in significantly lower data transfer rates (DTR).

An important part of the floppy disk is the cartridge with soft liners. It stabilizes disk rotation and protects it from mechanical damage. The liners (nonwoven fabric) clean the disk.

There is a relatively large variety of floppy disk drives, which differ by their application and interface type. Almost all types of interfaces can be found in the floppy disk drives: IDE, USB, SCSI, and so on.

In the floppy drive, a ceramic slider with a ferrite composite head slides on the the flexible disk. The disk consists of a 76 micron-thick polyethylene terephthalate (PET) coated on both sides with a micron-thick particulate magnetic coating, which is a bunch of magnetic iron oxide particles in the polymer matrix. The particles used are typically $Co\text{-}\gamma\text{-}Fe_2O_3$ with a relatively low coercivity of 630 Oe (compared, for example, to rigid magnetic disks with a coercivity of about 3,500 Oe). The thickness of magnetic coating is about 2 to 3 μm. To extend the life of the disk, the disk surface is lubricated. Figure 3–34 shows the design and dimensions of a micro-floppy disk.

Rotation of the flexible disk at about 300 RPM is achieved by clamping the disk at the center hole. The clamping is done by a magnet, which is moved into contact with the center hub when the disk is inserted. A pin on the drive spindle side interlocks with the center hole to provide repeatable positioning of the disk. The shutter opens on the insertion of the disk in the drive (shown open in the picture) and allows access to the media. When the disk starts rotating, two magnetic heads (one on each side) get positioned over the disk surface by a stepper motor. Magnetic heads slide over the disk surface to keep magnetic spacing as low as possible. The most popular data encoding scheme for floppy disk drives is a modified frequency modulation (MFM), which was discussed earlier in the chapter.

The future of the floppy disk drive as it is doesn't look promising. It is more-or-less obvious that with its inferior storage capacity and low data transfer rate it should be long gone. It is hard to predict for how much longer the floppy disk will exist as a standard component of the modern computer. The answer to this question could be in the next generation of removable media storage products, some of which are discussed next.

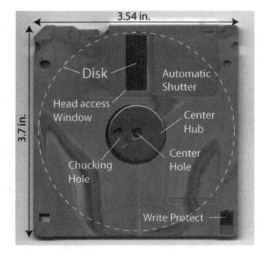

Figure 3–34
Floppy disk design.

HiFD 1.44/200 MB

High-density floppy disk drives were originally introduced by Sony, the original inventor of the 3.5" floppy disk. In 1999, better, modified HiFD drives became available from such manufacturers as Sony and IBM (Figure 3–35).

The idea behind this drive design is to introduce a new generation of larger and faster storage without losing the ability to read and write on a traditional 3.5" floppy disk. How was this achieved? By fitting two drives in one.

The new HiFD drives operate in two modes: with old 1.44MB/720 KB media and with the new 200 MB media. For example, when working with a 1.44 MB disk, the drive spins at 300 RPM only, while working with newer 200 MB disks (HiFD mode), it spins at 3000 RPM, which allows for a much higher data transfer rate (DTR)—up to 3.6 MB/sec. This is about 60 times faster than the traditional floppy disk drive (for the internal IDE version). Plus, the newer disks have a storage capacity of approximately 140-fold that of the older floppy disks. HiFD disk can, for instance, store more than 15 minutes of video in MPEG1 format or 45 minutes of stereo-quality audio recording. Thanks to high DTR, full motion video playback is also possible using the HiFD drives.

The HiFD drives are backward-compatible, meaning that one cannot use the newer disk in the older floppy drives but can use older disks in the newer drive. One advantage of the HiFD is that it fits right into the standard floppy drive bay, allowing for a relatively painless transition from the older floppy disk drive. The major characteristics of the HiFD drive are summarized in Table 3–9.

Figure 3–35
HiFD: High-density internal floppy disk drive (courtesy of IBM).

Table 3–9   Major Characteristics of the HiFD Drive

Parameter	HiFD
Company	Sony, IBM
Capacity, MB	1.44 and 200
Av. seek time (ms)	49 (HiFD mode)
Av. data transfer rate (read, MB/s)	3.6 (internal IDE) 0.6 (external parallel) 0.7 (external USB)
RPM	3600/300
Track density (TPI)	2822 (HiFD mode)
Bit density (kBPI)	72–91 (HiFD mode)
Head-disk interface	Flying head
Magnetic media	ATOMM, 86 mm in diameter
Head type	Inductive
Number of heads	2
Weight of external drives (g)	950 g
MSRP price	$149 (internal, IBM) $179 (parallel port, Sony) $199 (USB, Sony)

Sony has improved drive design since October 1999, adding some features such as a soft head loading mechanism for improved reliability and also has redesigned the disk shutter to better protect the media from dust and particulate contamination. Newer drives also feature an advanced PRML read channel to minimize read errors.

Unfortunately, the latest modifications have made newer HiFD drives incompatible with the older HiFD disks (purchased before November 1999). To deal with this issue, SONY provides free replacement for the older products.

The HiFD disks are more expensive than the 1.44 MB disks, but are reasonably priced at less than $15 per disk. Clearly, with 200 MB per disk, a user can transfer from one computer to another a relatively large data file: digital images, digital video, animated artwork, and so on. The only problem here is that there are not too many computers to exchange data with: the HiFD format is relatively new and isn't an industry standard like the 1.44 MB floppy disk drive. This is the main problem with all newer and better removable media storage products. But, since the drive comes in the external versions too (parallel and USB), it is possible to move the data along with the drive.

The USB interface allows for the problem-free connectivity with any modern (USB equipped) computer, making HiFD a good choice.

Superdisk (LS-120) 1.44/120 MB

The Superdisk from Imation (*www.imation.com*) also offers two drives in one body: a 1.44 MB floppy drive and a 120 MB drive (Figure 3–36). The drive comes in various configurations, such as IDE (internal), USB (external), and PC Card.

When operating in the high-density 120 MB mode, the drive is about 10 times faster than the traditional floppy drive. Clearly, to operate in the 120 Mb mode the Superdisk requires special disks.

In addition to the regular 120 MB disks, the Superdisk disks, with Secured Encryption Technology, are also available for protection of private data. Imation uses a "Blowfish" algorithm, which encodes the data 16 times over. These disks are easy to use and just require a password for accessing the data. Apparently, a lost password translates into lost data too. The same disk can be used to store both secured and unsecured information. The unsecured information will be visible to the user, while the encrypted file will be hidden.

The drive installation is easy. Drive operation is also easy with the single requirement of not ejecting the disk when the drive is operating. It is also recommended that the head be cleaned every once in a while, that is, approximately after about 40 hours of use. The main performance characteristics of the drive are summarized in Table 3–10.

Figure 3–36
IBM ThinkPad Superdisk LS-120 Drive (courtesy of IBM).

Table 3–10   Main Performance Characteristics of the Superdisk Drive

Model	Superdisk
Company	Imation
Capacity, MB	120
Av. seek time (ms)	65
Av. data transfer rate (MB/s)	0.55
RPM	720
Track density (TPI)	2490
Bit density (kBPI)	45
Head-disk interface	Sliding head
Magnetic media	MP
Head type	Inductive
MSRP price	$100 (USB, Hi-Val)

This standard of removable media storage finds its application in such products as digital cameras. For example, it is currently used in the Panasonic PalmCam Digital camera PV-SD4090, where it allows for storage of about 450 "super-fine resolution" images and about 1,500 images in "standard resolution." The advantage for those who already have a Superdisk drive on their computer is self-evident: pictures can be easily transferred from the camera, stored, swapped, and saved for printing, emailing, or posting on the web.

Even if you don't have the Superdisk drive on your computer, the data can be transferred to a regular floppy disk (or via USB port on the camera). Finally, the camera's drive may be utilized as an external storage device for a computer, since it has a complete Superdisk drive inside the camera.

Zip Drive 100/250 MB

Iomega 100 MB Zip drives (see Figure 3–37) are almost the standard for today's PCs. The latest iteration, a 250 MB Zip drive, could painlessly replace the 100 MB drives in the future, becoming the next "floppy drives." In fact, one 250 MB Zip disk is approximately equivalent in capacity to 174 floppy disks. DTR is also much faster (up to 2.4 MB/sec compared to 0.06 MB/sec for a floppy drive).

Zip disks can be used to store, back up, and move basic office application files, digital music, presentations, digital photos, digital video, and so on. Iomega characterizes

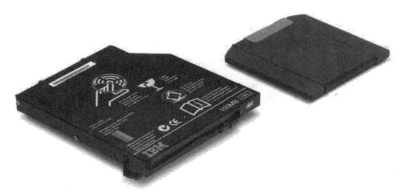

Figure 3–37
IBM ThinkPad Zip 100 MB UltraSlimBay drive and disk (courtesy of IBM).

this product as drives that "meet high capacity storage needs" for PC users. In reality, these products belong to the mobile storage category rather than to the backup category.

The Zip drive gained its popularity some years ago when the standard floppy was already too small in capacity, CD-R/RW was not cheap and common enough, and the Internet wasn't a simple alternative for data exchange. The advent of the Internet and the storage capabilities thereof is expected to impact the removable storage market.

Thanks to the fact that by 1999 Iomega had sold more than 22 million Zip drives (mostly 100 MB) and over 100 million Zip disks, compatibility is not an issue for this advanced floppy drive. For all external products, both the drive and the media can be moved, which is even easier now due to the availability of a special rechargeable battery pack capable of keeping the drive running for up to 2 hours. A good thing about the 250 MB drives is that they work with both 100 MB and 250 MB disks!

Zip drives come in all possible configurations, such as:

- Internal Zip
- Parallel port Zip
- USB (Universal Serial Bus) Zip
- SCSI Zip (for high-speed users)
- FireWire Zip (external)
- PC Card Zip (for laptops)

Table 3–11 compares basic performance features and prices of various Zip products.

Table 3–11   Performance Features and Prices of Various Zip Products

Product	Average Seek time (ms)	Data transfer rate (MB/s) (average)	Price ($) (Iomega)	Disk cost ($)
Zip 100 MB	29	0.79–1.40 MB/sec (Parallel)	99.95 (Parallel)	9.95
		1.2 MB/sec (USB)	129.95 (USB)	
		1.40 MB/sec (Internal ATAPI)	99.95 (Internal ATAPI)	
		0.79–1.40 MB/sec (SCSI)	99.95 (SCSI)	
		1.40 MB/sec (Notebook Zip)	199.95 (Notebook Zip)	
			220 (FireWire, VST Technologies, Inc.)	
			210 (PC Card, Addonics)	
Zip 250 MB	29	0.8 MB/sec (Parallel)	169.95 (Parallel)	19.95
		1.2 MB/sec (USB)	179.95 (USB)	
		2.4 MB/sec (Internal ATAPI)	169.95 (Internal ATAPI)	
		2.4 MB/sec (SCSI)	169.95 (SCSI)	
			280 (FireWire, VST Technologies, Inc.)	

It is evident from Table 3–11 that the ability to move data doesn't come cheaply: 1 Gigabyte costs about $200 to $400 if one includes the drive itself and the cost of disks needed to store 1 GB of data.

Parallel port Zip drives are the simplest in use—they are easily installed and connected to the printer port of the PC. A 250 MB SCSI Zip drive is about 50% faster than the 100 MB SCSI Zip drive, but both require the addition of a Zip Zoom SCSI accelerator card or some other compatible SCSI card (not provided with the drive). While being faster, SCSI is also more complex. Most Pentium computers have both PCI and ISA expansion slots to connect SCSI cards. One needs to check the documentation that comes with the computer to see what kind of expansion slots the computer has and buy a SCSI card that fits (it is better to use a PCI slot). There are also different numbers of pins on SCSI connectors (50-pin and 68-pin).

100 MB and 250 MB ATAPI internal Zip drives are not uncommon now on new computers. If you are planning to add one to your PC, make sure you have an available 3.5" or 5.25" drive bay and a free connection to the IDE controller. ATAPI (Advanced Technology Attachment Packet) is a type of interface used to connect additional hardware devices to a computer. This is an internal interface used to connect such devices as hard drives, CD-ROMs, tape drives, and so on.

Iomega Zip drives for notebook computers come in the 100 MB version (see Figure 3–37) only and are made specifically for the drive bays of a few leading notebook models on the market. A full list of supported notebook computers can be found on the Iomega web page. Iomega claims that its notebook Zip drive is 40% faster than the SCSI or ATAPI versions. In spite of this, its nominal data transfer rate (1.40MB/sec) does not differ from that reported for the 100 MB SCSI and ATAPI Zip drives.

The PC Card Zip drive (i.e., Microtech Mii SlimZip 100; *www.microtech-pc.com*) is also designed for laptop users and provides very reasonable performance comparable to that of the internal IDE Zip 100 MB and even the SCSI Zip 100 MB.

Let's now briefly discuss the Zip disk. Zip disks are made in a 3.5" form-factor and have a total thickness of 62 microns. The external dimensions of the Zip cartridges are $97 \times 98.5 \times 6$ mm. There is a small reflector window on the back side of each Zip cartridge, which is used by the Zip drive to identify a Zip disk so that it will not mistakenly engage the drive's read/write heads, thereby potentially damaging the drive. Since Zip disks only have this reflector, there is no danger of the drive engaging on a mistakenly inserted floppy disk, for example. The Iomega Jaz drive also uses a similar reflector mechanism.

A flexible disk inside the Zip cartridge spins at 2,940 RPM, creating a hard disklike slider-disk interface with the slider flying over the disk surface. The sliders (one for each side of the disk) are dynamically loaded on the disk surface after the system recognizes that the cartridge is inside the drive. When the cartridge is inserted, a special shutter arm moves the cartridge shutter aside, allowing access to the disks. This is done to prevent contamination of the disk and slider as much as possible, since contamination is the major possible cause of disk failure. The slider's air bearing is designed to be tolerant to abrasive particles passing in between the slider and the disk. Most particles on the disk are supposed to be swept away before/during the first read/write operations.

Warning!

Keep your cartridges clean and do not open the shutters of the cartridges to prevent atmospheric contaminants from entering it!

Typically, Zip disks are made using particulate media technology, similar to that found in magnetic tapes but not in modern hard drives. Nowadays, the most advanced Zip disks use the so-called ATOMM technology (Advanced super Thin-layer and height-Output Metal Media), developed in 1992 by Fuji Film. This media features a high-density, ultra-thin layer of magnetic material with a smooth, glossy finish on a base of a flexible polymeric media made of polyethylene terephthalate (PET). Very tough and smooth (but not as smooth as hard disks!), magnetic media is created during simultaneous coating of microscopic spherical particles in the nonmagnetic "titan-fine" lower layer. This layer is made of titan particles approximately one-sixth the size of magnetic particles, and creates a strong, flexible, and ultra-smooth foundation for a thin magnetic layer.

Magnetic particles inside the magnetic layer are kept together with a polyester-polyurethane binder. A thin layer of lubricant is applied topically on the Zip disks to improve durability.

Jaz Drive

The Jaz® 1 GB drive (Figure 3–38) was the first product of this type from Iomega, but is no longer manufactured. The newer Jaz 2 GB became the flagship of Iomega's removable storage products.

Figure 3–38
1 GB Jaz drive from Iomega.

Jaz disks can be used to store, backup, and move large office application files, digital music, presentations, digital photos, digital video, and to provide back-up for your OS. These products are much closer to the category of backup storage than the famous Zip drives and have a comparatively large storage capacity even by today's standards.

On the other hand, with the modern hard drive capacities exceeding 20 GB, back-up with Jaz 2 GB disks is too expensive. One will need to spend about $1,500 (including the cost of the drive itself) to back up a 20 GB hard drive. It is much cheaper to, for example, buy one extra hard disk drive and back up your data on it, or, alternatively, use a tape storage.

For the highest performance, Jaz drives come with an ultra-SCSI interface connector and require a separate SCSI card. They provide a "hard-drive-level" average seek time and a high data transfer rate. A good feature of 2 GB drives is that they work with both 1 GB and 2 GB disks!

Warning!

Do not use 2 GB disks with 1 GB drives! It may cause damage to the drive.

While admitting that the Jaz 2 GB drive is the correct and logical next step after the Zip drive, we have to mention that it is also somewhat of a step back in terms of compatibility. Unlike the 20 million Zip drives (mostly 100 MB) sold along with over 100 million Zip disks, Jaz 2 GB drives and disks are still relatively rare and they require a SCSI card (parallel and USB adapters for Jaz are also available now).

The Iomega Jaz drive is similar to the hard disk drive. It uses a hard, thin-film 3.5" magnetic disk (unlike Zip drives, which use flexible particulate media) that spin at a respectable 5,394 RPM. Jaz drives use the *load/unload* technique like the most advanced hard drives for mobile computers and servers. Still, in terms of their performance, Jaz drives fall behind real hard disk drives. Even if the Jaz drive's average seek time seems quite acceptable (10 ms read/12 ms write compared to, for example, 7.6 to 8.0 ms average seek time for Seagate Barracuda ATA IDE drives spinning at 7,200 RPM), its average data transfer rate (7.4 MB/sec) is below the level offered by newer hard disk drives (again, using a Seagate Barracuda ATA IDE Series drive as an example, its average sustained data transfer rate is above 15 MB/sec). On the other hand, we are talking about transferring 2 GB of data only—it may be done somewhat slower.

The Jaz drive's areal recording density is also relatively low by today's standards, providing only 1 GB per platter (disk) compared to a typical HDD of today with a storage capacity exceeding 5 GB per platter. Therefore, on a cost-performance basis, the Jaz drive became an expensive storage solution (see Table 3–12).

The main challenge for removable drives stems from contamination. Four magnetic heads in the Jaz 2 GB drive (one head per disk surface) are flying over the rigid magnetic disks at high velocities comparable to that in the fixed hard drives. However, the environment in which they operate is considerably dirtier. The durability of the head/disk interface depends strongly on the absence of particulate contamination in the disk atmosphere and on the surfaces of the disk and slider.

Table 3–12   Cost versus Performance of Jaz Drives

Product	Average Seek time (ms)	Data transfer rate (MB/s) (average)	Price ($)	Disk cost ($)
Jaz 1 GB SCSI-II	10 read/12 write	5.40 MB/sec (10 MB/s burst)	discontinued	89.99
Jaz 2 GB U-SCSI	10 read/12 write	7.4 MB/sec (20 MB/s burst)	349.95 (Iomega)	99.99

The high performance of Jaz drives allows for their use in various applications, and, even in the RAID-like environment on the so-called storage servers used for external storage solutions. In the case of, for example, Acentia's Kanga 7x Jaz Drive Rackmount Storage Server (*www.acentia.com*), up to seven Jaz drives are packed together along with an Ethernet card. The system has a capacity of 14 MB and may cost over $5,000.

Apparently, there is a need for fast, high-capacity removable media storage, such as a Jaz drive. This has encouraged other companies to start producing similar products. One of the best examples and a strong competitor to Jaz is discussed next.

Orb Drive

The ORB® 2.2 GB drive from Castlewood Systems (Figure 3–39) has an incrementally larger storage capacity than it's main rival—Jaz 2 GB from Iomega. Like the Jaz drive, ORB is designed for data backup and exchange.

Castlewood claims that their drive is faster and more reliable (see comparison in Table 3–13). It also comes in all thinkable configurations, such as internal (EIDE, SCSI) and external (Parallel, SCSI, USB, IEEE 1394 FireWire) and is available for both PC and Macintosh computers.

Similar to the Jaz drive, the ORB drive can be used to store, back up, and move large office application files, digital music, presentations, digital photos, digital video, and to provide partial backup for your OS. These products are much closer to the category of backup storage than the 100 MB and 250 MB Zip drives and have a relative-

Figure 3–39
2.2 GB ORB drive from Castlewood (courtesy of Castlewood).

ly large storage capacity even by today's standards. Table 3–13 compares the main parameters of Jaz 2 GB and ORB 2.2 GB drives.

Table 3–13 indicates that the ORB drive has some newer design features with specifications set to be better than those of a Jaz 2 GB drive. Comparison of the drive specifications shows that the ORB drive has approximately the same capacity and speed, but has the advantage in format time and weight. The ORB drive has a wider selection of interfaces, and is cheaper in price. The fact that you can buy EIDE, USB, or FireWire versions of the drive make it very attractive since these interfaces are much easier to use than the SCSI. The SCSI interface requires a special and relatively expensive adapter card.

One important fact to remember about ORB is that its use is not as widespread as the Jaz drive's. This may cause compatibility problems for the ORB users, unless they plan on traveling with their drives.

Castlewood has recently indicated that they are ready to release a newer high-end 5.7 GB version of the ORB drive. This capacity is large enough for a full backup of some computer systems.

Table 3–13   Comparison of Features of Jaz 2 and ORB Drives

Parameter	Jaz 2 GB (Iomega)	ORB 2.2 GB (Castlewood)
Capacity (GB)	2	2.2
Average seek time (ms)	10 read/12 write	10 read/12 write
Maximum (not average) sustained transfer rate (MB/sec)	8.7	12.2 (EIDE)
Burst transfer rate (MB/sec)	20	16.6 (EIDE)
Rotational speed (RPM)	5,394	5,400
Magnetic head type	MR (magnetoresistive)	MR (magnetoresistive)
Average start/stop time (sec)	15/15	20/10
Short format time (sec)	45	<1
Long format time with surface verify (minutes)	~55	9
Interfaces available	SCSI, parallel, USB	EIDE, SCSI, Parallel, USB, IEEE 1394 FireWire
Acoustical noise (dB)	< 45 dB	< 36
Weight (gm)	~900	426
Warranty (years)	1	1
List price (end of 2000)	$350—U-SCSI (external)	$150—EIDE (internal) $160—U-SCSI (internal) $180—U-SCSI (external) $200—USB (external)
Approximate disk price (end of 2000)	$100	$30

Iomega Clik! 40 MB Drives

The Iomega Clik! drive is an attempt by Iomega to enter a new market of portable electronic devices such as digital cameras, phones, handheld PCs, global positioning systems, and so on. With its 40 MB of storage capacity, the Clik! disk can hold approximately 40 mega-pixel images or hundreds of lower resolution images. For this, you will need to download the images from your camera's removable Flash memory card to the Clik! disk via the Clik! drive. Then, keep using the same memory card for more pictures. You can later download the pictures from the Clik! drive to your PC for editing, printing, and so on. Clik! drives cost about $200 and the disks are about $10.

As a storage device for data from digital cameras and palm-size PCs, Clik! is somewhat limited in its capabilities and seems to be just a temporary solution since "real" storage devices such as the IBM Microdrive (about the size of a Flash memory card and capable of storing from 170 MB to 1 GB of data) became available recently. The 340 MB Microdrive can hold 1,000 digitally compressed photographs, 6 hours of near CD-quality audio, or 300 hefty novels, the equivalent of more than 200 standard-size floppy disks. Its MSRP (manufacturer's suggested retail price) is about $500, which is expected to drop with time. Its weight is 16 grams. Table 3–14 summarizes the major characteristics of the Clik! drive.

Table 3–14   Major Characteristics of the Clik! Drive

Model	Clik!
Company	Iomega
Capacity, MB	40
Interface type	PC Card
Av. seek time (ms)	25
RPM	2941
Head-disk interface	Flying head
Head type	Inductive

External Hard Disk Drives

The removable hard drive is a simple and effective way to meet your need for a high-capacity removable storage and data backup system. The main reason the HDD is attractive for these applications is its high capacity and low cost.

An external hard disk drive is often an easy choice: it is faster then any other storage, it is large in capacity (allowing for a full-system backup), and it is cheap per gigabyte. Modern drives come in different form-factors, from a full-sized 3.5-inch drive to a tiny Microdrive with up to 1 GB (and larger in the future) capacity, the size of a Flash card, and a weight of 16 grams only.

On the majority of computers, the access to the port connector is on the back side, creating some inconveniences in the process of drive connection/disconnection. This is why there are several ways of connecting the external hard drive to a computer: using a *docking bay* (via IDE) on the front of the computer and using *existing ports* (parallel, USB, FireWire, PC Card). Sometimes, connection to a plug-in card (SCSI,

FireWire) may be necessary. Practically speaking, a removable drive may be the cheapest (per GB of data) option for the storage-hungry PC user with the need for high DTR (otherwise, one can opt with tape storage).

Let's now look at the drives that go inside the computer bay. For this, the hard drive is placed inside the special container (Figure 3–40), which is then inserted into a docking device on the front of the computer.

Assuming you have an unoccupied IDE connector and a free drive bay, installing the dockable drive is a relatively easy process. First, a special docking device is installed into a bay and connected to the IDE and power cables. Then, the drive is inserted, the computer is rebooted, and one can have a removable drive added to the system. And this is a real hard drive with its large capacity and fast data transfer rates. With today's low prices of HDDs, one can easily have about 10 mobile GBs for storage and backup for under $100–$150. Figure 3–41 shows the drive in the computer bay (courtesy of Datazone Corp.; *www.datazone.com*). This drive may offer the following advantages:

- Can be bootable (if the primary drive crashes, you can boot from this drive)
- Hot-swappable (until the computer is on; if restarted without the drive, a new reboot is needed). Therefore, one can remove the drive and plug it back or plug in another drive.
- Practical full-system backup or mirroring of the primary drive (in case of a crash)
- Data security (take the drive with you!)

Figure 3–40
Removable hard disk drive inside the docking device.

Figure 3–41
External hard disk drives: one attached to the laptop computer and another inserted into the computer bay (courtesy of Datazone Corp.).

Of course, a relative complexity of the installation and low popularity (compared to the Zip family) makes removable HDD a choice for users of storage-intensive applications, such as large graphic files, databases, data logs, and so on. A good application is data exchange between two or more of your own computers or computers within the same organization, since sending 3 GB of data over the intranet can be time-consuming.

The removable hard disk drive is also an excellent backup option, which allows updating information when necessary and stores large volumes of data at a low cost per GB. From the technical point of view, removable hard drives are just the same hard drives with a simplified access system to the controller connector and power cable, that allows swapping of the drives an easy task. The only requirement is the docking bay (about $35 to $100, depending on quality and interface type), a key (provided with the drive for security reasons), and a computer restart—and you have one extra hard drive! But what if that place you are going to deliver your data to doesn't have the right docking bay? Well, you can always connect your IDE drive to that computer directly, but the task now becomes more complex. This is where another configuration can be more suitable: an external hard disk drive.

External hard drives come in the following configurations:

- Parallel
- USB
- PC Card (for notebooks)
- FireWire
- SCSI

Some designs are interface independent (i.e., Datazone's Databook family), meaning that the drive can be used with the FireWire, USB, PCMCIA, and parallel port connections simply by changing the cable. It can be even used with the docking bay. Now, traveling with your drive is easy—one of the above interface options can be found almost anywhere. Of course, the DTR will be slower if you use a parallel connection versus, for example, the FireWire, but this is a small disadvantage compared to having almost unlimited connectivity, high capacity, low cost per gigabyte, and so on. Table 3–15 summarizes approximate DTRs for different connection types (according to Databook's specification).

Table 3-15   Approximate DTRs for Different Connection Types

Connection (interface) type	Sustained data transfer rate, MB/s
IDE (Docking bay)	9.0
Parallel port	0.8
USB	1.0
PC Card	2.0
FireWire	12.0

By adding special software, a user may add functionality to his external hard disk drive. For example, an automatic backup option can be used for desktop (via USB) or notebook computers (PC Card) (see CMS peripherals; *www.cmsperipheralsinc.com*). The storage options are limited by the drive capacity only and can be increased with time. Special software allows for automated full or incremental data backup. The data can be password-protected.

Summary

Only a few years ago, many of the discussed storage would have been called "backup systems," but this time is over. With hard disk drive capacities beyond 20 to 40 GB, one would need tens of Jaz disks for full system backup. Still, many useful applications such as documents, spreadsheets, and even medium-size databases can fit on 40 MB to 2 GB of removable medium.

The choice of removable magnetic storage can be quite straightforward and defined by the number "10." All of the data that needs to be stored should not exceed 10 storage disks of your choice.

More disks means more volume and more hustle, and it also means you should probably choose a system with higher storage capacity disks.

If the amount of data you are planning to move around could fit on 10 storage disks of your choice, you don't need larger, and generally speaking more expensive, storage. For example, if you are planning to move MS Word or Lotus documents, spreadsheets, or other similar documents, several 40 MB Clik! disks, 100 MB Zip disks, or 120 MB Superdisks will meet your needs. Increasing demand for storage will force you to migrate to a 250 MB Zip drive (which, by the way, can read 100 MB disks as well), and later, to a 2 GB Jaz or 2.2 GB Orb drive (*Again:* The 2 GB Jaz drive does not read 1 GB disks and could be damaged by them).

My personal choice is the following:

For daily backup and moving small files, such as Word and spreadsheet documents, I use 100 MB or 250 MB Iomega Zip drives. I have 5 Zip drives at work and one at home, and almost all of my friends have a Zip drive, making an exchange easy.

For the larger arrays of data, I prefer an external HDD, which allows for a complete system backup and also helps to move, say, 5 GB of digital pictures and video from one continent to another.

MAGNETIC STORAGE ON TAPE . . . .

Introduction

Unlike magnetic hard disk drives that follow strict standards in interface design, dimensions, and so on, a large variety of different tape storage systems is available today. These systems include 4 and 8 mm, 0.5"-wide helical drives as well as ¼-inch and ½-inch linear tape drives in different form-factors. Tape formats are developed based upon the conventions dictated by the organizations governing each particular tape format. As formats evolve toward higher capacity, better performance, and reliability, compatibility with all previous versions (at least, a "read-only" compatibility) is typically supported. On the other hand, there is often almost no compatibility between products from different makers even in the case of the same tape form-factor. The difference in technology, dimensions, capacity, performance, and price allows for each manufacturer to claim superiority and domination in the specified market segment.

In general, magnetic tapes exhibit slow performance and a lack of direct access to data. This is because data is stored linearly on magnetic tapes and therefore must be accessed linearly. At the same time, magnetic tapes are the cheapest storage solution per gigabyte of data (see the Table 3–16). This is why the tape drive market continues to grow and keeps adopting to new needs and new applications, and to migration of applications from the computer rooms to workstations and client/server architecture. The volume of data to store continues to increase, thus creating stable demands for higher performance, capacity, scalability, and reliability of tape storage.

Table 3–16   Cost per GB of Store

Storage system	Storage media type	Storage capacity (GB)	Cost of storage media (approximate)	~Cost of 1GB, $
Seagate Hornet/TapeStor 20 GB	Tape STTM20	20.0	$38	1.9
650 MB Rewritable CD	CD-RW	0.65	$2	3.0
7,200 RPM ATA-66 internal hard drive	Hard drive	20.4	$190	9.3
Iomega Jaz 2	Iomega Jaz 2	2.0	$100	50.0

The main applications of tape storage are summarized in Table 3–17.

Table 3–17   Main Applications of Tape Storage

Application	Purpose
Backup	Storage of the most critical data
Data transport	Moving large quantities of data
Offline/Near-line storage	Storing large, seldom-used files
Archive	Long-term data storage

Brief History of Magnetic Tape Storage

The history of digital tape storage started with the ½-inch tape and the first digital tape recorder called Uniservo I, which was developed in the late 1940s by the Remington Rand Corporation. This product was first shipped in 1951, and used a ½-inch metal (not polymer!) tape, which was considered at the time to be more robust. The capacity of the tape was on the order of a few megabytes. Nowadays, ½-inch tapes have native (uncompressed) capacity of 40 GB (DLT tape) to 110 GB (SuperDLT tape), and twice that when compressed. The Uniservo I was later integrated into the Remington Rand UNIVAC computer, thus becoming the first computer digital tape storage device. However, the metal tape caused excessive wear of the head and, subsequently, a more complex design using plastic tape running in between the head and another metal tape was proposed.

In 1953–55, IBM introduced its 726 and 727 series tape storage products, which used 10.5-inch reels and ½-inch tape, and became the *de facto* standard for scientific and commercial tape storage systems. The capacity per reel reached 6 MB in the 727 system.

The progress in integrated circuits (IC) and PC size minimization in the 1980s forced an introduction of smaller tape storage form-factors. First, IBM moved from the large 10.5-inch reels to much smaller 4 × 5 × 1-inch cartridges for ½-inch tape. The 10.5-inch reels at that time had about 80 m of tape with a storage capacity of about 150 MB. The new cartridges for the 3480 system held 18 m-long tape but had a capacity of 200 MB.

With a migration from mainframes to the personal computer, new, smaller formats such as DAT (digital audio tape) and 8-mm tape were introduced.

Philips was the first to introduce the compact cassette using a design with the head inserted inside the cassette for read and write operations. This design became the foundation for future low-cost, low-performance tape storage solutions.

In the mid-1980s, the first helical scan data recorder was developed by Honeywell using the popular VHS tape cassette. Despite its good performance, this system wasn't robust and reliable enough to capture the market.

In the late 1980s, Sony and HP first defined parameters for the 4-mm DAT format, which was later called DDS (digital data storage). DAT stands for digital audio tape and was designed for high-quality audio recording.

The first high-performance 8-mm helical scan tape drive was introduced in 1987 by Exabyte with technology based on a consumer 8-mm video cassette technology but with modifications. This eventually developed into the new helical scan drive, the Mammoth in 1996. The Mammoth became a successful product, with over 1.5 million units sold.

In the 1970s, the 3M Corporation developed the ¼-inch cartridge (QIC) format, which is now the dominant tape format for the low-end segment of the market with such well-known products as Travan.

In 1985, the Digital Equipment Corporation (DEC) developed and later sold to Quantum a low-cost ½-inch tape drive, the TK50, which gave birth to technology known today as the DLT, or digital linear tape.

Relatively recently, in 1996, a new 8-mm Format called AIT, or advanced intelligent tape, was introduced by Sony to target the mid-range server market. This format became available in a small 3.5" form-factor with a capacity of 25 GB per cartridge.

Finally, in 1998, IBM, Seagate, and Hewlett-Packard introduced the Linear Tape-Open, or LTO, technology, with scalable, open tape architecture for the mid-range to enterprise-class servers with up to 200 GB of data per cartridge. Open format is meant to enable compatibility between products from different vendors.

Tape Storage Technology

There are two basic configurations used in tape storage devices: linear and helical scan.

Linear tape is the same configuration used in consumer audio tape systems (Figure 3–42).

In the linear tape drives, the tape moves past the stationary magnetic read/write head(s), thus producing longitudinal parallel magnetic tracks that run along the length of the tape. When the track is completed, the drive reverses the direction of the tape. In the DLT7000 tape drive, for example, it takes 52 passes to fill the tape completely. The capacity depends on the number of tracks recorded on the tape, which is, in turn, a function of the number of heads. To achieve high DTR, the tape has to move by the head at high speed, with the newest linear tape drives moving tape at a velocity of about 4 m/s.

Helical scan is the same technology used in consumer VCR systems (Figure 3–43).

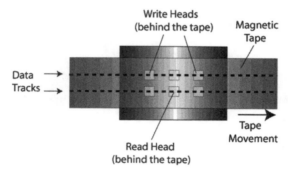

Figure 3–42
Linear tape configuration.

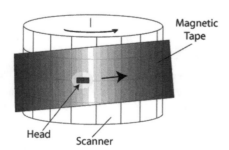

Figure 3–43
Helical scanner configuration.

In this tape drive design, a tape moves slowly around a fast-spinning scanner with several read and write heads. The read and write heads are placed apart around the scanner, for example, 90° apart. The head is slightly tilted relative to the tape, which results in a series of short tracks written across the tape. This allows for high recording density.

Traditionally, inductive read and write heads were used in the tape drives, but increased requirements for higher recording density forced a shift toward the magnetoresistive (MR) read heads—similar to those used in hard disk drives (HDD).

A recording density of magnetic tape drives has always been lower than that in the HDD, but it also always follows the HDD progress. At present, areal density is more than 5 MB/in² in linear tape drives (i.e., Quantum's DLT 8000), and more than 48 MB/in² for helical scan tape drives (i.e., HP DDS-3). This is much lower than recording densities of 10 GB/in² and higher achieved in the modern HDDs.

More tape drive technology issues will be addressed later in this chapter, where the most popular tape medium technologies and drive technologies are discussed, including the following:

- QIC (quarter-inch cartridges) format (Travan, DC2000, etc.)
- 4-mm DAT (digital audio tape) format (DDS)
- 8-mm helical scan tape (Mammoth II and AIT)
- DLT (digital linear tape) and SuperDLT (Quantum)
- LTO (linear tape open)
- Automated tape storage systems (stackers, autoloaders, libraries)

Tape Media Technology

MP (Metal Particle) and AMP (Advanced Metal Particle) Tapes

Most of the magnetic tapes we use are MP tapes—a mixture of metal oxide particles with a glue-like binder on a flexible polymer-base film made of polyethylene terephthalate (PET) (see Figure 3–44). This typically yields less than 50% of the film to be magnetic, with the rest being a nonmagnetic binder.

High-density magnetic recording needs smaller particles, and each generation of metal particle media features smaller and smaller magnetic particles and better magnetic properties. These particles are typically iron oxide, cobalt-doped iron oxide, chromium dioxide, barium ferrite, or pure iron. The particles are mixed with the binder (typically, polyester-polyurethane and lubricant to decrease wear).

The latest advancement in the world of MP media is the Advanced super Thin layer and high-Output Metal Media (ATOMM) film from Fujifilm.

ATOMM (Figure 3–45) is a thin ultra-smooth coating produced by simultaneously coating the magnetic layer over a nonmagnetic layer of titanium material. The titanium particles are approximately one-sixth the size of high density magnetic particles and are called "titan-fine" by Fujifilm. These "titan-fine" particles in the nonmagnetic lower layer create a strong, hard, and ultra-smooth platform for the upper magnetic layer. The resulting smoothness of the upper layer considerably improves head-to-media contact and reduces spacing loss to further enhance high-density recording. The film is also coated simultaneously on both sides. ATOMM technology is now used not only in magnetic tapes (DLTtape IV, DDS-3,4, etc.) but in other flexible storage media (Zip disk, HiFD disk).

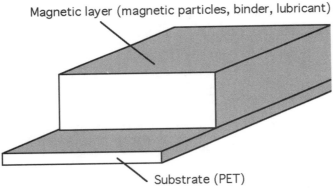

Figure 3–44
Design of the metal particle (MP) magnetic tape.

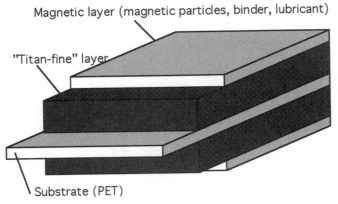

Figure 3–45
Design of the ATOMM tape.

Like all MP tapes, ATOMM uses the binder in both "titan-fine" and magnetic layer.

Fujifilm is using Advanced Metal Powder (AMP) to describe the "latest" smaller particles, which will be employed in future higher-density ATOMM products. These particles are not just smaller, they have a thinner and denser cobalt-ferrite protective coating. This improved passivation layer, which uniformly coats each particle, not only protects the particle in the traditional manner but also raises its magnetization.

Another variation of MP film is the AMP, or Advance Magnetic Powder, media film, used in the latest DLT and SuperDLT tape drives. The "Metal Powder" is just another term for "Metal particle" design. The difference in AMP design is that the backside of the AMP media is specially designed for storage of tracks for the optical servo. This design saves space on the tape's data zone and allows for higher storage capacity while eliminating preformatting.

ME (Metal Evaporated) and AME (Advanced Metal Evaporated) Tapes

Introduced for higher recording density, DTR, and durability, a metal evaporated (ME) tape uses very different design and technology. The films on the tape are produced in a vacuum chamber where a flexible tape substrate is exposed to a "vapor" of metal (nickel alloy). In order to turn solid metal into vapor, it is heated to temperatures at which the atoms start leaving its surface. Vacuum prevents oxidation of the metal. When the tape base is brought close to the source of metal atoms, some of the atoms are transferred onto the tape surface, thus forming a thin and uniform metal layer completely free of binder. This *nickel alloy* film has much better magnetic properties than the MP film with its metal oxide particles. The metal grains formed on the surface are quite uniform in shape and size and grow nearly perpendicular to the surface. One disadvantage of ME media is the fragility of its metal-evaporated film.

An even superior version of ME tape is called AME (Figure 3–46) and has a protective carbon coating on top of the magnetic layer (helps with ME fragility) and *pure cobalt* magnetic material (vs. nickel alloys used in ME tape design). This design is quite similar to that of the modern magnetic disks found in hard disk drives, but AME tape is flexible and is only about 7 microns thick. This design provides superior resistance to wear and tape durability combined with corrosion protection to the magnetic layer. AME is a data-grade tape, which stores more data per cartridge. Its anticorrosive properties improve tape durability and reduce tape wear, allowing the media to achieve a 30-year archival rating. AME media tape is used in 8-mm helical scan tape drives such as the Mammoth drive from Exabyte.

Finally, all of today's magnetic tapes are about 7 micron thick, but are expected to become thinner, near 4 micron in the near future.

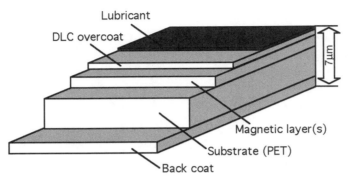

Figure 3–46
Design of the advanced metal evaporated (AME) tape.

Popular Tape Storage Technologies

QIC Linear Tape (Travan, DC2000, etc.)

QIC stands for quarter-inch cartridge. QIC technology is in more than 15 million drives worldwide, which is usually attributed to high reliability of this technology and products.

There is a wide variety of QIC standards. The most important QIC standards for the mini-cartridges are QIC-40, QIC-80, QIC-3010, and QIC-3020. These standards ensure compatibility between different platforms. For example, QIC-40/-80-compatible drives will be compatible with each other and must also conform to the QIC-117 interface standard. The QIC-80 format standard has eventually been replaced by QIC-3020, which achieves four times the storage capacity. But QIC-3020 drives, including Travan 3 devices, still read the earlier QIC mini-cartridges, because they were standardized. Drives using the newer cartridge recording format, QIC-5010, provide 13 GB of storage along with backward read compatibility with tapes of earlier QIC-2 GB, QIC-1000, QIC-525, and QIC-150/120 formats. Unfortunately, some tapes use proprietary software formatting and compression methods and aren't always compatible with other drives. Let's quickly review some of the popular QIC formats.

QIC-40/-80 • The oldest standard. QIC-80 tapes come in capacities of 80 MB, 120 MB, and 170 MB. QIC-80 drives are able to read from (but not write to or format) tapes written by QIC-40 drives (low-density tapes). Some drives also support the QIC-Wide standard.

QIC-3010/3020 • QIC-3010 and QIC 3020 drives use the same mini-cartridge size as QIC-40/80 but use a different recording head, which increases the tape's uncompressed storage capacity to 340 MB for QIC-3010 drives and 680 MB for QIC-3020 drives. Both drives can read QIC-40 and QIC-80 tapes and QIC-3020 drives can also read QIC-3010 tapes. Some drives also support the QIC-Wide standard.

QIC-Wide • Most QIC tapes are ¼-inch wide while QIC-Wide drives use a 0.315-inch wide tape. Native capacity for QIC-80 wide tapes is 210 MB, QIC-3010 wide tapes hold 425 MB, and QIC-3020 wide tapes hold 850 MB. QIC-Wide drives will read standard cartridges, but standard drives cannot read the wide tapes.

Travan • With capacity from 8 to 20 GB, Travan drives have a very large customer base and provide for better price/performance ratio than many other tape technologies, such as DAT, DC6000, and 8-mm. Travan mechanisms are known to be very reliable at a low cost point and are the perfect choice for high-performance PCs, NT workstations and small PC server environments. The main manufacturers of Travan drives are Seagate, HP, Iomega, and Sony.

Travan cartridges are similar in size and shape to standard DC2000 tape cartridges but are slightly wider and thicker (see Figure 3–47). Travan tape is 0.315-inch wide. Table 3–18 summarizes the main characteristics of Travan drives and specifies their compatibility for read or write (R/W).

Table 3–18   Characteristics of Travan Drives

Format	Capacity (native/ compressed), GB	Maximum DTR, MB/s	Compatibility
TR-1	0.4/0.8	0.125	QIC 40 (R), QIC 80 (R/W)
TR-2	0.8/1.6	0.125	QIC 3010 (R/W), QIC 80 (R)
TR-3	1.6/3.2	0.250	QIC 3010/3020 (R/W), QIC 80 (R)
TR-4	4/8	1.15	QIC 3080/3095 (R/W), QIC 3020 (R)
TR-5	10/20	1.80	TR-4, QIC 3220 (R/W), QIC 3095 (R)

Figure 3–47
Travan 20 GB tape cartridge (courtesy of Sony Electronics Inc.).

Figure 3–48
Ditto 2 GB tape cartridge (courtesy of Sony Electronics Inc.).

Ditto 2 GB • The Ditto 2 GB tape is an example of a proprietary tape format used exclusively by Iomega. This tape cartridge uses a 0.315"-wide tape and is 400 ft in length (see Figure 3–48). Native capacity for Ditto 2 GB tapes is 1 GB and capacity is doubled by compression. All Ditto 2 GB tapes come preformatted. The 2 GB tape drive can read and write to the 2 GB cartridge, but cannot format this cartridge. The 2 GB tape drive can read most other tape sizes.

Before 1983, the user's choice of tape drives consisted primarily of half-inch reel-to-reel drives and QIC tape drives. Nowadays, there is a much wider choice of tape storage technology for almost any PC, workstation, and network's backup. Development of QIC products will continue in the future.

DAT (Digital Audio Tape)

DAT stands for digital audio tape and this technology was originally designed for high-quality audio recording. Sony and HP were the first companies that defined parameters for the 4-mm DDS (digital data storage) format for DAT solutions, which was adopted in the late 1980s.

With capacity points from 4 to 40 GB, DDS is the industry standard in the workstation, PC, and mid-range server environments. Due to inexpensive DDS media, DDS drives are perfect for situations in which both capacity and media cost play a role.

DAT uses relatively inexpensive *4 mm tape* (Figure 3–49) and *helical-scan recording* technology with two read heads and two write heads mounted on a rotating drum. The drum's axis is tilted by 6 degrees relative to a vertical axis. The 3.5-inch form-factor mechanism of the DAT drives are easy to integrate into a PC.

Since the DDS standard was adopted, it became the only recognized DAT standard. Nowadays, all of the major manufacturers (HP, Seagate, Sony, Aiwa, etc.) of DAT products conform to the DDS standard, which was accepted as a standard by ANSI,

Figure 3–49
DAT 4 mm tape cartridge (courtesy of Sony Electronics Inc.).

ISO (International Standards Organization), and ECMA (European Computer Manufacturers Association). For example, DDS media must meet a specification that is set out in ISO/IEC 10777 (for 60 m DAT) or ISO/IEC 12247 (for 90 m DDS).

One of the big advantages of DDS is the compatibility of products from different manufacturers: one can record data with a drive from one manufacturer and read it back with a drive from another manufacturer. This is possible due to the adoption of specific physical formats for DDS-1, DDS-2, DDS-3, and DDS-4 cartridges, with a single method for compressing data.

The latest digital data storage format is the DDS-4, which provides for a large increase in storage capacity (up to 40 GB compressed) and DTR (up to 6 MB per second with 2:1 compressed data). The higher capacity of DDS-4 is achieved via reduced track pitch (from 9.1 μm to 6.8 μm), an increased number of tracks (from 12 to 16 over 1 mm of tape), and increased tape length (from 125 m to 155 m). The higher DTR of DDS-4 is achieved via improved read/write head, drum, media, and channel technology. For example, DDS-4 drum speed is increased. Increased recording density and capacity required new media capable of higher densities and also being thinner—to fit extra length inside the same cartridge. To allow for a reduction in track pitch on DDS-4, it has been necessary to develop new MP media capable of producing a greater output signal.

At the same time, DDS-4 retained the main technologies from DDS-3 such as PRML (Partial Response Maximum Likelihood) channel, Timed Tracking, and so on. The main advantage of DDS-1 are summarized below:

- 20 GB of data storage (uncompressed) or 40 GB with 2:1 compression ratio versus 12/24 GB for DDS-3

- DTR of up to 3 MB/sec (uncompressed) and up to 6 MB/sec (2:1 compression)

- Industry-wide compatibility and backward compatibility with earlier standards

- Read-after-write (RAW) technology with data being verified while it is being written, which eliminates the need for a further verification pass

In order to implement read-after-write (RAW) technology in a helical scan drive, two read heads (R1 and R2) are positioned on a helical scanner 180° apart from the two write heads (W1, W2) (see Figure 3–50). Two tracks are written and immediately read for each revolution of the scanner to make sure there was no error.

The main DDS-4 specifications are summarize below:

- 20 GB capacity (native)
- 6.8 micrometers track pitch
- 122 Kbpi linear bit density
- 90% format efficiency
- Error rate 10^{-15} or better
- Same group structure as DDS-3

DSS products are available in the following formats: DDS-1, -2, -3, and -4. With its relatively large, compressed capacity up to 40 GB (per cartridge), data transfer rate up to 6 MB/s, and high reliability, DAT is suitable for UNIX workstations and large PC servers. DDS standards and performance characteristics are summarized in Table 3–19.

Table 3–19   DDS Standards and Performance Characteristics

Standard	Capacity, GB (native/compressed)	Tape length, m	Maximum DTR, MB/s (native)
DDS-1	2/4	90	0.183
DDS-2	4/8	120	0.75
DDS-3	12/24	125	1.5
DDS-4	20/40	155	3.0

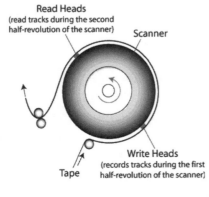

Read Heads
(read tracks during the second
half-revolution of the scanner)   Scanner

Write Heads
(records tracks during the first
Tape   half-revolution of the scanner)

Figure 3–50
Design of the DAT helical scanner implementing read-after-write (RAW) technology.

Apparently, DDS-4 is not the last standard adopted. All new technology incorporated in DDS-4 has created a solid platform for the future development of DDS-5 and beyond.

Exabyte Mammoth

The first high-performance 8-mm helical scan tape drive was introduced in 1987 by Exabyte. The drive technology was based on a consumer video technology with some modifications needed for higher data integrity and performance required for data storage and retrieval. For example, the RAW technology (discussed earlier) was used to minimize data errors.

In 1996, Exabyte introduced the new helical scan drive—the Mammoth. The Mammoth became an extremely successful product, with over 1.5 million units sold.

The Mammoth has about 40% fewer electronic components than previous 8 mm drives, is capable of self-calibration, and searches for and reports any errors. The Exabyte Mammoth system has the storage capacity of 40 GB and a sustained transfer rate of 6 MB/s (compressed), thus backing up 43 GB in less than two hours.

The Mammoth drives feature solid aluminum deck casting made for with accuracy and rigidity needed to maintain tight size tolerances in the drive. This design also protects the drive internals from contamination. The capstan-less drive design eliminates the traditional element of the tape drive, which accelerates tape wear. The design without a capstan prevents damage to the edge of the tape during repositioning. The tape path supports AME (Advanced Metal Evaporated) media, a thinner, more sensitive next-generation media. The Mammoth's scanner is also optimized for AME media. The smooth surface is a key element behind the Mammoth head's life specification of 35,000 hours.

Exabyte Mammoth-2 (or M2, see Figure 3–51) is the latest product in the line, which added lots of new technology and improved significantly both capacity and per-

Figure 3–51
Mammoth M2 drive (courtesy of Exabyte).

formance, and can back up 150 GB of data in less than 1.5 hours (vs. 43 GB in about two hours for the Mammoth). It is also backward compatible with previous Exabyte products.

In M2 products, Exabyte uses a so-called "power-on-rotor" technology with the signal pre-amplifiers placed on the rotating part of the scanner—as close to the heads as possible, which resulted in increased and almost equal strength of the read and write signals. This allowed for a newer "read-while-write" scheme to be implemented.

Read-while-write (RWR) technology makes possible to place write and read heads closer together on a scanner and also to increase the number of heads (see Figure 3–52). M2 has now two write channels (four heads W1–W4 in Figure 3–52) and two read channels (R1–R4). Earlier RAW technology required the heads to be 180° apart for alternative read and write operation. M2 uses the scanner design with heads mounted 90° apart. Each complete revolution of the scanner results in four tracks written while four previously written tracks are read and checked for errors.

Each channel of the scanner supports 6 MB/s, making a total DTR equal to 12 MB/s for both read and write operations. To improve performance and reliability of its read channel, Mammoth-2 uses an advanced PRML technique (discussed earlier in the chapter), similar to that used in the hard disk drives. Table 3–20 summarizes some characteristics of Mammoth tape drives.

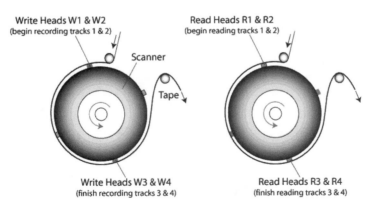

Figure 3–52
Mammoth M2 scanner design for read-while-write (RWR) technology. Second picture shows position after 270° rotation.

Table 3–20   Mammoth Tape Drive Characteristics

	Mammoth	Mammoth-2
Capacity (native/ compressed 2.5:1), GB	20/40	20/50; 40/100; 60/150
Sustained DTR (native/ compressed 2.5:1), MB/s	3/6	12/30
Maximum DTR (burst), MB/s	20	80 (LVD)/100 (Fibre Channel)
Interface	SCSI-2 Fast/Wide and Fast/Narrow; LVD SCSI	LVD SCSI/Fibre Channel
Compatibility	Mammoth (R/W), 8500/8500c/8200 (R) (except 8200 compressed)	Mammoth-2 (R/W), Mammoth-LT and Mammoth (R)
MTBF, hours	>250,000	>300,000

In the future, the 47 mm scanner may accommodate up to 16 heads (8 channels), making a DTR of about 80 MB/s a reality.

AIT (Advanced Intelligent Tape)

AIT is another 8-mm format used in helical scan tape drives. The AIT format was introduced to target the mid-range server market and to provide a combination of high reliability and data integrity, speed, and high capacity. To achieve these goals, newer, thinner magnetic media of AME tapes, new head technology, and a unique memory-in-cassette (MIC) technology were introduced.

The AIT format was developed by Sony and is available in a small, 3.5-inch form-factor. Sony AIT drives and tapes provide from 25 GB (native) to 50 GB (compressed) capacity on a single 8-mm tape cartridge with the linear (bit) density of 116 Kbpi. AIT-2 products double this capacity. AIT-4 quadruples it to reach 100/200 GB of storage (native/compressed).

The AIT technology relies on a helical scan recording scheme, which provided higher density of recording and allows for smaller and less expensive tape cartridges. Sony AIT drives use an Auto Tracking Following (ATF) technology for very accurate tape tracking, allowing to adjust for tape flutter and record data tracks much closer to each other.

Sony AIT systems feature a unique MIC (memory-in cassette) design with a 16 Kb memory chip built into the tape cartridge, which keeps the tape's system log. The

MIC chip stores all of the information usually found on the first segments of tapes in other tape technologies. Typically, the drive needs to rewind the tape to the beginning of the log to find a needed file. With the MIC design, this can be done much faster by reading data from the solid-state MIC.

Sony AIT drives also provide such useful features as head autocleaning, which is activated when the drive registers an increasing number of soft errors, which are associated with head contamination. The MTBF for Sony AIT drives is reported to be ~200,000 hours, and the magnetic head life is expected to last up to 30,000 hours.

Seagate is another manufacturer of AIT drives with its Sidewinder product series. The Sidewinder 50 drives are available in a 3.5-inch form-factor, a larger 5.25-inch form factor, and in external options.

DLT (Digital Linear Tape) and Super DLT

DLT and Super DLT are the 0.5-inch linear tape formats supported by Quantum. DLT technology was developed for client/server environments and network backup, and for mid-range computer systems and applications. DLT technology across the product line covers its target mid-range from the low end of the upper range through the high end of the lower range of products, and meets both ANSI and ECMA format standards.

The major elements of DLT technology include a low-tension linear recording path, multiple channel read/write system, high capacity, data integrity features, and the tape media and cartridge design (DLT tape). Backward compatibility is also supported through the generations of DLT tape products, thereby encouraging the user to stay with this proprietary format.

Figure 3–53 shows the basic design of a DLT tape drive. The 0.5-inch tape from the cartridge moves by the read/write head onto the take-up reel. Initially, the tape drive adjusts the tape tension, creating the lightest possible head-tape contact to reduce wear of both head and tape. There are six precision rollers, which guide the tape from the cartridge around the head-guide assembly in a smooth arc, and gently wraps it around the take-up reel in the drive.

The DLT tape cartridges are approximately 4 inches by 4 inches in size and are 1 inch thick. The cartridge contains only a supply reel of tape with the take-up reel being within the tape drive, which allows for larger cartridge capacity. The cartridge has a write-protect similar to that of a floppy disk.

As is conventional with the linear tape, the data is recorded linearly, forming multiple parallel tracks along the tape (Figure 3–54). This design allows for simultaneous reading of multiple tracks using a stationary read/write head.

The head design with self-regulating contours and outriggers creates a uniform contact pressure over the head surface to minimize wear. The head design also breaks

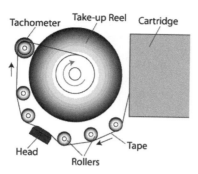

Figure 3–53
Basic design of DLT tape drive.

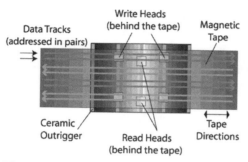

Figure 3–54
DLT tape is recorded linearly forming multiple parallel tracks along the tape.

down the air-cushion between the fast moving tape and the head surface to keep the physical (and magnetic) spacing as small as possible at the smallest possible contact pressure. A combination of tape-tensioning with the head design minimizes stress (while maximizing magnetic signal strength) and increases the head life (i.e., the DLT7000 tape drive offers a head life of 30,000 hours and the media has a demonstrated life of 500,000 passes).

DLT drives use half-inch-wide tape—the widest tape available today. The DLT7000 drive introduced the Symmetric Phase Recording (SPR) head, which writes adjacent tracks using an alternating angle (see Figure 3–55) and thereby eliminating cross-track interference and the need for guard bands. This also allows for narrower tracks and higher track density. This track density is the key to the DLT7000 tape drive's 35 GB per cartridge native capacity.

In 1994, the double-coated DLT digital tape media was introduced. Eventually, DLT technology incorporated high-grade metal particle (MP) tape in a half-inch for-

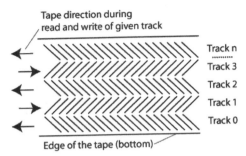

Figure 3–55
Symmetric Phase Recording (SPR) head in DLT7000 drive writes adjacent tracks using an alternating angle.

mat. A combination of both solid and liquid lubricants in the tape binder reduces tape and head wear while repelling airborne particles that might otherwise affect the read/write head performance and the self-cleaning feature.

The newer Quantum SuperDLT family of products is a scalable platform designed for multiple product generations. It is backward-compatible with earlier DLT drives, such as DLTtape 4000, 7000, and 8000 using DLT tape IV cartridges. While the DLT tape products target the mid-range Unix and NT server markets, the SuperDLT tape targets the networked Unix and large NT server systems running enterprise mission-critical applications.

The SuperDLT drives feature Quantum's Laser Guided Magnetic Recording (LGMR) technology, which includes magnetic recording (on the data side) and optical servoing (on the backside of the tape), and results in a significant increase in the number of data tracks. The SuperDLT also uses magnetoresistive cluster (MRC) heads for higher track density and lower cost, a PRML read channel, and advanced metal powder (AMP) media. Table 3–21 summarizes the main performance characteristics of the latest DLT and SuperDLT drives.

Table 3–21   Performance Characteristics of DLT and SuperDLT Drives

	DLT 7000	DLT 8000	SuperDLT
Capacity (native/ compressed), GB	35/70	40/80	110/220
Sustained DTR (native/ compressed 2.5:1), MB/s	5/10	6/12	11/22
Interface	SCSI-2 Fast/Wide (single ended and differential)	SCSI-2 Fast/Wide (single ended/LVD or HVD)	—
Compatibility	DLTtape III, DLTtape IIIXT, DLTtape IV, all previous DLT tapes (R/W)	DLTtape III, DLTtape IIIXT, DLTtape IV, all previous DLT tapes (R/W)	DLTtape IV
MTBF, hours	300,000	250,000	—

LTO or Linear Tape Open

In 1998, IBM, Seagate, and Hewlett-Packard have introduced the Linear Tape-Open, or LTO, technology, a new, powerful, scalable, open tape architecture to meet the growing storage demands of mid-range to enterprise-class servers with up to 200 GB of data per cartridge. An open format offers multiple sources of drives and media and enables compatibility between products from different vendors. Two different implementations of LTO were developed: Ultrium (see Figure 3–56) and Accelis.

Figure 3–56
IBM LTO Ultrium tape drive family (courtesy of IBM).

The Accelis tape format is optimized for fast data access, with high reliability and performance characteristics. It uses two-reel cartridges with loading at the middle of the tape to minimize access time. The Accelis format targets automated environments and a wide range of "on-line" data inquiry and retrieval applications. The Accelis migration path is summarized in Table 3–22, but the properties tabulated below are still subject to change (Generations 2–4).

Table 3–22   Accelis Migration Path

	Generation 1	Generation 2	Generation 3	Generation 4
Capacity (native)	25 GB	50 GB	100 GB	200 GB
DTR (native)	10–20	20–40	40–80	80–160
Encoding channel	RLL 1,7	PRML	PRML	PRML
Media	MP	MP	MP	Thin film
Access time, s	<10	<8	<7	<7

The Ultrium tape format is optimized for high capacity and performance with high reliability for either a stand-alone or an automated environment. The Ultrium uses a single reel cartridge (similar to DLT tape format) to maximize capacity and suites for backup, restore, and archive applications. The Ultrium migration path is summarized in Table 3–23, but still can be changed in the future (Generations 2–4).

Table 3–23   Ultrium Migration Path

	Generation 1	Generation 2	Generation 3	Generation 4
Capacity (native)	100 GB	200 GB	400 GB	800 GB
DTR (native)	10–20	20–40	40–80	80–160
Encoding channel	RLL 1,7	PRML	PRML	PRML
Media	MP	MP	MP	Thin film

An implementation of both LTO formats is available through open licenses to vendors wishing to participate in developing tape products that interchange between other vendors' products of the same format. The LTO format incorporates the best of several technologies in order to achieve the highest possible performance.

LTO is a linear serpentine technology that allows for a higher number of concurrent channels. The first generation of LTO enables up to eight channels, the future versions may have up to 16 channels.

LTO was also developed to take advantage of the best available servo and head technologies, needed for high track densities and, ultimately, for high areal recording density. As a result, LTO offers high recording areal density of 0.1 Gb/in^2.

Other features of LTO include improved data compression, new RLL code, dynamic rewrite of data written onto defective areas or written by a bad write head, dynamic stop of writing on any region of tape with unreliable servo, and LTO Cartridge Memory (LTO-CM, 4 KB of nonvolatile solid-state memory) to allow for fast data location. Finally, recording units are indexed precisely for rapid data search and simplified error and data recovery.

Automated Tape Applications

Estimates indicate that the amount of information stored on computer storage systems is steadily growing by 50 to 100% per year. Apparently, even large stand-alone tape drives cannot support even mid-sized networks unless a number of employers is assigned the task of swapping out tapes. This is why fully automated tape storage systems are the cost-effective data storage solution for high-volume storage systems.

The primary application for automated tape systems is data backup and archiving. It eliminates human error from the backup process (an incorrect tape loaded, scheduled backup is forgotten, etc.). Automated tape storage systems are also used in Hierarchical Storage Management (HSM), which is a system built around different types of media with high-demand data placed on hard disk drives and lower-demand information stored on optical disks or magnetic tapes. Managing data storage across media types is practically impossible without automation. Automated tape storage systems are also used as near-online storage, for archiving, for data collection, in tape arrays (RAID), and so on.

The basic idea of automated tape storage systems is simple: combine together robotics, tape drives, and provide controlling software to make the robotic device load, unload, and swap the tapes. An implementation of this idea may differ in the way they handle data backup and manage data access. There are three basic types of automated tape storage systems: *stackers*, *autoloaders*, and *libraries*.

Stackers represent the simplest type of automated tape systems used for small-scale backup and storage. Stackers are built around a single drive with tapes inserted and removed in a sequential manner by some kind of robotic device. A stacker typically starts the backup by inserting tape 0 and continues inserting and removing tapes until the task is completed or it runs out of tape cartridges. These systems are efficient, relatively inexpensive, and very inflexible.

Autoloaders are another type of automated tape storage also built around a single drive but capable of accessing any of their tapes upon request. This direct access feature allows for much more sophisticated applications such as small-scale network backup and restore or near-online storage. These systems are efficient, somewhat more inexpensive, but much more flexible.

Libraries are the third type of automated tape storage systems with functionality similar to that of the autoloaders, but built around multiple tape drives and with the ability to support large-scale backups, near-online access, user-initiated file recovery, and, what is impossible in stackers and autoloaders, simultaneous support of multiple users and hosts. While being much more flexible than stackers or autoloaders, libraries are also more complex and more expensive.

Automated tape libraries typically include:

- two or more tape drives
- robotic loader mechanism to move the tapes to and from the drive(s)
- separate library and loader controllers
- bar code reader to enable the software to track the inventory

To better understand what the automated tape library is capable of, let's consider the IBM Magstar 3494 Tape Library, which is one of the popular solutions for today's large storage requirements. The list of key features offered by the Magstar 3494 Tape Library (see Figure 3–57) are summarized next.

- *Increased attachments:* Connect up to 32 SCSI 2 Fast/Wide or Fibre Channel tape drives. With multiple ports it allows to add even more drives.
- *Performance*: Up to 610 cartridge mounts or dismounts per hour.
- *Flexibility*: Can use either the IBM 3490E tape drive, the Magstar 3590 tape drive, or both in the same 3494 library (but in different frames).
- *High data availability:* Designed to eliminate single points of failure.
- *Modular design*: Expandable from one to 16 library frames to handle from 160 tape cartridges up to 6,240 cartridges.
- *Expandable storage capacity*: Can be configured for up to 748 TB of tape storage.
- *Connectivity*: Supports a variety of server platforms such as zSeries, pSeries, iSeries, HP, Sun, and Windows NT, and allows multiple hosts to simultaneously share the library.

This impressive system is not cheap, of course: the price starts around $90,000. However, this is a cost-effective solution that provides high capacity, fast data access,

Figure 3–57
IBM Magstar 3494 Tape Library (courtesy of IBM).

and an incredible 748 TB (748,000 GB) of data storage, which is impossible to manage without proper automation.

Summary

I would like to summarize this chapter with a table comparing technologies discussed earlier.

The following definitions are used in Table 3–24 for the market segment:

- Low-end storage segment: *single* user, PC, high-end PC, low-end workstation, small PC server
- Mid-range storage segment: *2 to 129 users* in commercial environments of small and mid-size businesses, workstations, high-end NT servers, midrange enterprise servers
- High-end segment: *more than 129* users in enterprise environments, mainframes, high-end network servers, large network backup and data management

Table 3–24   Comparison of Drive Technologies

Format	Capacity (native/compressed), GB	Sustained data transfer rate (burst), MB/s	Storage market segment
QIC (Travan, etc.)	10/20	1/2	low-end
4-mm DAT (DDS-4)	20/40	3/6	low-end/mid-range
Mammoth	20/40	3/6	low-end/mid-range
Mammoth-2	60/150	12/30	mid-range/high-end
AIT-1	25/50	3/6	mid-range
AIT-2	50/100	6/12	mid-range/high-end
DLT	40/80	6/12	mid-range/high-end
Super DLT	110/220	11/22	high-end
LTO	100 (400 in the future)	20 (160 in the future)	mid-range/high-end
Automated library (i.e., Magstar)	up to 748,000	14/42 (drive dependent)	high-end and beyond

4

Optical Storage

In this chapter...

INTRODUCTION . . . .

The History of Optical Storage

As it was mentioned in the first chapter, the first optical recording technology was invented by the Sumerians of Mesopotamia back in 3500 BC. The logographic writing system they introduced consisted of numerous signs called logograms, representing complete words. This system was ambiguous and caused errors during data retrieval, or *reading*.

The more advanced optical recording technology—hieroglyphic and alphabetic writing systems, which allowed for storing, retrieval, and duplication of data *almost without errors* (except for misspellings and misreading)—was put forward by the Egyptians about 5,000 years ago.

Today's meaning of optical data storage refers to storage systems that use light for recording and retrieval of information.

Photography was the first example of optical data recording in the modern sense. The first photographs were developed about 200 years ago and represented analog optical storage, which has a limited application for information storage since it is difficult to interface analog data with digital machines, plus there is a continuous degradation of data at every step of reading and writing. Light can be easily used for digital information recording, especially since the invention of the lasers.

In 1972, Philips announced a method for storing audio signal optically. The technology they used was analog and was eventually rejected.

In 1977, the *optical* digital audio disk (DAD) was developed by Japanese companies Sony, Mitsubishi, and Hitachi. The disk was large, about 30 cm in diameter (like LP records). By 1978, Philips developed another version of DAD with much smaller—11.5 cm in diameter—disks. Eventually, in 1980, Sony and Philips defined the present CD design with a disc diameter of 12 cm and with 74 minutes of play-back time. Nowadays, the compact disc is the most popular media for high-quality digital audio playback.

In 1996, computer manufacturers, along with consumer electronics manufacturers and movie studios, accepted the DVD-Video standard. In 1997, the first DVD-Video players and more than 500 video titles became commercially available in the United States. DVD-ROM drives became an integrated part of many high-end computer systems from various manufacturers, with over 5 million drives sold by the end of 1999. At present, DVD looks like the next generation of optical storage product and future successor of the CD.

Optical recording was for a long time, and is still, considered a future replacement for magnetic recording. Optical recording systems potentially have much greater reliability than magnetic recording systems since there is a much larger distance between the read/write element and the moving media. Therefore, there is no wear associated with repeated use of the optical systems. However, there are other possible sources for trouble: the life and stability of the laser, mechanical damage to the relatively soft and exposed-to-the-environment media, mechanical damage due to shock and vibration, and so on. Another advantage of the optical recording systems over the best performing magnetic recording systems—hard drives—is their removability.

The main disadvantages of optical storage when compared to magnetic storage is slower random data access. This partially comes from the design of the relatively large (and heavy) optical heads. Moving 100 grams over the discs at the high acceleration and speed needed to match the 5 to 10 ms average access time for magnetic hard disk drives is a real challenge, since the effective weight of the moving parts of a hard drive's head-stack assembly (actuator arm with suspensions and sliders) is on the order of a few grams only. Plus, unlike the hard disk, an optical disk is usually removable, which limits rotational velocities and, correspondingly, limits access time. Increasing RPM causes the relatively loosely fixed CD-ROM disc to vibrate significantly compared to a stiff, fixed, and balanced hard disk.

Optical drives of all kinds operate on the same principle of detecting variations in the optical properties of the media surface. CD and DVD drives detect changes in light intensity; MO drives detect changes in the light polarization. All optical storage systems work with reflected light.

A convenient way to define tracks on the optical disks is by using grooves. These are created by etching, stamping, or molding the substrate. The bottoms of the grooves are used as a storage medium, and the grooves are separated by the lands. Lands could be also used as a storage medium, instead of, or together with, the grooves. The groove depth is based on the laser wavelength and typically equals 1/8 of the wavelength of the laser beam.

Another way to define tracks and provide servo information for the drive's electronics is to use a so-called sampled servo, where the tracks are defined by occasional marks placed on the substrate at regular intervals. The marks define the outer limits of the track and help to position the laser spot on the track.

Basic Optics for Optical Storage Systems

When the light reaches the surface of an opaque solid body, it can be reflected, refracted, transmitted, or absorbed. When it is reflected, it could be reflected in a specular way, in a diffusive way, or in a combination of both, shown in Figure 4–1.

If the surface is smooth, the light is reflected at the same angle as the angle of incidence, or in a *specular* way. The mirror has a very smooth surface and reflects most of the light specularly right back into your eyes with very little scattering.

If the surface is rough, the diffusive reflection takes place and the light is scattered all around. In spite of that, the law of reflection holds exactly over every local region of the surface small enough to be considered smooth. Rough mirror will send a portion of light away from the direction of incidence, making it miss your eyes and lowering the quality of the image.

When the light is reflected only partially, another part of it penetrates the surface and becomes refracted and absorbed (see Figure 4–2).

The index of refraction, n, is a measure of how much the material bends the light. It is expressed as a ratio of the velocity of light in a vacuum, c, to the velocity of light in a specific medium, v: $n = c/v$.

The index of refraction is typically greater than 1, but is a function of the nature of material and the wavelength of light. The refractive index of air is very close in value to that of a vacuum, and the refractive indexes of solids are practically measured relative to air rather than to a vacuum.

In optical design, the importance of the refraction phenomenon is that it bends the light when it passes between two materials, as shown in Figure 4–2.

Figure 4–1
When the light is reflected, it could be reflected in a specular way, diffusive way, or in a combination of both.

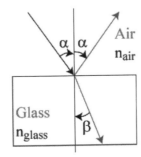

Figure 4–2
When the light is reflected only partially, another part of it penetrates the surface and becomes refracted and absorbed.

The so-called Snell's law of refraction allows you to calculate the degree of light bending as following:

$$n_{air} / n_{glass} = \sin\alpha / \sin\beta$$

There are some cases when the angle of incidence is such that all the light is reflected back inside the optically "denser" material or the material with a higher refraction index. This is called the *total internal reflection* and can be used to keep the light inside the optical cavity of the semiconductor laser diode or inside the optical fiber used in a Fibre Channel interface cable design or in the broadband data transmission lines. In the case of a glass-air interface, this phenomena occurs at the angles larger or equal to the critical angle of about 42° for visible light. This angle, at which the internal reflection starts, is called the critical angle of incidence and is defined as the following:

$$\alpha_c = \sin^{-1}(n_{glass} / n_{air})$$

The refractive index is affected by the wavelength of light, but this influence is small enough to be ignored in most cases (i.e., in optical fibers) as long as λ doesn't change appreciably. Table 4–1 summarizes refractive indexes of some known mediums.

Table 4–1   Refractive Indexes

Media	Index of refraction
Vacuum	1.0
Air	1.0003 ~ 1.0
Water	1.33
Glass	1.5
Diamond	2.0
Silicon	3.4

The depth at which the light can penetrate inside the material depends on the ability of the material to absorb this light. The absorption varies with the material and light wavelength. For example, the glass absorption is very small while metals have in general high absorption. In the case of metals, the penetration depth of light is on the order of nanometers, while in the case of glass it can be on the order of centimeters or meters, depending on the glass purity.

Therefore, for the optical element to be transparent, the penetration depth of light must be greater than the element's thickness. Otherwise, no light will reach the other end of the element and it will become nontransparent.

The amount of light transmitted through the material is determined from the following generic formula:

```
Transmission = 1 - Reflection - Absorption
```

The above is the energy balance equation for the incident light.

Lens and Light Focusing

The lens is the major element of the optical design of CD and DVD drives. The lens allows for light to be focused at small spots at the given distance f from the lens (the focal length). A basic design of the lens is shown in Figure 4–3.

For a thin lens, f is defined by the lens curvature and the refractive index of the material it is made of:

$$1/f = (n - 1)(1/R_1 - 1/R_2)$$

where R_1 and R_2 are the radii of curvature defined in Figure 4–3.

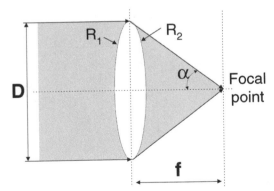

Figure 4–3
The basic design of the lens and light focusing.

The numerical aperture of the lens is a measure of the light-gathering power of the system. Current practice is to use lenses with a numerical aperture of about 0.5 to 0.6. The numerical aperture (NA) is defined as follows:

$$NA = n \sin \alpha$$

where α is the half angle of the cone of illumination (see Figure 4–3).

It is usually desired in optical recording to achieve the smallest laser beam spot possible, since the spot size is a measure of the bit size, which defines the areal density of the storage system. The spot size also affects the resolution of the system (smaller is better). An approximate spot size of the optical system is given by the following expression:

$$Spot \ diameter \sim wavelength \ of \ light \ / \ NA$$

The wavelength of the currently used GaAs lasers is in the range of 670–840 nm, which yields a minimum laser spot diameter of about 1 mm. These lasers are gradually replaced by those on the blue end of the spectra.

Another important parameter of a lens is the depth of focus, which indicates how much the lens can be moved away from the perfect focus and still maintain an acceptable focus. This is important since the storage media is spinning at high speed and has some vertical runout, which means that the distance between the data surface and the optical pickup of the drive is changing continuously. The depth of focus can be defined as follows:

$$Depth \ of \ focus \sim wavelength \ of \ light \ / \ NA^2$$

Assuming a wavelength of 700 nm and NA = 0.6, the depth of focus is about 1 micrometer. This means that the fast-spinning disk under the optical head has to keep the distance from its data layer to the objective lens within ±0.5 micrometers, which is almost impossible to get. This can be helped by using a fast auto-focus mechanism.

Diffraction Grating

When light waves pass by a sharp edge, those waves get scattered or diffracted, and the light no longer travels along a perfectly straight line. Diffraction gratings are surfaces with parallel, closely spaced narrow slots that are placed a few light wavelengths apart, which diffract incident light. The resultant interference of the diffracted waves makes them travel under some angle to the initial direction (Figure 4–4). This angle depends on the light wavelength and the slots period, and the diffraction grating can spread the light into a spectrum like a reflective prism.

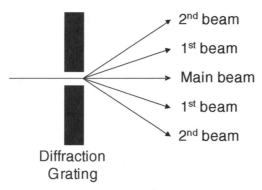

Figure 4–4
When light waves pass by sharp edges of the diffraction grating, those waves get scattered or diffracted, and the light no longer travels along a perfectly straight line.

Light Polarization

The light can be treated as a propagating *transverse electromagnetic wave* restricted to some *plane of vibration*. This plane of vibration can be constant or rotate along the propagation path of the light. The wave itself can be characterized by the *electric field vector* **E**, which indicates the direction of vibration, and the *propagation vector* **k,** which indicates the direction of propagation. To be precise, the electric field vector is a vector sum of two such vectors, say E_1 and E_2, restricted to orthogonal planes.

If the light has one plane of vibration, then it is considered to be *linearly polarized*. If the plane of vibration rotates around the propagation path, a *circularly polarized* light is obtained.

Any regular natural light source combines a large number of single, randomly oriented planes of vibration, and the overall polarization of the natural light is neutral. In other words, the natural light is *unpolarized*.

Let's imagine now that the beam of unpolarized light is shined upon the surface having a property of transmitting or reflecting light with *one plane of vibration* only. Thus, a *linear* light polarization will be achieved. An optical device that takes an unpolarized light and converts it into a linearly polarized light is called the *linear polarizer*. Linear polarizers and linearly polarized light are important elements of many optical devices. For example, magneto-optical devices (see Chapter 5) completely rely on polarized light in read operation when a small rotation of polarization plane (about 0.5° only) allows for detection of the media magnetization.

There are some natural materials, such as calcite ($CaCO_3$), that are the natural linear polarizers. The reason for that is that the calcite has a different index of refraction for two light polarizations, E_1 and E_2. Therefore, one polarization is bent more strongly than another, and one can separate those two components, thus creating linearly polarized light.

Even the regular glass can be used as a polarizer. If the natural visible light is shined upon the glass surface at some specific angle of 56.7° (called the Brewster's angle), then only one component of polarization, say E_1, will be partially reflected (about 15% of it), while another component, E_2, will be absorbed completely.

Beam-Splitter

As it follows from its name, the function of a beam-splitter is to divide the light into two parts: one transmitted and another reflected. A typical beam-splitter splits the light, creating two beams at a right angle onto another. Some beam-splitters act as polarizers by reflecting one light polarization and transmitting another polarization orthogonal to the first one. Since the beam-splitters are semi-transparent, the light intensity ration between the transmitted and reflected light can be controlled and made other than 1:1.

Light Collimator

The light collimator is an optical system (a mirror or a lens or a system of lenses) which is designed to create highly directional and parallel light beam. Such a system is also an important element of design of the optical storage systems.

The Laser Diode

All optical storage devices require a compact, reliable, and energy-efficient light source. Practically all light source types used in CD-like systems are semiconductor GaAs laser diodes. This type of laser diode is used not only for read operations, but also for writing and erasure of data. This laser diode is quite compact (about 0.3 mm × 0.1 mm × 0.05 mm) and allows to build small and relatively light optical heads. A simplified schematics of a GaAs laser diode is shown in Figure 4–5.

The active GaAs layer is surrounded by the doped n- and p- layers of GaAs and GaAlAs. Due to the fact that the refractive index of GaAs is greater than that of GaAlAs, this design confines the photons to the central GaAs layer.

When the external power source injects electrons and holes into the active GaAs layer, the electron-hole recombination takes place with the following release of energy and photon radiation. The wavelength of light emitted by the laser diode depends on the material energy gap between its conductor band and valence band.

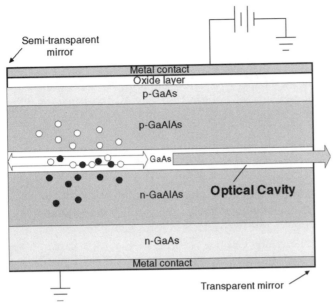

Figure 4–5
A simplified schematics of a GaAs laser diode.

The main feature of the laser diode is the optical cavity created by cleaving opposite ends of a chip into two highly reflective surfaces. Photons, created during recombination, become partially trapped within the cavity due to some degree of reflection from the cleaved ends. If the photon, on its way toward the end of the cavity, strikes an exited electron, this electron will immediately recombine and release another photon with the same direction, frequency, and phase. Therefore, trapping photons allows to stimulate emission of more and more identical photons. At the same time, a portion of photons is leaving the cavity via the end, thus creating a coherent beam of light.

The power of the output light of the laser diode can be controlled and modulated at high frequency by modulating external current.

Detector Arrays

Photodetector converts optical energy into electrical energy, thus making possible data reading in the optical storage systems. Modern photodetectors are typically semiconductor photodiodes (see Figure 4–6).

In the reverse-bias pn-photodiode, the carriers flow away from the p-n junction, thus creating a depletion region. There is very little current flowing through this junction.

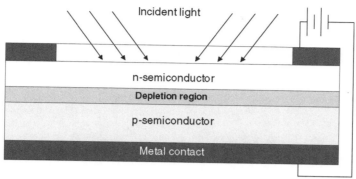

Figure 4–6
A simplified schematics of the semiconductor photodetectors.

When an incident light illuminates the surface of a photodiode, the absorbed photons create pairs of electrons and holes, particularly in the depletion zone. Those new carriers move quickly in opposite directions, and moving electrons create current in the external circuit. This completes the light-to-current conversion cycle.

Limitations of the Optical Data Storage

One major present and future limitation of the optical data storage is the data storage density. The reason for this is that diffraction phenomena limits the minimal possible size of recorded spot d_{min} to the wavelength of the light used, or

$$d_{min} \geq k\lambda \ / \ NA,$$

where λ is a recording or readout wavelength of light, NA is a numerical aperture, and k is an empirical coefficient that varies between 0.5 and 1.0.

Therefore, one needs shorter and shorter wavelength lasers to make a spot smaller. GaN In-doped lasers have already demonstrated high reliability at wavelengths as short as 370 nm and are considered to be a very promising future technology. Moving to lower wavelengths while providing required durability, small size, and low cost is the challenge for the future and the progress in this area will define the practical limits of the optical storage devices.

But durability, small size, and low cost is only a part of the problem. One important parameter of an optical system, such as the *depth of focus* (discussed earlier), is also affected by the reduction of the wavelength or decrease in the numerical aperture. As the depth of focus drops, it becomes more and more difficult to reliably focus on a moving surface of the optical media. Ultimately, it becomes impossible to keep a small spot in focus.

But, when the ultimate storage density limits of a "traditional" two-dimensional optical storage will be reached, there is a three-dimensional optical storage technology, called holography, which isn't cost-effective now, but may provide the only possible solution in the future. Another implementation of the idea of "data storage beyond one layer" is the two-layered design used in modern DVD drives that allows to effectively double recording density.

COMPACT DISC (CD) . . . .

Introduction

The history of the CD started with the videodisc in the form of Video Long Play (VLP) read-only systems. The videodisc did not become a commercial success—it was an analog storage system.

In about 1982, the CD-DA (compact disc-digital audio) was introduced to the market jointly by Philips and Sony. It stored high-quality stereo audio signal in a digital form. These systems became a huge success. In 1983, the compact disc system was first introduced in the United States.

In 1985, this technology was extended to computer storage, thanks again to cooperation between Philips and Sony. This was called a CD-ROM (compact disc-read only memory) and later became a standard ECMA-119, which specifies the CD-ROM physical format. The logical format of the CD-ROM is specified in the ISO standard 9660 and allows for data access through file names and directories.

The next step, CD-I (compact disc-interactive) was again created by Philips and Sony and announced in 1986. In the same year, Sony started shipping the first CD changer for cars.

The CD-ROM/XA (extended architecture) was introduced in 1988. Philips, Sony, and Microsoft specified digital optical formats for several media and published the specifications.

By the end of 1989, the number of CD-based hardware units sold in the United States exceeds 25 million. In the same year, Sony and Philips introduced the standard for CD-I, or CD interactive.

CD-WORM (write once read many times) technology was initiated in 1990, as well as CD-MO (magneto-optical).

By 1994, CD-ROM drives became a "standard" pre-installed feature in most desktop computers. New CD-Erasable and Enhanced Music CD (CD Plus) were introduced in 1995.

The main reason for the great success of CD-DA and CD-ROM technology is a set of standards jointly developed by Sony and Philips that, essentially specify the following:

- Macroscopic and microscopic physical structure and design of the disc
- Data format that specifies space for data, address information, and error correction codes
- Efficient error correction code (ECC) scheme, with room for additional data and ECC

CD-ROM standards, also created by Sony and Philips, use the same disc and scanning technology, and the same mastering and replication technique as used for CD-DA. The only difference between CD-DA and CD-ROM is in the data format, more powerful ECC, and more precise data addressing for CD-ROM.

CD: Basic Design

The compact disc is 12 cm in diameter, 1.2 mm thick, has a center hole 15 mm in diameter, and spins at a constant linear velocity (CLV) or constant angular velocity (CAV).

Unlike the hard disk or floppy disk, there is only one track on the optical disk and all data are stored in a spiral of about 2 billion small shallow pits on the surface (see Figure 4–7). There are about 20,000 windings on a CD—all part of the same track. This translates into about 16,000 track elements per inch (TPI) of track density and an areal density of about 80 MB/in^2. The total length of the track on a CD is almost 3 miles (~4.5 km).

Figure 4–7
Low-magnification (x 32) image of a CD showing an edge of the data zone.

A transparent polycarbonate (PC) polymeric substrate (layer) has data pits molded onto its surface. These pits are the coded data and carry information. The areas in between the pits, which are 0.9 micrometer to 3.3 micrometer long, are called "lands." The substrate layer is covered with a thin reflective layer of metal (aluminum) and with a protective layer of lacquer. On top of the CD sits the label layer.

Summarizing, the compact disc consists of:

- the label
- the protective layer
- the reflective layer
- the substrate layer

A schematic of an optical three-beam pick-up of a CD drive is shown in Figure 4–8, along with the laser beam route through the system.

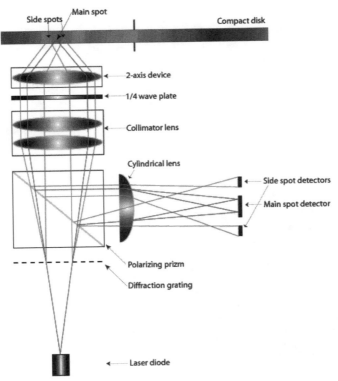

Figure 4–8
The schematic of an optical three-beam pick-up of a CD drive along with the laser beam route through the system.

The laser beam from the laser diode passes through the diffraction grating to produce two secondary beams needed to maintain correct tracking of the disc. Then, the beam passes a polarizing prism (beam-splitter) and only the vertical polarized light passes. The light beam is then converged into a parallel beam (by the collimator) and passes through the ¼-wave plate where the beam polarization plane is rotated by 45 degrees. The beam is then focused onto the disc surface by a lens and a servo-controlled mechanism called a 2-axis device. The polarization plane of the reflected beam is rotated by another 45 degrees, turning its initial vertical polarization into a horizontal.

After a few more reflections, all beams reach six photo detectors: four main spot detectors and two side spot detectors, enabling read-out of the pit information from the disc.

A laser beam of approximately 780 nm wave length is focused on the data side of the disc into a spot of about 1 mm in diameter. The laser moves in the radial direction over the fast-spinning disc and scans the data track for the intensity of the reflected light.

The data pits are about 0.12 micrometer deep and about 0.6 micrometer wide. The distance between the neighboring windings of the track is about 1.6 micrometers. The laser beam scattering occurs when it scans the pits, which translates into a slight drop in intensity of the reflected beam (see Figure 4–9).

A change in reflected light intensity occurs every time the laser spot moves from the pit onto the land and vice versa due to a partial scattering of light on pits (see Figure 4–10). The high-frequency modulated signal produced by these changes in light intensity represents the data stored on the CD.

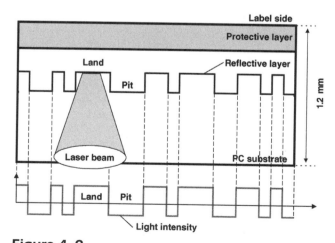

Figure 4–9
The laser beam scattering occurs when it scans the pits, which translates into a slight drop in intensity of the reflected beam.

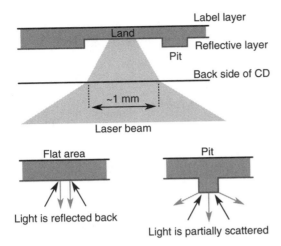

Figure 4–10
The light beam interaction with the disc features.

The main reason for high reliability of the CD is good protection of data from damage both inside and outside the CD drive.

Inside the drive, the disc and the drive's optics are separated by a distance of about 1 mm, making mechanical interaction and "crashes" even with wavy discs and imperfect clamping almost impossible.

Outside, the data layer is protected by the tough 1.2 mm thick layer of polycarbonate on one side and 10–20 micrometers of protective lacquer layer on the other side. Small scratches on the surface of a CD do not directly erase the data, but just create additional areas of light scattering. This can confuse the drive's electronics, which is also much less sensitive to radial scratches than to the circumferential ones. Gentle polishing of the scratch can (in many cases) make the CD readable again.

But, this is rarely necessary, thanks to the large size of the laser spot on the surface of the PC layer—about 1 mm. This large spot diameter "integrates" the signal over the large area, making the system much less sensitive to dirt and scratches on the disc surface. Then, the PC layer focuses the beam into a much smaller spot on the reflective layer.

Data Encoding

In a compact disc, every transition from a pit to a land and back is interpreted as "1." No transition means "0," and the length of each land segment represents the number of "0s" in the data stream. This principle is illustrated in Figure 4–11, which shows a stream of pits and lands and above it is the corresponding digital data stream.

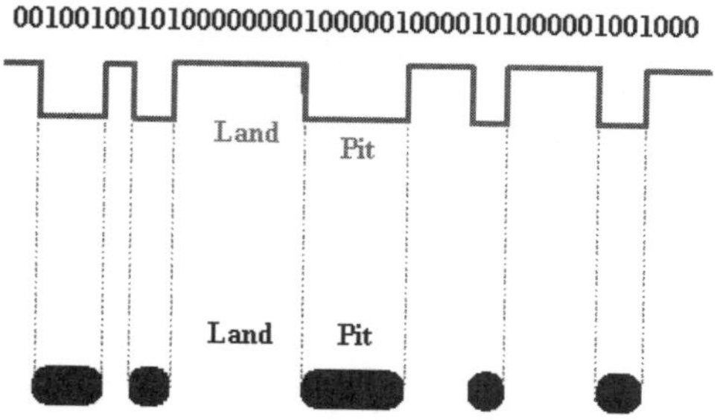

00100100101000000000100000100001010000010001000

Figure 4–11
The principle of data encoding in a CD-ROM with a stream of pits and lands and, above it, the corresponding digital data stream.

All codes needed to convert bits into their physical representation and back are called channel codes. The channel code for CD-DA and CD-ROM is called EFM: "eight-to-fourteen modulation." It interprets user's data along with the error correction data, address data, synchronization data, and other content into a stream of "channel bits." The "channel bits" are converted into a binary code and, eventually, turned into pits by the mastering machine.

During the playback, the EFM decoder of the CD-ROM works in the opposite direction, converting light modulations into a binary data stream, which is then cleared of any miscellaneous data by the drive's electronics.

Unfortunately, the resolution of the CD drive's optics is not sufficient to read directly a sequence of 1s or 0s following each other too closely, that is, 111111. Another limitation is the maximum length of a given pit or land, which is introduced in order to leave room for the clock (synchronization) data. Therefore, it was agreed to keep at least two 0s between two 1s and that the maximum length of lands and pits was limited to 10 bits in a row. These limitations led to the eight-to-fourteen conversion system which represents 8 user-bits with the (minimally required) 14 channel-bits.

Another problem appears if two 14-bit symbols follow each other, that is, "1" at the end of one symbol could be too close to "1" at the beginning of another symbol. To solve this issue, 3 special "merge" channel bits are placed between the 14-bit symbols. Thus, for each 8-bit user data, 17 channel-bits are used.

A basic unit of information stored on a CD is called a *frame*. The frame equals 24 17-bit symbols combined with the synchronization pattern, a control and display symbol, and 8 error correction symbols. Frames are grouped together to form blocks (also called sectors). Each block has 2,352 bytes of user data in the CD-DA standard or 2,048 bytes in the CD-ROM standards (due to tighter error correction technique and more error correction bytes). Figure 4–12 shows the structure of one CD-ROM block.

00	FF x 10	00	MIN	SEC	SECTOR	MODE	DATA	LAYERED ECC
12 bytes (synch)				4 bytes (ID)			2048 bytes	288 bytes
2352 bytes								

Figure 4–12
Structure of one CD-ROM block.

The first CD drives played back 75 blocks per second, which translated into the data transfer rate 1X, equal to about 0.15 MB/s.

Making a CD

One reason for the success of the optical disc technology is the ease and cheapness of replicating them in large quantities. The making of a CD includes two main steps: *premastering* and *mastering* (see Figure 4–13).

Premastering involves data preparation for recording. The data is indexed, organized, reformatted (possibly with some ECC), and transferred to the magnetic tape. Now, the data is ready to be imprinted onto the CD.

Mastering involves physical transfer of the data into the pits and lands. First, a layer of light-sensitive photoresist is spin-coated onto the clean glass master disc from a solvent solution. Then, the photoresist is heat-cured and exposed to a modulated beam of short-wavelength light, which carries the encoded data to be recorded on a CD. Next, the master is developed in a wet process by exposing it to the developer, which etches away exposed areas, thus leaving the same pattern we will find later on the CD.

Next, the master is coated (using a electroplating technique) with a thin layer of silver and then with a thick (about 300 micrometers) layer of Ni to form a father-stamper—a negative replica of the disc. The photoresist layer is destroyed during this process, but the much more durable stamper is formed and can be used for CD replication. Usually, a stamper can be used to produce a few tens of thousands CDs before it wears out. Therefore, more stampers than one are needed. These stamper-mothers are produced by electroplating the father itself. Then, the mothers can be used to make many actual stampers for making CDs.

Finally, the process of injection molding is used to produce the surface of the CD. Hot plastic (PC) is injected into a mold, and then is pressed against the stamper and cooled, resulting in a CD. Other processes than injection molding could be used, but they all involve pressing the hot plastic against the stamper. Finally, the pits and lands

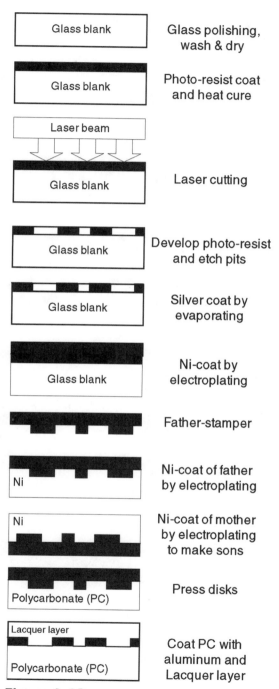

Figure 4–13
The process of making a CD.

on the surface of a CD are coated with a thin reflective metal layer (aluminum), then coated with lacquer, the center hole is punched, and the disc is supplied with a label. Packaging usually finishes the process of making a CD.

Spin Rates and Data Transfer Rate

The X ratings of CD-ROM drives are based on a comparison with the very first generation drives with the data transfer rates of 150 KB/s or 1X. Today's drives operate at more then 32X, boosting data transfer rates beyond 4.8 MB/s, and the improvement has mostly come from the increase in spin rates. The other components have mostly remained unchanged. It seems at this point that further increase in spindle speed may be impractical due to vibration and following loss in drive performance.

At first, CD-ROM drives were designed using the constant linear velocity (CLV) principle, where the angular speed of the drive (rpm) was continuously adjusted following the read head to keep the laser spot moving over the disc surface at constant velocity. This provided uniform spacing of the pits along the track and a constant data transfer rate independent of head positioning over the disc. At some point, this principle was sacrificed to keep up with the need for faster and faster motors, which is much easier to achieve with the constant-angular speed motors.

Therefore, many (but not all) newest CD drives operate on a constant angular velocity (CAV) principle, like hard disk drives, for example. For CAV, the transfer rate is a function of the data radius. This means that the *average data transfer rate* (DTR) of the drive is much lower than the *drive's maximum rate specified by its X-rating*. The first 1X CD-ROM drive had the data transfer rate equal to 0.15 MB/s. Therefore, 2X drives had 0.3 MB/s rate, 4X drives had 0.6 MB/s, and so on up to 12X. For faster drives, which operate on CAV principle, one needs to specify two data transfer rates: minimum and maximum. Table 4–2 summarizes this and shows the slowdown in the average DTR in spite of continuously increasing nominal drive speed.

Table 4–2   Data Transfer Rates for CD Drives

Drive speed rating	Design	Minimum DTR (MB/s)	Maximum DTR (MB/s)	Average DTR (MB/s)
1 X	CLV	0.15	0.15	0.15
2 X	CLV	0.30	0.30	0.30
4 X	CLV	0.60	0.60	0.60
6 X	CLV	0.90	0.90	0.90
8 X	CLV	1.20	1.20	1.20
10 X	CLV	1.50	1.50	1.50
12 X	CLV	1.80	1.80	1.80
12 X to 20 X	CAV	1.80	3.00	2.40
12 X to 24 X	CAV	1.80	3.60	2.70
12 X to 32 X	CAV	1.80	4.80	3.30
12 X to 48 X	CAV	1.80	7.20	4.50

Interfaces

Most CD-ROM drives come with ATAPI Interface (enhanced IDE), which can be directly connected to the motherboard. External CD-ROMs use parallel, SCSI, USB, or FireWire interfaces. Read more about interfaces in Chapter 2.

TrueX Multibeam CD/DVD Technology

Traditional CD and DVD drives employ a single laser beam directed at one data track, which forms a continuous spiral on the disc.

Instead of illuminating a single track on the surface of a CD-ROM or DVD-ROM disc, the technology, proposed by Zen Research, illuminates multiple tracks, detects bits simultaneously, and reads them in parallel (see Figure 4–14). This technology can be used without changes to the CD or DVD disc standards or basic drive design, and works with both CAV (Constant Angular Velocity) and CLV (Constant Linear Velocity), which is preferred by Zen Research to deliver constant data transfer rates across the disc. Multibeam technology at CLV enables optical drives to read and transfer data from the disc at a constant speed, which corresponds to the drive's true spin X-rating.

An increase in the data rates is due to the multibeam approach which allows for the reduction of disc spin rates which decreases vibration and noise associated with high speeds.

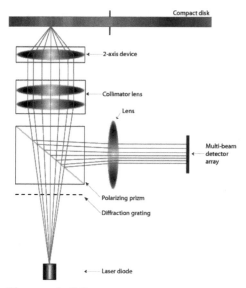

Figure 4–14
Instead of illuminating a single track on the surface of the discs, the multi-beam technology relies on illumination of multiple tracks, detecting bits simultaneously, and reading them in parallel.

The TrueX Multibeam method uses a conventional laser beam sent through a diffraction grating, which splits the beam into seven evenly spaced beams (see Figure 4–14). These beams illuminate seven different tracks simultaneously. On their way to the disc surface, beams pass through a beam-splitting mirror to the objective lens toward the disc surface. Focus and tracking are performed using the central beam. Three beams on each side of the central beam are readable by a detector array if the center beam is in focus and on track. On the way back, the reflected beams reach the multiple beam detector array, which consists of seven discrete detectors—one for each beam.

By reading seven tracks at once, the TrueX Multibeam drive achieves much higher data transfer rates than a conventional drive spinning at the same rate. Similarly, the TrueX Multibeam drive, operating at a lower speed, can achieve the same data rate as a conventional drive and keep vibration and noise at a lower level. Currently, Kenwood Technologies Inc., a subsidiary of Kenwood Corporation, offers a Zen-enabled TrueX Multibeam CD-ROM drive with an effective spin rate of up to X 72.

Recordable CD (CD-R)

A CD-R disc looks almost like a CD-ROM, but is gold on the label side and dark green on the data (recordable) side, unlike the silver coloring of a regular CD. The CD-R disc acts like a CD-ROM during reading, but also allows for data recording (once!) if used in special CD-R or CD-RW drives.

A typical CD-R structure and the data reading process are shown in Figure 4–15.

Initially, a CD-R is blank. The structure of the disc is somewhat different from that of a CD-ROM, but they both have a similar substrate layer, protective layer, and reflective metal layer. The difference is really in the organic dye layer. The CD-R drive is different from the regular CD-ROM drive since its laser can operate on different power levels. The highest level burns the pits on the disc surface, the lowest reads the pits and lands without damaging the disc surface. The recording spiral starts, like in CD-ROM, from the inner radius of the disc and continues toward the outer edge of the disc until all required data is recorded or the data limit is reached.

To simplify the head positioning mechanism, a special pre-groove is usually created on a blank CD-R. The laser beam can follow this groove during both data reading and writing. Standard CD-R discs are relatively inexpensive (less than $1–$2) and accommodates about 650 MB of data (or 74 minutes of audio recording).

During recording, the data marks—pits—are formed inside the light-absorbing organic film and look like holes. The thermal conductivity of the organic material is very low (much lower than that of metals) and very high temperatures can be achieved during less than a microsecond of heating by the drive's laser. Even if the output of the laser is relatively small, focusing the laser beam on a very small area results in high

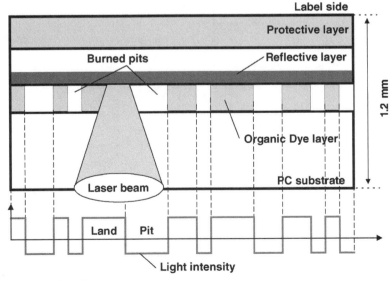

Figure 4–15
A typical CD-R structure and the data reading process.

power density, and the surface temperature can be increased by hundreds or even thousands of degrees, depending on the thermal properties of the materials.

The energy absorbed by that organic layer dissipates in the form of heat, causing local material ablation and the pit formation where the ablated material changes its roughness and, therefore, optical properties.

The design of the CD-R itself makes them write-once media, since it is impossible to erase the pits from the disc surface using the same laser. This is why the CD-R is a relatively inexpensive option for permanent data archiving and backup.

Note

If you have a CD-R or CD-RW drive that records at 8X or higher speeds, pay attention to the discs you are buying: you need to buy correspondingly fast-rated discs with fast-acting dyes.

ReWritable CD (CD-RW)

A CD-RW disc looks almost like a CD-ROM and is distinguishable by its metallic gray color. CD-RW acts like a CD-ROM during reading, but also allows data recording for thousands of times.

Many materials can exist in more than one phase (water is a good example), and different phases may have different mechanical and physical (in particular optical) properties. Often these materials could be switched from one phase to another by supplying the heat. This phenomena is used in CD-RW discs.

The typical phase-change alloy for optical recording has a stable, crystalline phase and a metastable amorphous phase with different optical properties. Recording on a CD-RW is accomplished by locally melting the recording material, which is then being cooled quickly enough to quench in its amorphous phase. The cooling rate is apparently a strong function of thermal properties of the layer and surrounding layers, in particularly, their thermal diffusivity $k = c/pa$, where c is the specific heat, p is the material density, and a is material thermal conductivity. In general, the time t required for heat to diffuse a distance l in a material could be expressed as:

$$t \sim l^2 / k$$

To return amorphous material to its initial crystalline state, a process of annealing is used, when material is heated slightly below its melting temperature. Fast data erasure could be achieved if the annealing rate is very high and the temperature is slightly below the melting temperature.

These are the most important basic requirements for a successful erasable phase-change material:

- Different refractive index for crystalline and amorphous phases
- Low melting point (for low laser power)
- Moderate thermal conductivity (for fast cooling and quenching)
- Rapid annealing below melting temperature (for single-pass erasure)

A typical structure of the CD-RW disc and the data reading process is shown in Figure 4–16. The structure of the CD-RW disc is somewhat similar to that of a CD-R, with a similar polycarbonate substrate layer, protective layer, and reflective metal layer, plus two dielectric layers and a layer of phase-changing metal alloy. The dielectric layers prevent overheating of the phase-changing layer during the data-recording process. The data marks—the pits—are formed inside the light-adsorbing phase-changing film and have different optical properties and different light reflectance.

To simplify the head positioning mechanism, like in other CD storage systems, a special pregroove is usually created on a blank CD-RW. The laser beam of the servo mechanism can follow this groove during both data reading and writing.

The CD-RW drive is different from the regular CD-ROM drive since its laser can operate on different power levels. The highest level causes phase transitions in the recording material and is used for data recording. The medium level is used for annealing or data erasure. And the lowest level of laser power is used for data reading—scanning the pits and lands without damaging the disc surface.

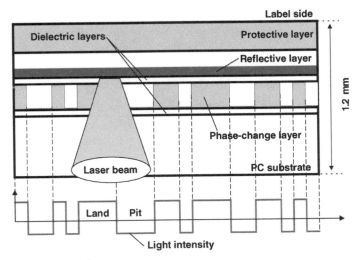

Figure 4–16
A typical structure of the CD-RW disc and the data reading process.

Today's CD-RW uses a so-called direct overwrite (DOW) method when the new data are just written on top of the old data. A standard CD-RW disc is more expensive than CD-R and typically accommodates about 650 MB of data (or 74 minutes of audio recording).

The design of CD-RW itself makes it a perfect-writable storage, which is inexpensive and mobile. On the other hand, the distant future of CD-RW technology is unclear since the new technology—DVD-RAM—is gaining momentum. With its much higher storage capacity and data rates, DVD-RAM could become the "CD-RW/R killers" in the near future, when the price of these relatively new systems will go down substantially.

CD Performance Comparison

Let's now look at a few representative high-end CD-ROM and CD-RW drives. Table 4–3 summarizes their main performance characteristics.

Table 4–3   Performance Characteristics of Some CD-ROM and CD-RW Drives

Drive and type	Average seek time, ms	Sustained DTR, MB/s	Comment
Compaq Deskpro TrueX 52X CD-ROM, internal	100	7.8	Estimated using the X-factor
Kenwood True-X 72X CD-ROM, internal	100	10.8	Estimated using the X-factor
Ricoh Media Master MP7120A 12X/10X/32X CD-RW, internal	120	4.8 (read) 1.8 (write) 1.5 (rewrite)	Estimated using the X-factor
Plextor PlexWriter 12/10/32A CD-RW, internal	150	4.8 (read) 1.8 (write) 1.5 (rewrite)	Estimated using the X-factor
Zip 100/250	29	<1.40/<2.4	
Jaz 2 GB	10 (read) 12 (write)	7.4	
HDD IBM Deskstar 75 GXP	8.5	37.0	(75 GB, desktop class, 7200 rpm. ATA-100)

Table 4–3 shows the following:

- The DTR of CD-ROM drives is comparable or better than that of the best removable magnetic storage systems but cannot compete with the HDD data transfer rates.
- Random seek is a weakness of the CD-ROM/RW drives and is much slower than that of removable magnetic storage systems.

Therefore, the main advantage of the optical CD-ROM/CD-RW drives is in the cost of media, which is on the order of a few dollars per disc, as compared to $10–$25 (Zip 100/250 MB) to $100 (Jaz 2 GB) for removable magnetic media.

Understanding the CD Drive's Specifications

Finally, let's take a look at the CD drive specifications (from *www.cnet.com*) and try to interpret them. Tables 4–4 and 4–5 describe the CD-ROM drives, one of which is a standard fast drive, and the second is the drive using multibeam technology (discussed earlier). Table 4–6 describes the characteristics of an internal rewritable drive.

Table 4–4   Compaq Deskpro TrueX 52X CD-ROM

Characteristic		Comments
Platform(s)	PC	Meant for PC only
Internal or external	Internal	Mounted inside the PC
Data transfer rate (read)	52X	The maximum DTR; approximately, 52×0.15 MB/s = 7.8 MB/s
Rotation method	CLV	Constant linear velocity, changing angular velocity. DTR is constant and independent on the radius.
Avg. access time	100 ms	The interval between the time of a request made by the system and the time the data is available from the drive. Includes the seek time, latency time, and command processing overhead time 100 ms is an average number for the CD-ROM drive.
Avg. sustained transfer rate	6.75–7.8 MB/sec	The DTR the drive can sustain over the substantial period of time.
Interface(s)	EIDE	Or ATA with UDMA access (see chapter 2)

Table 4–4 (continued)

Characteristic		Comments
IDE/EIDE type	ATAPI	From the practical point of view—same as ATA (see Chapter 2)
Compatible media (read)	CD-R, CD-RW	Reads from the recordable and rewritable media.
Format(s) supported (read)	CD-ROM, CD-XA (additional hardware necessary), CD-I, PhotoCD, multisession, CD audio	Reads media with these data formats.
Chassis and Power Supply Weight	3 lbs.	
Base warranty	1 yr.	

Table 4–5 Kenwood True-X 72X CD-ROM

Characteristic		Comments
Platform(s)	PC	Meant for PC only
Internal or external	Internal	Mounted inside the PC
Data transfer rate (read)	72X	The maximum DTR; approximately, 72×0.15 MB/s = 10.8 MB/s
Rotational speed	5200 RPM	CAV or constant angular velocity drive. DTR varies as a function of the data track radius.
Avg. access time	100 ms	100 ms is an average number for CD-ROM drives.
Interface(s)	EIDE	Or ATA with UDMA access (see Chapter 2)
IDE/EIDE type	ATAPI	From the practical point of view—same as ATA (see Chapter 2)
Media Format(s) supported (read)	CD-ROM, CD-R, CD-RW, Photo CD, CD-Audio, Video-CD	Reads from the following media types.

Table 4–5   (continued)

Characteristic		Comments
Software Drivers included	Windows 95, 98	Drivers for installation are included.
Chassis and Power Supply Portable?	No	Also means internal
Dimensions (W × H × D)	5.9" × 1.7" × 7.9"	
Input/output ports	Headphone out	Has an output socket for the headphone.
Sound controls	Volume	
Loading mechanism	Tray	As opposite to a "slot"
Drive mounting	Horizontal or vertical	The disc can be inserted when the drive is mounted either horizontally or vertically.
Base warranty	1 yr.	

Table 4–6   Yamaha CRW2100EZ (16X/10X/40X)

Characteristic		Comments
Platform(s)	PC, Mac	Meant for both PC and Mac
Drive type	CD-RW	Rewritable drive
Internal or external	Internal	Mounted inside the PC
Avg. access time	160 ms	160 ms is slow
Buffer	8 MB	Larger buffer (cache) memory is better and allows to speed up data transfer.
Data transfer rate (read)	40X	Approximately $40 \times 0.15 = 6$ MB/s
Data transfer rate (write)	16X	Approximately $16 \times 0.15 = 2.4$ MB/s
Data transfer rate (rewrite)	10X	Approximately $10 \times 0.15 = 1.5$ MB/s
Interface(s)	EIDE	Or ATA with UDMA access (see Chapter 2)
Cable included?	Yes	Internal 40-pin IDE cable
Media included	1 CD-R	
Compatible media (read)	CD-ROM, CD-RW, CD-R	
Compatible media (write)	CD-RW, CD-R	Writes to the following media types

Table 4–6   (continued)

Characteristic		Comments
Format(s) supported (read)	CD-DA, CD-ROM, CD-ROM XA (both Photo CD and Video CD), CD-I, CD-Digital, CD-Bridge, Audio CD, CD-Extra, and Video CD	Reads from the following media types
Software included	Adaptec DirectCD, Adaptec Toast for Macintosh, Adaptec Easy-CD Creator, Adobe PhotoDeluxe BE, Neato CD Labeling, MusicMatch JukeBox, and Earthlink Internet Access	
Chassis and Power Supply Dimensions (W × H × D)	5.8" × 1.6" × 8 in.	
Weight	3.92 lbs.	
Input/output ports	Headphone out	Has an output socket for the headphone
Sound controls	Volume	
Loading mechanism	Tray	As opposite to a "slot"
Drive mounting	Horizontal only	The disc can be inserted when the drive is mounted horizontally only.
Base warranty	1 yr.	

DVD . . . .

Introduction

DVD initially stood for Digital Video Disk but now stands for Digital Versatile Disc. Like a CD, DVD is an optical storage system for read-only, recordable, and rewritable applications. But, being similar to a CD in many ways, DVD is considered to be a CD future replacement.

The main differences between the CD and DVD are summarized in Table 4–7 and also in Figure 4–17.

Table 4–7   DVD versus CD-ROM

Feature	DVD	CD-ROM
Substrate diameter/thickness (mm)	120/1.2	120/1.2
Sides	1 or 2	1
Layers per side	1 or 2	1
Capacity (GB)	4.7, 8.54, 9.4, or 17	~ 0.7
Track pitch (micrometers)	0.74	1.6
Min. pit length (micrometers)	0.4–0.44	0.83
Linear velocity used for scan (m/s)	3.5–3.84	1.3
Laser wavelength (nm)	635 or 650	780
Numerical aperture	0.6	0.45
Modulation	8 to 16	EFM (effectively: 8 to 17)
Error correction code (ECC)	RSPC	CIRC
Durability and dust/scratch	Same as that of a CD	high

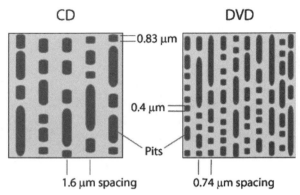

Figure 4–17
Comparison of the main features of the CD and DVD discs.

The main features of the DVD formats (Table 4–8) can be summarized as follows:

- Backward compatibility with current CD media (at least the newest models of DVD drives).
- Physical dimensions identical to the compact disc with a total thickness equal to 1.2 mm, but with a capacity at least 7 times larger than that of a CD.
- Capacities of 4.7 GB, 8.54 GB, 9.4 GB, and 17.08 GB, depending on the disc structure.
- Single-layer/dual-layer and single/double-sided options.
- DVD replication process is similar to that used for compact discs.
- A disc-based format means fast random access like in hard drives and CDs and unlike tapes.
- Designed from the outset for video, audio, and multimedia. Meets the requirement for 133 minutes of high quality video on one side of a disc.
- DVD-ROM for enhanced multimedia and games applications.
- DVD-Video for full-length high-quality movies on one disc.
- DVD-Audio for higher quality music, surround sound, and optional video, graphics, and other features.
- All formats use a common file system.
- Copy protection built into standard.

DVD Formats

Table 4–8   DVD Formats

Format	Application	Status
DVD-ROM	High-capacity computer ROM storage, capable of replacing multiple CDs Multimedia, computer games, interactive systems, databases	Available today
DVD-Audio	High-quality surround-sound music with increased playing time	Available today
DVD-Video	High-quality multi-lingual movies on one disc with random-access to episodes and surround-sound audio	Available today
DVD-RAM and DVD-R	Very large (compared to CD) direct access data storage	Limited availability; variety of standards

DVD Configurations and Basic Design

CD players and CD-ROM drives use lasers working at a wavelength of 780 nanometers. Since the wavelength is one of the parameters responsible for the beam diameter and spot size, new DVD players and DVD-ROM drives use red lasers working at 650 nm and 635 nm wavelengths. Another parameter, important for smaller and denser bits, is the numerical aperture (NA) that was increased in DVD drives by refining the laser assembly.

DVD's digital modulation and ECC (error correction code) were designed to support increased storage capacity. The 8 to 16 (EFM PLUS) modulation scheme (8 to 17 is used in a CD, see earlier in the chapter) is very efficient and provides backward compatibility. Also, the RS-PC (Reed Solomon Product Code) error correction code is about 10 times more robust than that currently used in CD systems.

Unlike a CD, DVD is a bonded disc, made of two 0.6 mm substrates joined together. Although they are similar in appearance, some substantial differences between the CD and DVD are revealed under the surface.

The DVD format provides several configurations (see Table 4–9) of data layers, moving from two-dimensional storage toward a three-dimensional storage. Each configuration is designed to provide additional storage capacity.

Table 4–9   DVD Format Configurations

Name	Media structure	Capacity (GB)
DVD-5	Single side/single layer	4.7
DVD-9	Single side/dual layer	8.54
DVD-10	Double side/single layer	9.4
DVD-18	Double side/dual layer	17.08
DVD-R	Single or double side/single layer	3.95/7.9
DVD-RAM	Single or double side/single layer	2.6/5.2

All DVD-5 to DVD-18, like a CD, store prerecorded information, which cannot be changed. DVD-5, shown in Figure 4–18, is basically a sandwich of two layers of 0.6 mm thick, one of which has the data and another is blank. A thin metal layer reflects the laser beam back to the detector in a way quite similar to a CD. The difference here is in a smaller spot size, smaller bits, and tighter tracks. The label is attached to the label side in a fashion similar to a CD label.

The similarity between the DVD and the CD gets smaller with the next configuration used, DVD-9, which utilizes two layers to store the information and two laser beams to retrieve the data. Although 4.7 GB stores more data than seven compact discs, even higher storage capacity (8.54 GB) is achieved in DVD-9 by going three-dimensional.

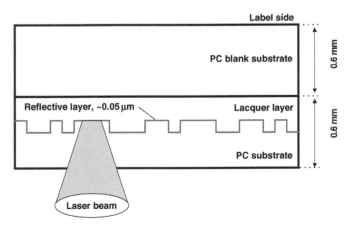

Figure 4–18
Schematics of the DVD-5. Single side, single layer disc (4.7 GB).

The first layer in a DVD-9 disc is semireflective (see Figure 4–19), which allows the second beam to reach the second layer, which is fully reflective. The disc is made by bonding together two 0.6 mm-thick substrates using transparent (with no internal defects or bubbles) UV-cured (UV = ultra-violet) lacquer. This disc design allows for almost twice as much data to be stored as that on a DVD-5. Labels are printed on the other side of the disc conventionally.

A further improvement on CDs—a double-sided disc design—is introduced in DVD-10 and DVD-18, shown in Figures 4–20 and 4–21.

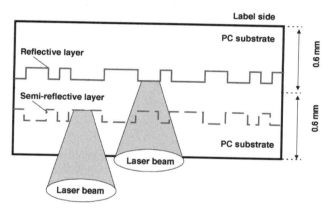

Figure 4–19
Schematics of the DVD-9. Single side, double layer disc (8.54 GB).

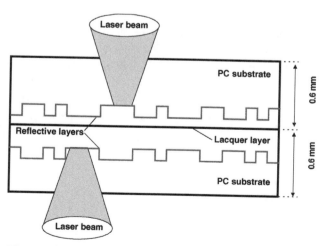

Figure 4–20
Schematics of the DVD-10. Double side, single layer disc (9.4 GB).

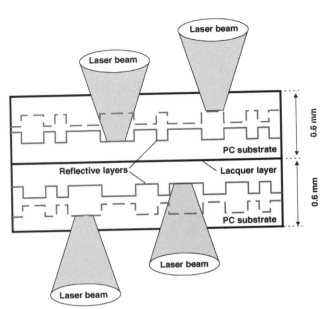

Figure 4–21
Schematics of the DVD-18. Double side, double layer disc (17.08 GB).

DVD-10 (Figure 4–20) is made of two metalized substrates with fully reflective layers bonded together. The binder does not need to be transparent because the data is read by the laser beams from both sides of the disc. This type of disc is much more difficult to make. Also, there is no place for a conventional label, which is now restricted to an area within the disc hub on both sides of the disc. Finally, since half of the data is on the second side of the disc, it requires either flipping the disc or having a DVD drive/player capable of two-sided playback. One obvious advantage of this design is the doubled capacity to 9.4 GB (compared to DVD-5), but almost the same value could be achieved using a one-sided DVD-8 design.

DVD-18 discs (Figure 4–21) are also made of two substrates bonded together with each having two data layers and allowing for double-sided data retrieval. This design is even more complex than that of a DVD-10, and shares all the advantages and disadvantages of a DVD-10.

DVD-R and DVD-RW or RAM

There is a lot of confusion associated with various recordable and rewritable DVD formats. Table 4–10 summarizes those competing formats and also shows DVD-ROM for comparison.

Table 4–10   Comparing Competing DVD Formats

Format	DVD-ROM	DVD-R	DVD-RAM	DVD+RW	DVD-R/W	ASMO
Media	Pressed track (read only)	Dye-polymer (write once)	Phase change (rewritable)	Phase change (rewritable)	Phase change (rewritable)	Magneto-optical (read/write)
Capacity, GB (for one side/one layer)	4.7	3.95	2.6	3.0	3.95	6.0
Track format	Land (no groove)	Groove	Land and groove (wobbled)	Groove (wobbled)	Groove (wobbled)	Land and groove
Supporters	DVD Forum	DVD Forum	Hitachi, Matsushita, Toshiba, and DVD Forum	Hewlett-Packard, Mitsubishi, Philips, Ricoh, Sony, and Yamaha	Hitachi, Maxell, JVC, Mitsubishi, Pioneer, and TDK	ASMO Group (Founders: Fujitsu, Hitachi, Imation, Olympus, Philips, Sanyo, Sharp, and Sony)

Recordable and rewritable DVD drives are clearly more complex than the DVD-ROM drives, since they require lasers with different power levels for reading, erasing, and writing.

DVD-R media operates on a principle similar to CD-R. The laser burns marks in a special dye layer and locally changes its reflectivity. Since the DVD-R uses a shorter-wavelength laser, it is incompatible with the green recordable media of CD-R, and another laser is required to solve this problem.

In the case of rewritable DVD, compatibility problems occur with the laser power-levels, since the drive needs different laser powers to record (cause phase transformation in the media), read ("measure" the reflectance), and erase (anneal the media) for both DVD and CD media.

Some of today's DVD players can read all of the most important formats, such as DVD-RAM, DVD-ROM, DVD-Video, DVD-R, CD-Audio, CD-ROM, CD-R, CD-RW, and video CD but are, understandably, quite expensive.

ASMO (for Advanced Storage Magneto-Optical Technology) discs are the same size as CDs and ASMO drives are supposed to read CD-ROM and DVD discs. But, since they use magneto-optical principles instead of a phase-change process, the ASMO drives will not be able to record DVD-RAM discs.

DVD-ROM

Like a CD, a DVD-ROM is a prerecorded disc. DVD-ROM is used to store general data, as well as video and audio information needed for multimedia applications and computer games.

DVD-ROM satisfies the following requirements:

- Backward compatibility with CD-ROMs
- Forward compatibility with future recordable (R) and rewritable (RW) discs
- Single format for computer and TV applications
- Single file system for all data types and media types

The backward compatibility of the DVD drives means that it will read both CD-ROM and CD-audio, which makes them a great replacement for CD-drives. Because of a higher bit density and other advantageous features, even a 5x-speed DVD drive will read a CD at a rate equivalent to about 40x for the regular CD drive. This positions DVD-ROM as the computer storage of the near future, especially for databases, multimedia, games, interactive video, and so on.

For now, DVD drives are, in general, more expensive, and require special MPEG-2 hardware or software decoders to read compressed data. To have the best video quality, the hardware approach is better unless the fastest processors are used.

DVD-Video and DVD-Audio

One of the reasons for the success of DVD technology is the DVD-Video formats. DVD video application is strongly dependent on data compression, since at the bit rate of 167 Mbps (which corresponds to the video rate specified by the CCIR-601 digital video standard), the 4.7-gigabyte capacity of a standard DVD would be enough to store roughly 4 minutes of digital video. The data compression provides for the nominal 133 minutes of playing time for DVD-5. Longer movies should use a dual-layer technology (DVD-9). The data on the first layer start at the inside of the disc and end at the outside, where the data on the second layer start at the outside, thus providing uninter-rupted playback.

Two types of video compression standards could be used for DVD: MPEG-1 and MPEG-2, but only MPEG-2 video data can be copy protected and region coded (MPEG stands for the Moving Picture Experts Group). Therefore, the same techniques of copy protection currently used for CDs are being adopted for DVD.

Like all compression algorithms (WinZip is one example), MPEG-2 analyzes repetition in the video signal, called redundancy, and tries to get rid of it. MPEG-2 is capable of "filtering" about 97% of the data in the video signal without significantly degrading the quality of the picture. This allows for recording of 133 minutes on a 4.7 GB disc at a much lower bit rate than required by the digital video standard.

DVD-Video may have up to eight (typically, three) tracks of mono, stereo, or multichannel surround sound, which makes it much better than the VCR. The audio encoding formats include Dolby Digital (5.1 channel surround sound), MPEG (up to 7.1 channels), LPCM (number of channels is hardware-dependent), and DTS (only in addition to one of the other formats).

DVD's direct data access allows interactivity and direct access to the movie episodes or other information of the disc. DVD also allows subtitles (up to 32 sets in different languages), making any DVD really universal. On the other hand, to provide additional copy protection, most DVDs have a so-called regional coding, making it impossible to play the same disc in different regions, since most DVD-Videos are made for a specific region or country and not for free worldwide use. There are six regions (see Table 4–11) used for DVD-Video coding.

Table 4–11   DVD Region Codes

Region codes	Countries/geographic regions
1	USA, Canada
2	Europe, Japan, Middle East, South Africa
3	Southeast Asia, Taiwan
4	Australia, New Zealand, Central and South America, Mexico
5	Russia, India, Pakistan, part of Africa
6	China

Red Laser versus Blue Laser

Current DVD drives use red lasers (630 to 650 nm), and the "easiest" way to increase areal density is to switch to shorter-wavelength lasers, that is, blue or violet lasers with wavelengths as low as 400 nm. This will make possible about 15 GB of data per layer per side. To achieve, say, 45 GB of data per side per layer, even shorter UV range lasers will be needed. Still, compact, reliable, and inexpensive short-wavelength lasers are hard to make.

Three primary blue-laser technologies are available now:

- ZnSe lasers
- GaN lasers
- second-harmonic generation (SHG) lasers

ZnSe lasers brought the first success to the field, but these lasers have a relatively short lifetime at required power levels, and are also at the green end of the blue range (460 to 520 nm).

GaN In-doped lasers have already demonstrated high reliability at wavelengths as short as 370 nm and are considered to be a very promising future technology.

SHG lasers offer the best durability at the moment. This technology either doubles the frequency of a given infrared laser or directly generates a second harmonic in the blue portion of the spectrum. For example, for a given infrared laser with a wavelength of 850 nm, this technology will double the laser light frequency (using a so-called distributed Bragg reflector, or DBR) and produce blue light at 425 nm.

Another issue is manufacturing tolerances for 120 mm DVD discs, which are already very high. Blue lasers with smaller bits will make this issue even more complex.

Also, servo-control with smaller spot size and higher (potentially) spin rates is another issue.

Performance Comparison

Table 4–12 compares performance characteristics of high-performance DVD-ROM and DVD-RAM drives with some other optical and magnetic storage systems.

Table 4–12   Performance Comparison of Storage Systmes

Drive and type	Average seek time, ms	Sustained DTR, MB/s	Comment
HiVal 10X DVD-ROM	70 (CD-ROM)/ 90 (DVD-ROM)	6.0 (CD-ROM)	Estimated from the X-factor
AOpen DVD-1240 DVD-ROM	N/A	6.0 (CD-ROM)/ 16.6 (DVD-ROM)	
DVD-RAM: La Cie DVDAM52	95 (CD-ROM)/ 120 (DVD-ROM)	3.0 (CD-ROM)/ 2.77 (DVD-ROM)	
Sony SMO-F551/S, internal	25	5.0	On 5.2 GB media
Compaq Deskpro TrueX 52X CD-ROM, internal	100	7.8	Estimated from the X-factor
Kenwood True-X 72X CD-ROM, internal	100	10.8	Estimated using the X-factor
Ricoh Media Master MP7120A 12X/10X/ 32X CD-RW, internal	120	4.8 (read) 1.8 (write) 1.5 (rewrite)	Estimated from the X-factor
Plextor PlexWriter 12/10/32A CD-RW, internal	150	4.8 (read) 1.8 (write) 1.5 (rewrite)	Estimated from the X-factor
Zip 100/250	29	<1.40 / <2.4	
Jaz 2 GB	10 (read)/ 12 (write)	7.4	
HDD IBM Deskstar 75 GXP	8.5	37.0	(75 GB, desktop class, 7200 RPM. ATA-100)

Table 4–12 shows the following:

- The DTR of DVD drives is comparable or better than that of the CD-ROM and CD-RW systems (when DVD-ROM is compared with CD-ROM and DVD-RAM is compared with CD-RW), and can compete with the removable magnetic storage systems, but is still significantly lower than that of the HDD.

- The random seek of DVD drives is better (shorter) when compared to CD-ROM and CD-RW devices. The random seek of DVD drives is three to four times longer when compared to the MO device. It is also significantly longer than that of the Zip drive and is much longer than that of high-end Jaz 2 GB and real HDD.

Understanding the DVD Drive Specification

Finally, let's take a look at the DVD drive specifications (from *www.cnet.com*) and try to interpret them. Table 4–13 describes the DVD-ROM drive and Table 4–14 describes the DVD-RAM drive.

Table 4–13   Hi-Val 10X DVD-ROM Drive (Hardware Decoding)

Characteristics		Comment
Platform(s)	PC	Meant for PC only
Drive type	DVD-ROM	Read-only
Internal or external	Internal	Mounted inside the PC
Data transfer rate (read)	10X DVD, 40X CD	For CD: approximately 40×0.15 MB/s $= 6.0$ MB/s
Avg. seek time	90ms DVD, 70ms CD	Characterizes speed of access to randomized data; 70 ms is very good for CD-ROM
Avg. access time	110ms DVD, 80ms CD	The interval between the time of a request made by the system and the time the data is available from the drive; includes the seek time, latency time, and command processing overhead time; 80 ms is good for CD
Buffer	512K	Larger buffer (cache) memory is better and allows to speed up data transfer.
Interface(s)	EIDE	Same as ATA with UDMA access (see Chapter 2)
IDE/EIDE type	ATAPI	Same as ATA

Table 4–13   (continued)

Characteristics		Comment
MPEG-2 decoding	hardware	The drive comes with a plug-in MPEG-2 decoder card for higher quality; it is recommended and is better (and more expensive) than the software decoders.
Media Format(s) supported (read)	DVD-ROM, DVD Video, DVD-R, DVD-RW, CD-ROM, CD-ROM/XA, CD-R, CD-RW, CD-Extra (CD+), and Photo-CD	Reads from the following media types and formats
Chassis and Power Supply Portable?	No	Means internal
Dimensions (W × H × D)	5.8" × 1.7" × 8.8"	
Weight	3.2 lb.	
Input/output ports	Headphone out	Has an output socket for the headphone.
Sound controls	Volume	
Loading mechanism	Tray	As opposed to a slot
Drive mounting	Horizontal only	The disc can be inserted when the drive is mounted horizontally only.
Base warranty	1 yr.	

Table 4–14   La Cie DVD-RAM IEEE 1394

Characteristics		Comment
Platform(s)	PC, Mac	Meant for both PC and Mac
Drive type	DVD-RAM	Recordable/rewritable
Internal or external	External	Attached to the PC with the cable
Data transfer rate (read)	6X	
Avg. seek time	120 ms DVD-RAM, 95 ms DVD-ROM	95 ms is good for DVD-ROM and 120 ms is good for DVD-RAM.

Table 4–14   (continued)

Characteristics		Comment
Interface(s)	IEEE 1394	FireWire interface provides for easy connection and up to 40 MB/s DTR; may require a plug-in PCI card for older computers.
Compatible media (read)	CD-R, CD-RW, DVD-ROM, DVD-RAM, DVD-Video, and PD cartridge	Reads from the following media types and formats
Compatible media (write)	DVD-RAM, PD cartridges	Writes on the following media types
Software included	DVD writing software for Mac and PC Mac	Application program for PC and Mac is included.
Input/output ports	Headphone out	Has an output socket for the headphone.
Sound controls	Volume	
Loading mechanism	Tray	As opposed to a slot
Drive mounting	Horizontal only	The disc can be inserted when the drive is mounted horizontally only.
Base warranty	1 yr.	

5

Magneto-Optical Storage Systems

In this chapter...

INTRODUCTION ·······················

Magneto-optical storage is a dynamic, changing field and it is difficult to predict its future. At present, it is based on a mature technology that is being consistently improved with newer techniques, that is, *direct overwrite* (DOW) or *magnetically induced super-resolution* (MSR) to achieve higher speed and higher storage density. MO technology is also quite popular among the major players in the field of data storage, which can be seen from this alphabetical list of major manufacturers of MO products:

- Fujitsu
- Maxell
- Nikon
- Olympus
- Philips
- PDO Media
- Sony
- Verbatim

Erasability always implies that the recording media can undergo a very large number of write/erase operations without any loss in recording/reading quality. There are two main media designs for rewritable optical systems: MO (magneto-optical) media and phase-change media (known as CD-RW).

The MO systems include basic principles of both magnetic and optical storage systems: MO systems write magnetically (with thermal assist) and read optically. This is why MO storage occupies a special chapter of this book.

Presently, there are two standard form-factors used for MO systems with 5.25-inch (130 mm) and 3.5-inch (90 mm) disks that are placed inside a hard envelope. These standards are defined by the ISO (International Standards Organization).

The standard for the first-generation 5.25-inch MO drive (325 MB x2 or double-sided) was introduced in 1988 (ISO/IEC 10089) in a 650 MB/600 MB capacity. The next generation of MO drives—the 3.5-inch drive (128 MB)—was introduced in 1991. Since then, much faster and larger in capacity MO products became available with the first MO drive with capacity exceeding a gigabyte, introduced in 1991 (5.25-inch, 1.3 GB, 2X original capacity). Later, 2.6 GB/2.3 GB (4X original capacity) and 5.2 GB/4.8 GB/4.1 GB (8X original capacity) drives were introduced without losing their backward compatibility with the previous generations. The latest 5.2 GB capacity drive can read disks written on first-generation 650 MB capacity drives. At present, the 3.5-inch MO drives have a capacity of 1.3 GB.

Figure 5–1
4.8 GB MO disks from Sony (courtesy of Sony Electronics Inc.)

Each capacity group uses a different size of the data sector. The latest 8X capacity disk, 5.2 GB, is based on 2,048 bytes/sector; 4.8 GB (see Figure 5–1) uses 1,024 bytes/sector, and 4.1 GB is based on 512 bytes/sector. Certain operating systems such as MS DOS and some varieties of UNIX® will only support a specific recording sector size, such as 512 bytes/sector.

One remarkably successful MO product comes in a 2.5-inch (about 64 mm) form-factor, called the MiniDisk, and became the first recordable optical system for both consumer and data applications with its unique data compression and direct overwrite (DOW) technologies. MO drives apply MFM data encoding, which is already being successfully used in the audio sector—in the form of the MiniDisk.

In spite of all the recent advances, the MO products are losing popularity in the last years due to the successful development of competitive products, such as CD-ROM/R/RW and DVD-ROM/RAM. Yet, MO manufacturers keep emphasizing the following advantages of MO products:

- low cost per megabyte for a large storage capacity
- high storage capacity
- high speed (data access and DTR)
- safety of data

Table 5–1 shows the number of removable media units and the approximate cost of backing up one CD, and demonstrates that MO media provides the cheapest way per MB of data (source: *www.mo-forum.com*).

Table 5–1   Approximate Cost of Backing Up One CD

Product	Number of media required	Back-up time (min)	Price per medium ($)
Floppy disk	450	240	450
Zip 100 MB disk	6	15	150
Jaz 1 GB disk	1	4	140
MO 230MB disk	3	15	45
MO 640MB disk	1	8	30

Of course, the above example is somewhat misleading since the best and cheapest way to back up a CD is, perhaps, to use another CD-R or CD-RW, which costs a few dollars only.

The storage capacity of the latest MO products is still quite impressive, and, so far, can be rivaled (in the world of rewritable removable media storage) only by the high-end magnetic storage systems, such as Jaz 2 GB and Orb 2.2 GB, and by the newest DVD-RAM drives. For example, the latest 5.25-inch MO drives have a storage capacity of 5.2 GB on a rewritable media. The 3.5-inch MO drives have also reached the capacity of an impressive 1.3 GB. In addition, all these products are backward compatible with the older products. It seems that the *high storage capacity along with rewritability* could be one future advantage for MO products over other optical and magnetic removable storage media products. According to some recent announcements, the 5.25" MO product with 9.1 GB (double-sided) and the 3.5" MO product with 2.6 GB (single-sided) will become available very soon.

Another possible advantage is the speed of read, write, and random seek, which is in the range of 19 ms to 30 ms. The MO drives spin at high RPM of 3,300 to 4,500 RPM and have a low latency of about 8 ms to 9 ms.

Therefore, it seems at the moment that the *major advantage* of the MO drives is in *performance* when compared to other rewritable optical systems. Table 5–2 summarizes the main performance characteristics of a few representative high-end CD-RW and DVD-RAM drives along with some magnetic storage devices.

Table 5–2   Performance Characteristics of Various Storage Devices

Drive type	Average seek time, ms	Sustained DTR, MB/s	Comment
Sony SMO-F551/S, internal	25	5.0	On 5.2 GB MO media
Ricoh Media Master MP7120A 12X/10X/32X CD-RW, internal	120	4.8 (read) 1.8 (write) 1.5 (rewrite)	Estimated using the X-factor
Plextor PlexWriter 12/10/32A CD-RW, internal	150	4.8 (read) 1.8 (write) 1.5 (rewrite)	Estimated using the X-factor
DVD-RAM: La Cie DVDAM52	95 (CD-ROM)/ 120 (DVD-ROM)	3.0 (CD-ROM)/ 2.77 (DVD-ROM)	
Zip 100/250	29	<1.40/<2.4	
Jaz 2 GB	10 (read)/ 12 (write)	7.4	
HDD IBM Deskstar 75 GXP	8.5	37.0	(75 GB, desktop class, 7200 RPM. ATA-100)

Table 5–2 demonstrates the following:

- The DTR of MO drives is comparable or better than that of the best removable magnetic storage systems but cannot compete with the HDD data transfer rates.

- The random seek time of MO drives is much better (shorter) when compared to other optical storage devices, including CD-RW and DVD-RAM. It is comparable to that of a Zip drive and "only" two to three times slower than that of a high-end Jaz 2 GB and a "real" HDD.

Finally, let's look at the *MO data safety* argument. Since the design of all the optical storage systems is quite similar with the optical head being separated from the media by about 1 mm, the reliability of all these systems—CD-ROM, CD-RW, DVD-ROM, DVD-RW, and MO—should be about the same. It becomes apparent when the nominal (announced) reliability is compared in terms of MTBF (mean time before failure). The example of MTBF data for some CD-RW, DVD-ROM, and MO drives is shown in Table 5–3.

Table 5–3   MTBF Data for Some CD-RW, DVD-ROM, and MO Drives

Product	MTBF, hours
Sony SMO-F551/S 5.25-inch MO drive	100,000
AOpen DVD-1240 DVD-ROM	100,000
AOpen CD-952E CD-ROM	100,000

One thing beneficial for the MO media is that it is enclosed within the rigid jacket that protects the disk from dust and mechanical damage much better than the ordinary CD or DVD media are protected.

A reliability comparison with the hard disk drives is more difficult since the reliability of HDD is usually expressed in contact start-stop cycles or power-on/power-off cycles. But, it is true that the optical drives have potentially higher reliability due to lack of mechanical interaction between the media and the read/write head.

It should also be mentioned that some of the principles of the MO technology (i.e., thermally assisted magnetic recording) may find their way into the most advanced magnetic storage devices of the future. Plus, one of the latest rewritable DVD implementations—called the ASMO (see Chapter 4)—is based on magneto-recording principles allowing us to speculate about a possible merger of these two popular storage technologies.

BASICS OF MO RECORDING . . . .

All magnetic materials have a characteristic temperature, called the Curie temperature, above which they lose magnetization due to a complete disordering of their magnetic domains. At the same temperature they lose all the data they had stored before. More importantly, the material's *coercivity*, which is the measure of material's resistance to magnetization by the applied magnetic field (see Chapter 3), decreases as the temperature approaches the Curie point, and reaches zero when this temperature is exceeded. For the modern magnetic materials used in MO systems, this Curie temperature is on the order of 200°C. It is important (since this is a multiply erasable system) that the only change to the material when it is heated and cooled is the change in magnetization, with no damage to the material itself.

The fact that the material's coercivity drops at higher temperatures allows for thermally assisted magnetic recording with relatively weak magnetic fields, which simplifies the drive design. Even a relatively weak laser can generate high local temperatures when focused at a small spot (about 1 micron in case of MO systems). When the material is heated, and its coercivity is low, a magnetization of the media can be changed by applying a magnetic field from the magnet. When the material is cooled to room temperature, its coercivity rises back to such a high level that the magnetic data cannot be easily affected by the magnetic fields we encounter in our regular daily activity. The basic schematic of this recording process is illustrated in Figure 5–2.

When the disk is inserted into the drive, the label side will face the magnet, and the transparent side will face the laser.

The direction of magnetization in the thin magnetic films (on magnetic rigid disks, for example) can be parallel to the surface (longitudinal recording) or perpendicular to the surface (perpendicular recording). The latter has potential for higher density of magnetic recording. Most of the magnetic hard drives nowadays utilize longitudinal recording, while the MO systems use the perpendicular direction of magnetization.

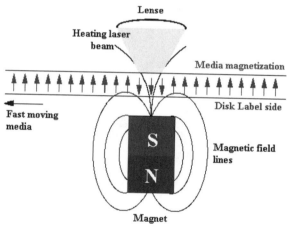

Figure 5–2
The basic schematic of MO recording process.

BASICS OF MO READING · · · · · · · · · · · · · · · · · ·

Unlike traditional magnetic recording systems, which use currents induced in the magnetic heads by the changing magnetic fluxes on the disk surface to read the data, MO systems use polarized light to read the data from the disk. The changes in light polarization occur due to a presence of magnetic field on the surface of the disk (the Kerr effect). If a beam of the polarized light is shined onto the surface, the light polarization of the reflected beam will change slightly (typically less than 0.5°) if it is reflected from a magnetized surface (see Figure 5–3). If the magnetization is reversed, the change in polarization (the Kerr angle) is reversed too.

The magnetized areas—bits—cannot be seen in a regular light, but only in a polarized light. The change in direction of magnetization could be associated with numbers 0 or 1, making this technique useful for binary data storage.

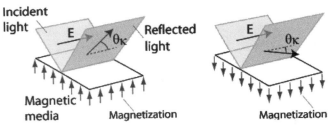

Figure 5–3
An illustration of the Kerr effect. E is the polarization vector.

MO SYSTEM: BASIC DESIGN . . . .

The MO drive's optical design is quite similar to that of the CD drive and DVD drive (see Figure 5–4) but, it is optimized for measuring slight changes in the light polarization upon reflecting from the disk. The differential detection system is the basis of the MO system's readout. A so-called "leaky" beam-splitter channels half of the reflected light away from the laser and toward the detectors. The polarizing beam-splitter splits the beam into two reflected components of the polarized beam: parallel and perpendicular to the direction of incident polarization. In the absence of media magnetization—and in the absence of the Kerr effect—both beams coming out of the polarizing beam-splitter will receive the same amount of light. If the media is magnetized, and the returned beam's polarization was slightly rotated, this rotation will be detected as a difference in the amount of light received by detectors 1 and 2 (Figure 5–4). This design is sensitive to very small changes in the angle of polarization.

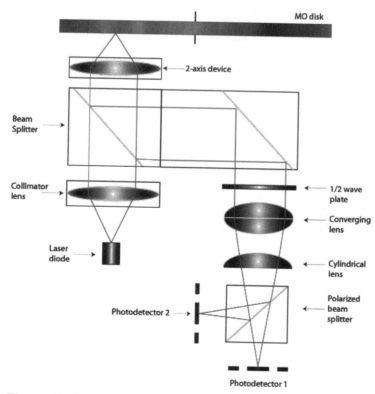

Figure 5–4
Simplified optical design of the MO drive.

The servo tracking system of MO drives differs from that used in CD and DVD drives, which use pits to derive the tracking error. In case of MO storage systems, which have no pits, the spiral grove is preformed on the substrate to obtain the tracking error signal and to allow the system to position on the data track. The popular tracking system used in MO drives is called a "push–pull" tracking servo, and uses light beam diffraction on the edges of the grove. When the light is diffracted, the light intensity profile of the returned beam changes, and it becomes asymmetric if the beam drifts away from the center of the grove. The servo tracking keeps the beam spot in the center of the grove by keeping the beam asymmetry as small as possible.

Figure 5–5 shows the basic design of the quadrilayer magneto-optical disk.

Thermal properties of the optical disk can be changed if the active magneto-optical layer is combined with thin optimizing layers, which may also improve the protection and signal-to-noise characteristics of the medium. These layers are usually designed in such a way that they increase light absorption by the active layer, and thus are called "antireflection layers." For example, let's assume a smooth metal surface reflecting back about 50% of the incident light. With the help of antireflecting layers on that surface, the light reflection can be reduced down to 20% and less, thus decreasing needed laser power. So-called *quadrilayers* are usually used in the design of MO disks. The aluminum layer can play the roles of both light reflector and heat sink (to minimize lateral heating of the active layer).

Amorphous rare earth-transition metal alloys are typically used for the MO media. The general structure of this alloy is TbFeCo, where iron (Fe) and cobalt (Co) are transition metals and terbium (Tb) is the rare earth element, which makes about 80% of the alloy. The rare earth elements are very active chemically and have poor cor-

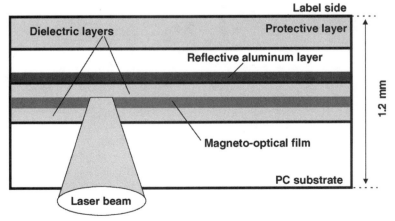

Figure 5–5
Basic design of the quadrilayer magneto-optical disk.

rosive resistance and thus require protective layers. The layers on the disk are typically deposited by sputtering from one alloy target or from several single-element targets simultaneously.

Finally, the materials for MO recording should meet the following major criteria:

- Have amorphous structure (smooth surface and domain's boundaries to decrease system's noise)
- Low thermal conductivity (to limit lateral heating to the recording layer itself)
- High melting point at about 200°C–300°C (for media stability and accidental data loss prevention)
- Rapid drop of coercivity near the Curie temperature (for sharp recording threshold)
- High coercivity at room temperature (for media stability and accidental data loss prevention)
- Vertical anisotropy (for perpendicular magnetic recording)
- Chemical stability (for constant material's properties under repeated heating–cooling)

DIRECT OVERWRITE (DOW) . . . .

Direct overwrite is an extremely important technology for the MO drives since it allows to roughly double the speed of the rewrite operation. A more traditional rewrite operation includes two steps (and two disk rotations):

- Irradiation and heating of the selected bit for overwriting to exceed the Curie temperature, forcing its coercivity to drop to zero, and then reversal in magnetic field for erasure.
- Second irradiation with magnetic field applied to write a new information into the bit.

The above process requires two passes over the same bit. The DOW technology allowed to erase and rewrite the new data in one pass.

There are two techniques used for DOW: the magnetic field modulation DOW, called (MFM-DOW), and the light intensity modulation, called LIM-DOW. Both techniques are used today in the MO drives with the light intensity modulation direct overwrite (LIM-DOW) allowing to achieve faster data overwriting.

The MFM-DOW technology is used in such popular products as the MiniDisk, and have some advantages over the LIM-DOW in terms of system stability and the margins between the disk and the optical head. MFM-DOW involves changing directions of the magnetic field and allows to change the media's magnetization during one heating action of the laser. The MiniDisk drive design uses a flying magnetic head on the opposite side of the disk (opposite to the laser side), which is separated from the media by a few micrometers. The frequency of magnetic field modulation in the MiniDisk drives is 720 kHz.

The LIM-DOW is achieved using special media with two operating temperatures, unlike the ordinary MO media with one operating temperature only. This special media is called an exchange-coupled multilayered (ECML) MO media. The ECML has one temperature T_L for erase and another, higher temperature T_H for recording. If the laser beam intensity is modulated in such a way that the temperature of the ECML media is modulated between T_L and T_H, the sequential erasure and rewrite occurs at once in the same direction of magnetization required for writing. The MO disks using LIM-DOW technology are called DOW-MO disks.

MAGNETICALLY INDUCED SUPER RESOLUTION (MSR) . . . .

MSR is another critically important technology for MO storage and it is also unique to *magnetic* storage technology and cannot be used in *purely optical* storage devices. The reason for using MSR is the desire to achieve higher recording density by going with smaller written marks—smaller than is allowed by the diffraction limit of the system (see explanation in Chapter 4). The diffraction limit of the optical system is the function of the numerical aperture (NA) of the objective lens and the wavelength of the laser. The MSR uses a kind of "masking" complete area of the laser spot using the principles of thermomagnetic recording.

There are two parts to MSR: *recording* of small densely packed bits, and *reading* those bits. Interestingly enough, the resolution of the system is limited not by the recording process, but by the optical readout.

Let's first look at how to record the magnetic bits smaller than the laser spot size. Magnetic materials have their properties, that is, coercivity H_c, dependent on the temperature. Therefore, by changing the laser power, and correspondingly, the temperature of the recording layer, one can control the coercivity value to bring it to a desired level H_{rec} at the prespecified temperature T_{rec}. When the laser beam heats the surface, the temperature profile it forms isn't quite uniform and decreases in the direction away from the center of the spot. Therefore, the coercivity of the MO media is decreasing in the same direction too. If the recording magnetic field is adjusted in such a way that it requires coercivity H_{rec} and lower (or, temperature T_{rec} and higher) for media magnetization, then only a part of the heated area with the $T = T_{rec}$ will become magnetized (see Figure 5–6). Therefore, a recording mark smaller than the laser spot can be made.

The problem with the readout of small bits is the following: If the bits are smaller than the laser spot size, then to increase the recording density, they can be placed closer to each other (otherwise, no density advantage is gained), resulting in multiple recording marks being illuminated simultaneously *by the same laser spot*. Clearly, measuring light polarization change from several bits at once isn't practical. Therefore, some kind of "masking" is required here to limit the readout signal to one desired bit only.

The MSR reading process, therefore, consists of the following sequence:

- The laser spot moves on the disk surface toward the bit it is about to read. On its way, it heats the surface up to a temperature high enough to demagnetize the bits it is passing over.

- When it reaches the desired location, it has several bits inside the light spot, but all bits but one—the one it is about to read—are already heated and demagnetized. Therefore, the only bit inside the spot that remains magnetized contributes to the light polarization change is the needed bit.

- An optical pickup detects the light polarization change and interprets the bit as "0" or "1."

- All previously erased bits restore (!) their original magnetization by themselves, thanks to a special multilayered magnetic film design. This film is the key to MSR technology.

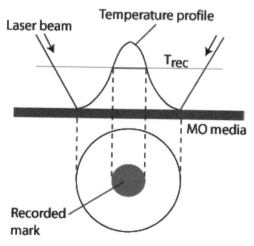

Figure 5–6
Magnetically Induced Super Resolution (MSR): recording magnetic bits smaller than the laser spot size.

The first MO drive using MSR technology was the Fujitsu MCD3130SS drive, which also became the first 3.5-inch MO drive to achieve a 1.3 GB storage capacity. The MSR implementation in the drives do not, luckily, require changing the optical head.

UNDERSTANDING MO DRIVE SPECIFICATIONS . . . . .

Finally, let's take a look at the high-end 3.5" and 5.25" MO drive specifications (from *www.cnet.com*) and try to interpret them (see Tables 5–4 and 5–5).

Table 5–4   HP SureStore 5200ex 5.2 GB Magneto-Optical Drive (5.25")

Characteristics		Comment
Platform(s)	PC, Mac	Meant for both PC and Mac
Drive type	Magneto-optical	
Internal or external	External	Mounted inside the PC
Max. capacity	5.2 GB	Means the maximum formatted capacity of the media
Rotational speed	3,000 RPM	Constant angular velocity (like HDD)
Avg. seek time	25 ms	Characterizes speed of access to randomized data; 25 ms is good for the MO drive
Avg. access time	35 ms	The interval between the time a request is made by the system and the time the data is available from the drive; includes the seek time, latency, and the processing overhead time.
Buffer	2 MB	Larger buffer (cache) memory is better and allows to speed up data transfer.
Interface(s)	SCSI	
SCSI type	SCSI-2	Burst DTR of 10 MB/s, 8 supported devices, 3 m cable length (see Chapter 2)
Controller card included?	No	May need a plug-in PCI SCSI card
Media		
Media included	5.2 GB MO	

Table 5–4   (continued)

Characteristics		Comment
Compatible media (read)	5.2 GB MO, 2.6 GB MO, 1.3 GB MO, 650 MB MO	Reads from the following MO media formats
Compatible media (write)	5.2 GB MO, 2.6 GB MO	Writes to the following MO media formats
Software		
Drivers included	Windows 3.1.1, Windows 95, Windows 98, Windows NT 3.5.1, Windows NT 4.0, Macintosh	Comes with the drivers for installation procedure
Chassis and Power Supply		
Weight	11.22	
Both 110 V and 220 V operation?	Yes	Can be used both inside and outside the US
AC power supply included?	Yes	
Length	11 in.	
Width	6.5 in.	
Height	3.9 in.	

Table 5–5   **Fujitsu MCD3130SS 1.3 GB Magneto-Optical Drive (3.5″)**

Characteristics		Comment
Platform(s)	PC, Mac	Meant for both PC and Mac
Drive type	Magneto-optical	
Internal or external	Internal	Mounted inside the PC
Internal drive size	3.5 in.	Approximately equal to the disk diameter
Max. capacity	1.3 GB	Means the maximum formatted capacity of the media

Table 5–5   (continued)

Characteristics		Comment
Rotational speed	3,214 RPM	Constant angular velocity (like HDD)
Avg. seek time	28 ms	Characterizes speed of access to randomized data; 28 ms is good for the MO drive
Avg. access time	35 ms	The interval between the time a request is made by the system and the time the data is available from the drive; includes the seek time, latency, and the processing overhead time.
Avg. sustained transfer rate	4.6 MB/sec	The DTR the drive can sustain over a substantial period of time
Buffer	2 MB	Larger buffer (cache) memory is better and allows to speed up data transfer.
Interface(s)	SCSI	
SCSI type	SCSI-2	Burst DTR of 10 MB/s, 8 supported devices, 3 m cable length (see Chapter 2)
Media		
Media included	None	
Compatible media (read)	1.3 GB MO, 640 MB MO, 540 MB MO, 230 MB MO, 128 MB MO	Reads from the following MO media formats
Compatible media (write)	1.3 GB MO, 640 MB MO, 540 MB MO, 230 MB MO, 128 MB MO	Writes to the following MO media formats
Chassis and Power Supply		
Dimensions (W × H × D)	4" × 1" × 5.9"	
Weight 1.50		
Warranty		
Base warranty	1 yr.	

6

Nonvolatile Solid-State Memory

In this chapter...

INTRODUCTION . . . .

Memory is the place where a computer can store data and programs and execute them. PC Main memory is a random access solid-state memory (RAM), which enables the computer's CPU (central processing unit) to access instructions and data at a high speed. The reason for the CPU to keep all the important information in RAM is that solid-state memory is much faster than all other computer data storage technologies, such as the hard disk drive, CD-ROM, DVD, and so on.

As was mentioned in Chapter 1, people sometimes confuse the terms *storage* and *memory*, since both of them are used to describe computer devices that store information.

One difference here is that *storage* is designed for less frequently used data or data that could be accessed at a *relatively slow speed*. The *memory* is the place where the computer keeps its most needed and frequently used data, which it can access at a much *faster speed*. An analogy with the file cabinet (storage) and the work desk (memory) is sometimes used to illustrate this difference. One keeps the materials he uses frequently right in front of him on top of the desk, while all other materials are kept in a large file cabinet. Clearly, if one keeps too much data on the desk, it becomes increasingly difficult to locate the needed item, and the data access speed decreases. This is one reason why computer memory is typically much smaller than storage.

Another difference between storage and memory is that storage is *always nonvolatile*, while memory is *mostly volatile*. This means the following: when the power is turned down, nonvolatile memory (hard disk drive, tape, CD, Flash chip, etc.) retains all the information stored while volatile memory (DRAM, SRAM, etc.) loses all the information stored.

In some border cases, a device used for data storage can still be called "memory," thanks to tradition. For example, in the Palm Pilot personal digital assistant (PDA), there are two distinct types of semiconductor memory used: larger volatile RAM and smaller nonvolatile ROM (read only memory). The data in RAM are available for as long as the power is supplied to the system. The data in ROM—which is based on Flash memory technology—is permanently stored and is independent on electric power. The ROM stores the program code, which becomes available upon request and expands into RAM for high availability and fast access. Therefore, the semiconductor ROM here performs a function of a storage device while another semiconductor memory is used purely as the memory device.

Sometimes, the same function can be performed by both the semiconductor memory device and another type of storage device. For example, in some of the newest personal digital assistants (PDAs, see Chapter 7), the same function of ROM can be performed by either the Flash *memory* card or by a small hard disk drive, which is a magnetic *storage* device.

When thinking about "perfect" computer memory, it is relatively easy to assemble a list of desired characteristics:

- Nonvolatility
- High storage density (high capacity/small volume)
- Fast read, write, and erase operations
- In-system rewritability (by the user, not by the manufacturer only)
- Durability
- Low power consumption
- Low cost
- Single-power supply (for solid state memory)
- Scalability (easy to upgrade to a higher capacity)

In reality, there is always a compromise between the capacity, data access rate, and volatility, as was shown earlier (see Chapter 1) in the computer memory and storage hierarchy. Another important parameter here is always cost.

The solid-state memory is typically very fast, with an access time of 50 to 100 ns compared to more than 5 ms for a hard disk drive, and more than 100 ms for a CD-ROM drive. But the cost one pays for this speed gain is on the order of a magnitude higher (per unit storage capacity) than that of a hard disk or a CD-ROM. This is why different tasks require different types of memory and storage.

There is a large variety of semiconductor memories that differ in speed, cost, storage density, writing/rewriting methods, and volatility. Table 6–1 compares memory and storage attributes for some popular semiconductor memories and magnetic storage devices.

Table 6–1　Comparison of Memory and Storage Attributes

Attribute	Flash	DRAM	SRAM	EEPROM	UV-EPROM	Hard disk drive	Floppy disk
Nonvolatility	Y			Y	Y	Y	Y
High density	Y	Y			Y	Y	
Low power	Y			Y	Y		
In-system rewritability	Y	Y	Y	Y		Y	Y
Fast read	Y	Y	Y	Y	Y	Y	
Fast write	Y	Y	Y	Y	Y	Y	

Table 6–1   (continued)

Attribute	Flash	DRAM	SRAM	EEPROM	UV-EPROM	Hard disk drive	Floppy disk
High endurance	Y	Y	Y	Y		Y	Y
Low cost	Y	Y			Y	Y	Y
Single-power supply	Y	Y	Y	Y		Y	Y

Figure 6–1 illustrates the features of some solid-state memory technologies.

It seems that Flash memory is best positioned and combines high storage density with nonvolatility and electrical rewritability. This is why this chapter of the book *reviews* computer RAM memory, but *concentrates* on the nonvolatile solid-state (or semiconductor) memory, namely, Flash memory.

From many points of view, Flash memory is the perfect medium for nonvolatile and rewritable storage. Like all other types of solid-state memory, Flash doesn't have moving parts, is compact, is tolerant to a high degree of mechanical shock and vibration, and has low energy consumption.

However, magnetic and optical disk drives still offer much higher cost efficiency, with Flash memory being cost-effective for some specialized applications only, where lost time translates into lost human life or money. In addition, the data rewrite operation within Flash memory is much slower than the read operation, and is slower than that in the modern hard disk drives.

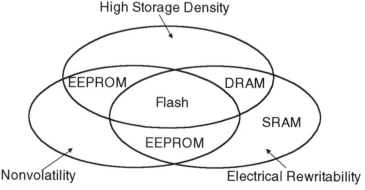

Figure 6–1
Features comparison for some solid state technologies.

Because of its higher cost per unit storage, flash memory is still mostly limited to those storage applications where the advantages of flash still outweigh the cost disadvantage. These applications, that is, digital cameras, PDAs, and so on, typically operate with a small storage capacity, making the total cost of the storage unit less dramatic.

Let's now look at the technology of semiconductor memory devices.

BASICS OF SEMICONDUCTOR MEMORY TECHNOLOGY . . . .

Semiconductors

Silicon and germanium are two basic materials for semiconductor devices. When found in their pure crystalline form, they have a diamond-cubic, perfectly regular lattice with four valence electrons per atom. These electrons interact with other electrons within the lattice and are not free to move, turning these materials into insulators. But, when implanted with a small amount of certain impurities, both germanium and silicon can conduct electricity.

The impurities are of two basic types: donors and acceptors. The donors, created by implanting antimony, arsenic, phosphorus, and so on, contribute excess electrons to the crystal, while the acceptors (gallium, indium, etc.) create electron deficiencies called holes. Under applied voltage, the holes behave as positive charges and move in the direction opposite to that of the electrons.

The semiconductors with excess electrons are called negative or n-type, while the acceptor-type semiconductors are called positive or p-type.

Bipolar Junction Transistor

The bipolar junction transistors are made of three layers of silicon or germanium doped with boron (p-type) or phosphorus (n-type). In the result of placing p- and n-type materials next to each other, the boundary between the layers forms a junction with the property of allowing current to flow in one direction only: from p to n.

The main applications of a transistor are switching and amplification. Both of these applications are possible because of its ability to quickly fluctuate between two states: conduction and isolation. The next figure explains how a transistor can instantly change from a conductor in Figure 6–2a to an insulator in Figure 6–2b.

Figure 6–2 shows the transistor being a conductor with a positive voltage applied to the base (B) and current flowing from the emitter (E) to the collector (C). But, as soon as the negative voltage is applied to the base (B), the electrons in the base region are repelled by the similar charge (moving electrons in a current), and form insulation boundaries. At that moment, the current flow from point E to point C stops and the transistor changes its state from a conductor to an insulator.

The amplification function is illustrated in Figure 6–3.

First, when there is no input signal, the base (B) is negative and the *npn* junction works as an insulator and blocks the current flow.

When the input signal appears, it translates into a positive voltage applied to the base, which opens the *npn* junction and allows the current, which is much stronger than the input signal current and is its precise replica, to flow through the circuit, thus effectively amplifying the input signal. The amplification depends on the circuit design, and can increase the input signal by 10 or even 1,000 times.

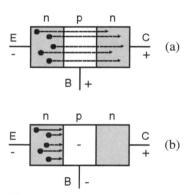

Figure 6–2
An illustration of how a transistor can instantly change from a conductor (a) to an insulator (b).

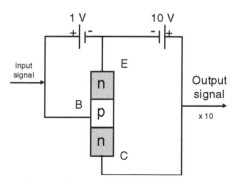

Figure 6–3
The principles of signal amplification by a bipolar junction transistor.

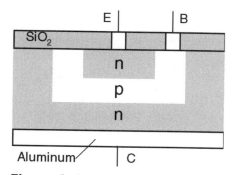

Figure 6–4
A practical design of a typical npn-bipolar junction transistor.

Figure 6–4 shows the design of a typical npn–bipolar junction transistor, with silicon dioxide used to protect metalized surfaces from corrosion, and with metal contacts made of aluminum.

MOSFET (Meta-Oxide-Semiconductor Field-Effect Transistor)

The Metal-Oxide-Semiconductor Field-Effect Transistor (MOSFET) is a four-terminal semiconductor device that is the basis for a large variety of digital integrated circuits (IC) and semiconductor memory devices.

The MOS transistor differs from the bipolar junction transistor (npn- or pnp-type) in the following ways:

- The current flow through MOSFET is controlled by an electric field rather then by a base (B) current.
- This gives MOSFET a very high input resistance and thus requires very small input currents.
- MOSFET is a unipolar transistor and relies on the majority carrier current only.

The MOSFET is, in fact, a voltage-controlled switch. It can amplify the signal as well, but is less efficient than the bipolar transistors.

Let's now look at the MOSFET design. The n-type MOSFET consists of a source and a drain made of conductive n-type semiconductor regions. A metal or poly-crystalline gate is separated from the semiconductor by the gate oxide layer. Figure 6–5 shows the n-type or n-channel MOSFET fabricated on a p-type Silicon substrate. N-type and p-type silicon is produced by implantation.

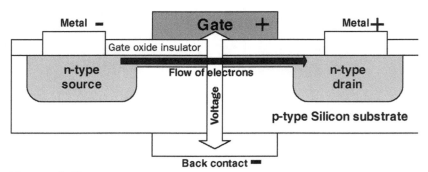

Figure 6–5
The n-type MOSFET fabricated on a p-type silicon substrate.

When a positive voltage between the gate and the back contact exceeds the specific threshold level, the electrons become attracted to the interface between the gate oxide insulator and the substrate, thus forming a narrow conductive channel, its thickness on the order of 10 nm, which connects the source and the drain. The transistor instantly turns on and a current flows between the source and the drain. Therefore, the flow of electrons through the channel, called an inversion layer, is controlled by the gate voltage.

There is no need in the current flow between the gate and the back contact to create the inversion layer. When the gate is connected to the source or is negative with respect to the source, the resistance between the source and the drain is on the order of 10^{10} ohm, making electrons stop flowing that way and the channel to disappear.

When the gate voltage is higher than the threshold voltage, the source-drain connection acts like an open circuit, and conducts only when the gate voltage is more negative than the threshold voltage.

There are two types of MOSFET, which behavior is opposite to each other: n-type (shown above) and p-type, which uses p-type silicon for source and drain and n-type silicon as a substrate. Sometimes, these two types of MOS transistors, are called NMOS and PMOS. The PMOS transistor operation is the same as for the NMOS transistor, with the polarity of the gate voltage reversed.

The typical schematic representations of the NMOS and PMOS transistors are shown in Figure 6–6.

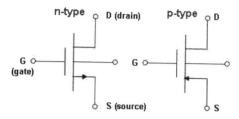

Figure 6–6
The typical schematic representations of the NMOS and PMOS transistors.

COMPUTER RANDOM ACCESS MEMORY (RAM) . . . . .

Let's first look at the part of a computer where the real action takes place: the cache and the Main memory.

In order for the central processing unit (CPU) to run an application, this application must reside in the memory, which is called the Main memory or System memory. When a specific application is needed for an operating system, the system will find it on the storage device (*i.e.*, hard disk drive) and then transfer it to Main memory. Figure 6–7 shows the memory structure in a computer system with high-speed cache memory (L1) integrated into the processor, high-speed secondary cache (L2) included in the system to boost performance, and a relatively large Main memory, which is significantly slower and has a large access time penalty.

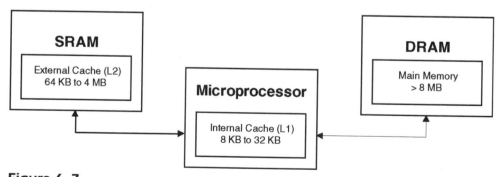

Figure 6–7
A memory hierarchy with high-speed cache memory (L1) integrated into the processor, high-speed secondary cache (L2) included in the system to boost performance, and a relatively large and slower main memory.

Main memory is built of DRAM chips and is connected to the CPU via the memory bus. For the Intel Pentium class systems, the memory bus is a 64-bit data bus that runs at 50, 60, or 66 MHz (depending on the CPU speed). The Pentium II memory bus can run at up to 100 MHz. The Pentium III memory bus runs at 100 MHz and at 133 MHz, and Pentium 4's bus is 400 MHz. The speed of the memory bus is, typically, a ratio of the CPU speed, which is referred to as the clock ratio. If the CPU runs at 450 MHz and the memory bus runs at 100 MHz, the clock ratio is 4.5.

DRAM (Dynamic RAM)

MOS (metal oxide semiconductor) random access memories are dynamic or static. Static memory is able to store the recorded information as long as the power is on. A dynamic MOS memory cell is a circuit that needs the signal to be periodically refreshed. Refreshing requires special timing signals and extra power supplies, which make dynamic memory more complex (one of its disadvantages). On the other hand, dynamic memories dissipate less power and also allow for more bits per chip than static memories.

Every DRAM memory cell is made of a pass transistor and a storage capacitor, with a single transistor chip used for each single bit of data. It is done to reduce the size of memory units and make it cheaper. In DRAM, the capacitor is built using a MOSFET device operating in the inversion region. Nowadays, the trenches filled with dielectric material are used to create the capacitive storage element of a cell.

The DRAM chips are large, rectangular arrays of memory cells that support logic that is used for reading and writing data in the arrays, and refresh circuitry needed to prevent data degradation. The memory arrays are organized in rows and columns of memory cells called *wordlines* and *bitlines*. To find the cell, each of them is assigned a unique address created by an intersection of a row and a column.

The charge stored at the MOSFET gate represents the data. This charge leaks with time, and the data will be lost if not refreshed frequently. This is *why* the content of DRAM has to be *refreshed continuously* using a special nonstop "DRAM refresh" process (unless a PC is turned off and all content is lost).

Cache

In 1969 IBM Corporation introduced the 360/85 computer, which contained a 16 KB bipolar cache memory. This manifested the beginning of the practical use of semiconductor memory.

Cache memory is random access memory that a CPU can access more quickly than the regular RAM. In fact, when the microprocessor works with data, it first looks for it in the cache memory.

Level-1 Cache

High-speed cache memory, integrated into the microprocessor, is used to temporarily store frequently used instructions and data. Since this memory is integrated into the chip, it is limited in size. Cache memory interfaces with the microprocessor via a zero wait-state interface, typically varies in size from 8 KB to 32 KB, and is called level 1 (L1)-cache, primary cache, or internal cache.

Level-1 cache is Static RAM (SRAM) that uses two transistors per bit to maintain its state and hold the data. SRAM circuit is also known as a flip-flop circuit.

A flip-flop circuit can maintain a binary state indefinitely (as long as power is delivered to the circuit) until directed by an input signal to switch states. One may think of a flip-flop as consisting of two NOT-circuits connected serially, as shown in Figure 6–8.

If one assumes binary variables on inverted inputs, the flip-flop must be in one of the two indicated states: "0" or "1," "off" or "on." These two conditions are stable and the flip-flop remains in one of the assumed states. Thus, level-1 cache memory doesn't need to be refreshed unless the data should be changed.

Level-2 Cache

High-speed level-2 cache memory is integrated into the system to compensate for performance differences between the processor and memory bus. Secondary cache has a goal similar to that of the primary cache: to supply data to the processor with minimal

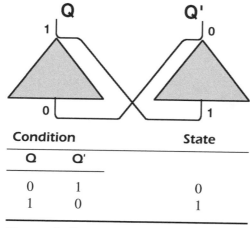

Condition		State
Q	Q'	
0	1	0
1	0	1

Figure 6–8
A flip-flop device schematics.

delay. Secondary cache is also implemented using a SRAM technology with the static RAM (SRAM) acting as a buffer between the CPU and the memory.

Cache memory typically uses two (and sometimes four) transistors per bit, which is the main reason why it is used in small quantity: the DRAM can store up to four times more data in the same volume, which makes it up to four times less expensive to make. Still, when you need the very fastest possible RAM, SRAM is the best choice.

Computer Memory Chips

Memory chips are generally placed inside ceramic or plastic packages by the time they leave the factory. This protects the structure of the chip from mechanical damage, moisture, electro-static discharge, and so on. Several memory chips, when mounted on a special printed circuit board (PCB), form a memory module.

Memory modules were adopted in the mid-1980s. At that time, computer memory consisted of dual in-line packages (DIPs), which were soldered to the motherboard or installed in the DIP sockets. This memory occupied lots of onboard space and was difficult to upgrade.

The first memory module was the 30-pin single inline memory module (SIMM), similar to that shown in Figure 6–9. It offered a low-cost pluggable memory solution. This design was widely adopted in the late 1980s.

The next memory module design was the 72-pin SIMM, which was a little bit larger than the 32-pin SIMM. This module design was popular through 1995 and is shown in the Figure 6–10.

Current memory module design, the 168-pin dual inline memory module (DIMM) was developed based on SIMM design to better balance low cost with reliability and performance. DIMM is the design used in modern PCs and is shown in Figure 6–11.

Figure 6–9
30-pin SIMM. Older memory module design. (3.5" x 0.75")

Figure 6–10
72-pin SIMM. (4.5" x 1.0")

Figure 6–11
168-pin DIMM. Current memory module design. (5.37" x 1.0")

Figure 6–12
72-pin SODIMM. (2.375" x 1.0")

Figure 6–13
144-pin SODIMM. (2.625" x 1.0")

There are two different types of 168-pin DIMM modules: the buffered memory modules and nonbuffered memory modules. The buffered memory modules represent the first generation of 168-pin DIMMs and have memory chips mounted horizontally on the printed circuit board (PCB).

Laptop computers require physically smaller memory modules. Those found in laptop computers are 72-pin and 144-pin SODIMM modules, shown in Figures 6–12 and 6–13.

Even cache memory is now available in modules called Cache-On-A-Stick (COASt).

FLASH MEMORY . . . .

The potential of metal-oxide semiconductors (MOS) technology to lead to high density and high performance of the memory devices became known in the mid-1960s. Then, chip makers started thinking hard on how to solve the main problem associated with the MOS memory concept—its volatility.

The Main memory (RAM) is most responsible for handling operating and application needs. Unfortunately, being a *volatile memory*, RAM loses all data when the system is powered down.

Another type of memory is called ROM, or Read Only Memory. ROM has data permanently stored even when the system is off, and represents a *nonvolatile* semiconductor memory (NVSM) technology.

The first solutions for the volatility problem came in 1967 in the form of a floating gate concept and the metal-nitride-oxide-semiconductor (MNOS) memory device. An ultraviolet (UV)-erasable programmable ROM (PROM/EPROM) of 1 Kb became widely available in 1971. In 1983, 16 KB EEPROM were introduced.

There are three major types of ROM: PROM (Programmable ROM), EPROM (Erasable PROM), and EEPROM (Electrically Erasable PROM).

PROM cannot be changed after being recorded once. EPROM allows the manufacturer to remove one set of instructions in exchange for another set. EEPROM is upgraded by "flashing" the chip and is called Flash ROM.

Flashing is done with the help of a special software program that stores new data on the chip. The term "Flash" refers to the fact that the entire content of the memory chip is erased in one step. In fact, current generation of Flash memory devices differs from both EEPROM and EPROM in that the "erase" operations of the Flash chip can be done in blocks.

Flash, as well as EPROM and EEPROM, must be erased before it is written to. Whole EPROM chips are, for example, erased at once by UV light. EEPROM is erased automatically before the "write" operation. The Flash chip can be erased all at once (bulk erase flash) or in blocks (boot block erased flash).

Therefore, Flash memory is both *nonvolatile* and *easy to reprogram*. This is why Flash memory is often used for data storage in digital cameras and camcorders (still image option), digital cellular phones, PC cards for laptop PCs, audio digital recorders, PDAs, GPS, answering machine sets, and so on (see Chapter 7).

Basics of Flash Memory Technology

All nonvolatile semiconductor memory devices store the data in a form of electric charges in the gate insulator of a MOSFET.

As was mentioned earlier, Flash memory is called so because the entire sections of the microchip are erased at once (or flashed). The erasure is caused by the so-called Fowler-Nordheim tunneling of electrons from the floating gate back to the substrate during the *erase* cycle.

Flash memory devices (see Figure 6–14) is built on a poly-silicon structure floating-gate MOSFET. The control gate is connected to the *wordline* and is isolated from the

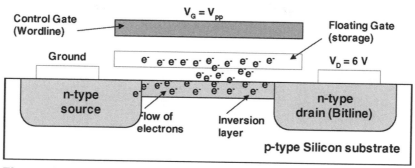

Figure 6–14
An illustration of the Flash cell writing process.

floating gate by the dielectric layer. The floating gate, which is the effective storage medium in a flash device, is isolated from the substrate by a thin oxide layer of about 10 nm thick. This isolation is needed to enable the floating gate layer to store charges.

Flash write operation is based on *hot electron injection* into the floating gate when the *high programming voltage* (V_{pp} = 12V) is applied to the control gate. This voltage creates the inversion region in the p-substrate and allows the electrons from the source to start flowing toward the drain. The electrons are then accelerated by the drain voltage and gain enough energy to "jump" or be "hot-injected" into the floating gate.

After the write cycle is completed, it forms a negative charge on the floating gate, which raises the flash cell's threshold voltage above the so-called wordline *logic 1 voltage*, used by a sense amplifier for detection of the cell current. If the flash cell is written, it corresponds to a "0," and the cell with no negative charge on the floating gate is interpreted as "1." When the wordline of this cell is brought higher than the threshold voltage during read operation, this cell will not "turn on" and conduct the current, thus allowing interpretation of its state as "1."

Flash erase operation (see Figure 6–15) uses the Fowler-Nordheim electron tunneling to remove the charge from the floating gate by applying *high programming voltage* (V_{pp} = 12V) to the source. The high positive voltage on the source makes the electrons move from the floating gate to the source. This changes the state of the cell back to "1." When the wordline of this cell is brought higher than the threshold voltage during read operation, this cell will "turn on" and conduct more current, thus allowing interpretation of its state as "0."

Flash memory cells are organized arrays and are connected via the wordlines and bitlines.

During the *read* operation, the wordline voltage is brought to a voltage higher than the threshold voltage of the erased cell. This turns the erased cells on, which allows for current to flow from drain to source. At the same time, all written cells (with

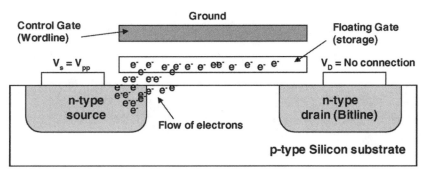

Figure 6–15
An illustration of the Flash cell high-voltage source erase process.

electrons "sitting" on the floating gate) will stay in the off state with almost no current flowing from drain to source. The cell current is then detected by the sense amplifier, allowing interpretation of its state.

Flash Memory Cards

Flash memory card loses power when it is disconnected from the PC, yet the data stored in it is retained indefinitely, until it is rewritten. Flash memory cards use flash memory chips to store and retrieve data. There are two basic types of cards: PC cards (linear cards) and ATA Flash PC cards.

PC cards, also called linear cards: PC cards are typically connected directly to the PC bus and have direct access to the CPU (or CPU has direct access to the card). This mode of operation is called "execute in place" (XIP) mode and is a method of directly executing the applications from the card's ROM without loading the application into DRAM. XIP requires high-speed random access during read operation. This type of application is typically needed for internal PC storage of the system data, the boot code, BIOS, fonts, and so on.

ATA Flash PC cards: PC cards that are connected to the CPU via the ATA interface, similar to that used by other storage devices such as hard disk drives. The interface could either belong to the computer or to the PC card. CPU in this case treats the ATA Flash PC card just as a solid-state equivalent of the hard disk drive (HDD) and the card must be capable of addressing (rewriting) data using 512-byte blocks—the way HDD does it.

Figure 6–16 shows how the PC cards of two different types communicate with the CPU. Linear cards communicate directly with the CPU in XIP mode. ATA Flash PC cards use DRAM (Dynamic Random Access Memory) to communicate with the CPU.

Generally, the linear cards use DINOR and NOR flash chips logic, while ATA PC cards use AND and NAND flash chips logic. Those chips are electrically pro-

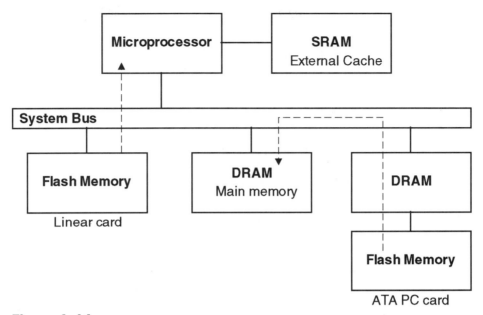

Figure 6–16
PC Card communication with the CPU.

grammable and reprogrammable nonvolatile solid-state data storage devices. Next is the explanation to the different logical designs used in Flash cards.

NOR

The logic of NOR is shown next and should be understood as follows (for the first row):

If A = 0 and B = 0, then C = 1.

A	B	C
0	0	1
0	1	0
1	0	0
1	1	0

NOR represents the earliest flash design. NOR flash memory has a large sector size and cell size, high-speed rewrite, and high-speed random data access. NOR devices use energy consuming hot electron injection for data writing and tunnel release for erasing. One disadvantage of NOR is that they are difficult to scale up to higher capacities.

NAND

The logic of NAND is shown next:

A	B	C
0	0	1
0	1	1
1	0	1
1	1	0

NAND flash chips are serial access devices with high storage capacity, single voltage (3.3V or 5V) operation, small block size, small cell size, and high durability. NAND use tunnel injection for writing and tunnel release for erasing, which is a power-saving technique.

DINOR (Divided Bit-Line NOR)

DINOR flash chips (introduced by Mitsubishi) have high random data access, single voltage supply (3.3V or 2.7V), fast block erase, large block size, multi-sector erase capabilities, and low power consumption using tunnel injection/tunnel release for write and erase. Storage capacity (called density) for DINOR is currently in the range from 1 MB to 2 MB.

AND

The logic of AND is shown next:

A	B	C
0	0	0
0	1	0
1	0	0
1	1	1

The AND Flash chip (first introduced by Hitachi) is a serial access device combining the best of NOR and NAND devices. It has fast erase, single voltage supply operation, very high capacity, low power consumption (writing by tunnel injection and erasing by tunnel current release), and small block size. It offers multiblock erase and auxiliary byte redundancy for ECC. AND flash chips are optimized for high-capacity storage devices such as ATA Flash PC cards. Devices with more than 32 MB of storage capacity are available.

FLASH MEMORY CARD FORMATS . . . .

Initially, Flash memory cards were made according to the PC Card Standard, which provides physical specifications for three types of PC Cards. All three card types have the same length and width and use the same 68-pin connector. The only difference between the card types is the thickness. The thickness is 3.3, 5.0, and 10.5 millimeters for Type I, Type II, and Type III cards, respectively.

Increasing competition among flash memory chip makers, along with their desire to enter new markets of such devices as PDAs, digital cameras, sound recorders, and so on (see Chapter 7), resulted in newer card formats being introduced. There were about six formats introduced in recent years, with cards being even smaller than the Type I PC Card, but having adapters, which allow most of them to be connected to the standard PC Card socket. This miniaturization trend is quite reasonable because of a continuous growth in storage density of Flash memory cards. Most of the newer card formats have smaller than 68 connector contacts, meaning the shift from parallel data exchange toward serial or parallel with narrower bus width.

Table 6–2 summarizes available Flash memory card formats.

Table 6–2   Available Flash Memory Card Formats

Name	Original developer	Dimensions (mm)	Number of contacts
SmartMedia	Toshiba	$45 \times 37 \times 0.76$	22
CompactFlash	SanDisk	$43 \times 36 \times 3.3$	50
Miniature card	AMD and Intel	$38 \times 33 \times 3.3$	60
Serial flash module	NexFlash Technology	$15 \times 45 \times (< 1)$	2–4
MultimediaCard	Siemens and SanDisk	$32 \times 24 \times 1.4$	7
Memory Stick	Sony	$21 \times 50 \times 2.8$	10

In spite of using the same storage principles, different Flash cards have different architectures, storage capacity, and physical dimensions. The reason is manufacturers believe that the higher cost cards (like the CompactFlash card) will eventually self-limit their market applications and market share. Then, the Compactflash card can be used, for example, for high-end digital cameras, while a smaller Miniature card can be used in cheaper cameras for the general consumer.

Let's now take a look at some of the most popular card formats.

SmartMedia

The SmartMedia card (see Figure 6–17) is an ATA (parallel) card using an external controller and was originally developed by Toshiba (see *www.toshiba.com*). It weighs only 2 g.

Each SmartMedia™ card features an embedded NAND-type flash memory chip, and thus is less costly than other types of memory cards. SmartMedia cards are now available in capacities of up to 64 MB.

CompactFlash

Volume shipments of the CompactFlash card, developed by SanDisk (see Figure 6–18), began in 1995. CompactFlash card is an ATA (parallel) card with an embedded controller chip. It is thicker and heavier than the SmartMedia card. But, CompactFlash cards have a superior storage capacity of up to 192 MB for Type I cards and up to 300 MB for Type II cards. Unlike the SmartMedia cards that use one voltage level of 3.3V for all required operations, CompactFlash cards utilize 3.3V/5V read/write operation. The 50-pin CompactFlash card can be easily inserted into a passive 68-pin Type II adapter card that fully meets PC Card electrical and mechanical interface specifications.

Figure 6–17
SmartMedia card.

Figure 6–18
CompactFlash card from SanDisk (courtesy of SanDisk).

Miniature Card

Miniature Card (see Figure 6–19) is a linear memory card developed jointly by Intel and AMD for low-cost consumer needs. Being a linear card, the Miniature Card requires no microcontrollers or hardware overhead. The low-cost connector reduces card cost by requiring no connector on the card and no ejection mechanism on the host side. Nowadays, Miniature Cards have a storage capacity of up to 64 MB.

Miniature Card supports 3.3V/5V read/write operation, automated program suspend capabilities, and has integrated power-down modes for extended battery life.

Serial Flash Module

Serial Flash modules (see Figure 6–20) from NexFlash (*www.nexflash.com*) are designed to be a small form-factor solution for storage of data, voice, and images for systems constrained by power, available pins, physical dimensions, and performance. The capacity of the modules ranges nowadays from 128 KB to 4 MB. Because they have room for only a few pins and don't have space for an internal controller, the tiny new Flash cards necessarily have serial I/O formats.

This family of products offers a 4-pin Serial Peripheral Interface (SPI) or a 2-pin NXS (NexFlash Serial) interface. The devices operate using a single 3V or 5V power

Figure 6–19
Miniature card.

Figure 6–20
Serial Flash Module from NexFlash (courtesy of NexFlash Technologies)

supply with a current as low as 5 mA active and 1 µA at standby, making them attractive for battery-powered applications. Other features include erase/write rates over 100 KB/S, 16 MHz clocks, on-chip SRAM, write protection, electronic ID, and small DOS-compatible sectors that simplify file-system implementation.

MultiMediaCard

Like most other Flash memory cards, the SanDisk MultiMediaCard serial memory card (see *www.sandisk.com*) is also designed for the ultra-portable devices market where small size, low cost, and simplicity of the interface are key requirements (see Figure 6–21). The MultiMediaCard is a card with a low-cost 7-pin connector.

The SanDisk MultiMediaCard is available now in storage capacities ranging from 8–64 MB.

Memory Stick

The last small Flash memory card format discussed is the Memory Stick serial card from Sony (see Figure 6–22). As the name suggests, the card has a long and narrow shape (50 × 21 mm) and looks like a stick of chewing gum.

Figure 6–21
The SanDisk MultiMediaCard serial memory card (courtesy of SanDisk).

Figure 6–22
The Memory Stick serial card from Sony.

The data in the card are organized in large 8-KB blocks, which make it easier to manage audio and video data, unlike those cards using 512-byte blocks. For example, a compressed digital image requires an average of 60 KB (and more), and 1 minute of compressed sound requires about 100 KB. Therefore, very small blocks add unnecessary complexity to the file management.

Current storage capacity of the Memory Stick card reaches 64 MB.

SOLID-STATE HARD DISK DRIVES

These storage devices have the form-factors (2.5", 3.5", etc.) and the interface of a typical hard disk drive, but store data using solid-state memory technology. Since solid-state memory costs more than magnetic storage, solid-state drives are available in much smaller capacities (for example, for SanDisk FlashDrives, the maximum capacity is 1.2 GB).

There are different names used for this technology at the moment. Quantum, for example, calls the solid-state memory drive a "solid state disk" (SSD). SanDisk called it a FlashDrive. The solid-state drives are now available with the same most popular interfaces as used by the ordinary drives, namely, IDE and SCSI.

The main advantages of solid-state drives are summarized next:

- Quiet operation: no moving parts translate into no sound coming out of the drive. The noise level of the solid-state drive is virtually equal to zero.
- Much faster data access during "read" due to virtually eliminated seek and latency delays (typical for rotating magnetic or optical media).
- High vibration and shock resistance: no moving parts lowers the risk of mechanical damage.
- Low power consumption, since now energy is spent on moving and rotating parts.

At present, there are two types of solid-state drives:

- volatile, based on DRAM technology
- nonvolatile, based on Flash technology

Nonvolatile Flash memory drives are just the same Flash memory cards but made to the standard HDD size, and equipped with the standard drive interface, such as IDE in the case of SanDisk's FlashDrive. FlashDrives range in capacity from 32 MB to 1.2 GB with the price (at the time of writing this book) ranging from $130 (for 32 MB) to an impressive $3,775 (for 1.2 GB).

Table 6–3 compares a 2.5-inch solid-state drive (from SanDisk) with 2.5" HDD and 1-inch Microdrive from IBM.

Table 6–3   Comparison of Solid-State Drive, HDD, and Microdrive

Characteristic	2.5" FlashDrive (SanDisk)	2.5" HDD Travelstar 18GT (IBM)	1" IBM Microdrive
Total capacity, GB	1.2	18.1	1.0
Interface type	IDE	EIDE (ATA-4)	IDE and PC Card
Latency, ms	0	7.1	8.33
Seek time, ms	1.25	12	12
Operational temperature	0°–60°C	5°–55°C	0°–65°C
Shock	1000 G (operating) 1000 G (nonoperating)	150 G (2 ms half sine wave, operating) 500 G (2 ms half sine wave, nonoperating)	175 G (2 ms half sine wave, operating) 1500 G (2 ms half sine wave, nonoperating)
Vibration, G	15 (peak-to-peak)	1 G (operating, zero-to-peak @ 5–500 Hz)	1 G (operating, zero-to-peak @ 5–500 Hz)
Acoustic noise, dBA	0	27	27
Error rate (nonrecoverable)	$< 10^{-14}$	$< 10^{-13}$	$< 10^{-13}$
Power requirements	+5/+3.3 VDC	+5V VDC	+5/+3.3 VDC
Power consumption, W	0.6 (read/write) 0.0025 (sleep)	2.1/2.2 (read/write) 0.1 (sleep)	0.825 (read/write) 0.067 (sleep) (at +3.3VDC)
List price, $	3,775	495.00	< 500

The volatile drives (see *www.quantum.com*) use memory units that require continuous power to retain information, which may be implemented using a battery back up. Another way to back up the data (to safely shut the drive down) is to combine batteries with the nonvolatile magnetic hard disk drive.

Considering the high cost of the solid-state drives, what is the possible market for them?

Apparently, solid-state drives are the best for applications where performance, especially read performance, is the major issue, the data volumes are limited, and cost isn't an issue.

As an example of these applications one may think of military hardware, space technology, commercial data processing, and on-line transaction processing applications. In all those cases the tangible costs of lost lives or money readily justify investment in solid-state technology.

On the other hand, the high price per MB of storage will limit application of Flash technology to smaller capacity devices, such as PDAs, digital cameras, and so on.

SUMMARY . . . .

The main trends observed by comparing solid-state technology and magnetic or optical storage technologies are about the same:

- Miniaturization and increasing storage density
- Continuous price erosion
- Expansion into the new and nontraditional markets

Solid-state technology is, for example, attempting to capture some market share from the magnetic storage devices by entering the HDD market with solid-state drives. At the same time, HDD technology has started competing with Flash technology in the field of hand-held devices with products like IBM Microdrive. It seems at the moment that the cost of storage will determine the future outcome of this battle.

7

New Applications of Storage Devices

In this chapter...

This chapter discusses new applications of data storage devices.

MP3 PLAYERS ·

A subsystem of the MPEG-2 data compression system that deals with sound compression is called *MPEG audio Layer-3,* or *MP3*. MPEG is the acronym for Moving Picture Experts Group, the same group that developed compression systems for video, such as the MPEG-2, used in DVD movies.

The MP3 format is a compression system for music. This format helps to reduce the size of a song while keeping its quality close to that of the original. The goal of the MP3 format is to compress the music file by a factor of 10 to 14 without losing the CD sound quality. A 32 megabyte (MB) song on a CD can be compressed down to about 3 MB on MP3, while providing an acceptable quality. This lets you download a song in minutes rather than hours, and you can store 10 to 20 songs on an MP3 player using a relatively small amount of on-board memory.

The history of MP3 technology goes back to 1987, when a German company, Fraunhofer Gesellschaft, developed the original algorithm now used in MP3. This algorithm was patented in Germany in 1989 and in the United States in 1996. By now, there are over 500,000 songs from 80,000 artists available in MP3 format.

The main reason for the success of MP3 technology is its high compression. For example, a 3-minute CD-quality song takes approximately 32 MB of space. The same song with *about the same quality* in MP3 format requires only about 1.6 MB. This creates possibilities for portable music players, fast download from the Web, and so on.

Major manufacturers of MP3 players at the moment are:

- Rio (*www.riohome.com*)
- Sony (*http://64.14.40.118/products/index.jsp*)
- Philips (*www.philips.com*)
- Samsung (*www.samsungelectronics.com/products/yepp/yepp.html*)
- Audiovox (*www.audiovox.com*)
- Rave (*www.ravemp.com*)

MP3 players typically use computers to download and upload music. For example, a song from a CD can be converted into MP3 format (compressed) and downloaded onto a portable player. The same song, already in MP3 format, can be downloaded from the Web to the computer and then to the player. There are thousands of web sites with MP3 music available for download, with one, *www.MP3.com*, being the largest.

The player can be connected to the computer using one of the traditional interfaces: for example, parallel or USB (see Chapter 2). Special software will allow you to just drag and drop files into the player's storage. The players could be portable or stationary (much larger).

Nonvolatile storage is a critical element of MP3 player technology, along with the micro-processor, DSP processor, display, power supply, audio and data ports, and so on. There are two major types of nonvolatile storage used in MP3 players today: solid-state Flash memory and magnetic recording storage. The next list summarizes the main storage types used:

- Internal Flash memory
- CompactFlash memory card
- SmartMedia Flash memory card
- Memory Stick (Sony)
- HipZip drive (from Iomega)
- Hard disk drive (including IBM Microdrive and larger drives)

Solid-state Flash memory is faster during "read" than magnetic or optical storage, and has a much higher vibration and shock resistance, but is also much more expensive (per unit storage). This is why it comes in small quantities (like 32 or 64 MB).

Magnetic storage devices are somewhat slower then flash memory, but fast enough to do the job (in fact, the HDD is many times faster than needed to do the job!), and are much cheaper per unit storage. MP3 players equipped with magnetic storage are typically capable of storing 10 to 100 times more music.

Several examples of MP3 players with solid-state and magnetic memory are presented here.

MP3 Player with Built-In Flash Memory and External SmartMedia Memory Card

The YP-NEP/NEU MP3 player (Figure 7–1) from Samsung has 32 MB to 64 MB built-in Flash memory and allows for additional memory with the SmartMedia card. The player uses USB or Parallel interfaces for communication with the computer.

Figure 7–1
YP-NEP/NEU MP3 player (courtesy of Samsung Group).

MP3 Player with Memory Stick

The VAIO Music Clip™ Personal Network Player from Sony (Figure 7–2) plays up to 120 minutes of MP3 files with its 64 MB built-in Flash memory (60.8 MB available for storage). The player uses a USB interface for data upload to and download from the computer.

MP3 Player with a Clik!

This MP3 player from Iomega (Figure 7–3) is built around a known storage technology called Click!, which is based on small flexible (Zip-like) magnetic disks. One PocketZip™ disk ($10) has 40 MB of storage capacity—enough for 80 minutes of MP3-compressed music. The HipZip™ is also called a PocketZip™ storage device and allows for download and transport of computer data, images, and more. The player uses a USB interface to communicate with the computer. The re-chargeable internal lithium ion battery provides up to 12 hours of continuous play. The player costs around $300.

Figure 7–2
VAIO Music Clip™ Personal Network Player from Sony (courtesy of Sony Electronics Inc.).

Figure 7–3
HipZip™ digital music player from Iomega (courtesy of Iomega Corp).

MP3 Player with Magnetic Hard Disk Drive

The Jukebox 6000 MP3 Player from Archos (*www.archos.com*) obviously doesn't belong to a category of mobile MP3 players but allows storage of about 100 hours of MP3-quality music on an internal 3.5" IDE hard disk drive (see Figure 7–4). With its 6 GB of storage capacity, the Jukebox 6000 allows you to create and manage a larger music collection—the equivalency of over 150 CDs!

The player communicates with PC and Mac computers using a USB interface and a simple drag-and-drop file system (using MS Explorer). Clearly, this kind of MP3 player allows you to build an extremely large collection of songs. The list price of this player is $350.

Mobile Phone/MP3 Player

Samsung's SGH-M100 (Figure 7–5) is the world's first MP3 GSM mobile phone with a built-in MP3 player. The SGH-M100 combines the best in mobile technology with the best in music technology inside its slim 19.3 mm and 97 g body. The phone/MP3 player uses 32 MB of solid-state Flash memory, which allows about 8 MP3 songs. The data can be downloaded from the computer over the parallel interface.

Figure 7–4
The Jukebox 6000 MP3 Player from Archos (courtesy of Archos Technology).

Figure 7–5
Samsung's SGH mobile phone with a built-in MP3 player (courtesy of Samsung Group).

Figure 7–6
FinePix40i from Fujifilm is the high-resolution digital camera with the built in
MP-3 music player (courtesy of Fuji Photo Film U.S.A.).

Digital Camera/MP3 Player

This is another hybrid of MP3 technology with some other digital technology, namely,
the digital camera. The FinePix40i from Fujifilm (Figure 7–6) is the world's smallest
high-resolution digital camera with 4.3 million pixel pictures (2400×1800) and a
built-in MP3 music player. Communication with the PC is done via a USB port.

DIGITAL CAMERAS . . . .

Traditional (analog) photography means expensive film and long and often inconve-
nient processing. To download pictures to your computer one needs a scanner and this
process results in a degraded picture quality. Digital still cameras eliminate the need
for film and film processing and make duplication, distribution, processing, copying,
and so on, an easy task. Most cameras allow for instant replay of the image and, if you
are not happy with the result, you can erase it and try again as many times as you wish.
Further development in the field of inexpensive high-quality home printing will eventually lead to the complete elimination of traditional film-based analog cameras.

Digital cameras differ from their traditional analog counterparts in almost everything: the way they acquire, process, and store images is fully digital. They also allow
for in-house picture printing using high-quality photo-printers. Unfortunately, to obtain
a high-quality digital equivalent of the analog image, the high sampling frequency (see
Chapter 1) or, in other words, a large number of pixels, is required. As a result, the
newest high-quality digital cameras are capable of acquiring images with more than 5
million pixels. The next obvious question is how to store and subsequently transfer
such a large amount of data.

Since digital cameras don't use film anymore, they have to rely on high-capacity
digital data storage that is small in size, and low in both weight and cost. Many differ-

ent types of storage systems are being tried in digital cameras by different makers. The following storage technologies can be found in many of the digital cameras available on the market today:

- Solid-state Flash memory (CompactFlash, SmartMedia, etc.)
- Miniature hard disk drive (IBM Microdrive)
- Clik! Drive systems (Iomega)
- Superdisk 120 MB systems (from Imation)
- CD-R systems (from Sony)

There is also an issue of fast and painless data transfer to the computer. Modern digital cameras most often use the USB interface because of its high DTR, hot-plug-in capabilities, and small convenient connectors.

Let's now consider some examples of the modern digital cameras with different storage systems.

The application of the 120 MB Superdisk in digital cameras has already been discussed in Chapter 3, using the Panasonic PalmCam Digital camera PV-SD4090 as an example. This technology allows for storage of about 450 "super fine resolution" and about 1,500 "standard resolution" images. Even if one doesn't have a Superdisk drive on their computer, the data can be transferred onto a regular floppy disk or directly to the computer via the USB port on the camera.

Digital Camera with Solid-State Memory

First, there is a QV-8000SX digital camera from Casio (Figure 7–7) that features $1,280 \times 960$ images and uses 8 MB CompactFlash solid-state memory cards for data storage. With the use of the special Photo Loader, the camera automatically transfers images from the camera or from an optional CompactFlash reader to your PC via a USB interface.

Figure 7–7
QV-8000SX digital camera from Casio (courtesy of Casio Computer Co.).

The 8 MB memory is sufficient for 13 images or 25 seconds of a movie in AVI format. The cost of the camera is about $700.

Digital Camera with a Hard Disk Drive

An example of a digital camera with a hard disk drive is the QV-2300UXPlus from Casio (Figure 7–8). This camera comes with the 340 MB IBM Microdrive, which allows for up to 400 images in high resolution ($1,600 \times 1,200$) and 2,054 in economy mode (800×600). The camera can be connected to a computer via a USB interface (IBM PC) or a serial port (Macintosh). The camera costs about $1,000.

Digital Camera in a Watch

The next example shows the WQV1-1CR: a digital camera integrated into a wristwatch (Figure 7–9). In this case, the Microdrive clearly is too large and power hungry, so a

Figure 7–8
QV-2300UXPlus Digital Camera from Casio uses the IBM Microdrive (courtesy of Casio Computer Co.).

Figure 7–9
The WQV1-1CR is a digital camera integrated into a wrist watch (courtesy of Casio Computer Co.).

tiny Flash memory is best suited for the job. The camera has 1 MB of Flash memory, which is sufficient for storing 100 digital images.

The world's first wrist-type wearable digital camera from Casio measures just 40.0 (W) × 52.0 (H) × 16 (D) mm, weighs 32 g, and hardly differs from the regular digital watch. Yet, it is always ready to capture images digitally whenever the need arises. Images can be played back on the camera's own screen. To transfer your photos to the desktop, you have to use the optional Wrist Camera Software Package, which includes Wrist Camera Software and an infra-red (IR) wireless adapter. When transferred to the computer, the images will be converted from the proprietary Casio format into BMP or JPEG formats. The camera costs about $200.

Digital Camera with Multiple Recording Media

The FinePix S1 Pro from Fujifilm (Figure 7–10) is a good example of a high-quality professional digital camera with an ultra-high resolution imaging system and with high-storage capacity for images with up to 6.1 million pixels (3040 × 2016). To address this issue, the camera is made compatible with three different types of storage: SmartMedia, CompactFlash, and IBM Microdrive.

To transfer those large files to the PC, a USB interface is used.

Digital Camera with a Memory Stick

DSC-S70 camera from Sony (Figure 7–11) has superb multicoated optics from Carl Zeiss® Vario-Sonnar and a superb image sensor with 3.34 mega-pixel resolution. The digital data can even be saved in the TIFF file format, which preserves every bit of res-

Figure 7–10
The FinePix S1 Pro from Fujifilm is a professional digital camera with up to 6.1 million pixels per image (courtesy of Fuji Photo Film U.S.A.).

Figure 7–11
DSC-S70 camera from Sony uses Memory Stick for data storage (courtesy of
Sony Electronics Inc.).

olution. As a storage device for large image files, the DSC-S70 uses Memory Sticks
from Sony. It comes with 8 MB Memory Stick media, but supports 8 MB, 16 MB, 32
MB, and 64 MB Memory Stick media. In fact, one can save up to 1,000 images on a
single 64 MB Memory Stick media card, which is more than 40 rolls of traditional film.
Also, sharing the images with all your other digital devices is easy by transferring the
Memory Sticks. Optional features include a Memory Stick printer and Memory Stick
floppy disk adapter. Communication with the PC is done via a USB interface. The camera costs around $800.

Solid-State Memory-to-Floppy Disk Adapter

To make data transfer from a digital camera to the computer easier and more flexible,
solid-state memory-to-floppy disk adapters are often used. For example, the SmartMedia
Floppy Disk Adapter FD-A2 from Fujifilm (Figure 7–12) allows for easy transfer of the
images from a SmartMedia memory card to the PC. The card is just inserted into the

Figure 7–12
SmartMedia Floppy Disk Adapter FD-A2 from Fujifilm (courtesy of Fuji Photo
Film U.S.A.).

adapter, which is shaped like a 3.5-inch floppy disk. The adapter is then inserted into the floppy disk drive. The adapter is compatible with both Windows and Macintosh.

Digital Camera with a Clik!

This mega-pixel Agfa ePhoto CL30 Clik! digital camera (Figure 7–13) has a built-in PocketZip drive from Iomega, which uses 40 MB magnetic disks that can store up to 60 high-resolution and 360 low-resolution pictures per disk. The $10 disks are quite inexpensive, compact, and convenient. They are somewhat similar in technology to the well-known Zip disks, but are much smaller in size. For a direct camera-to-PC connection, a USB interface is used. The camera's cost is about $500.

Digital Camera with a CD-R

The MVC-CD1000 2.1 from Sony (Figure 7–14) has a high-powered 52 mm 10x optical zoom lens added to a 2.1-megapixel image sensor with high resolution. What is different

Figure 7–13
Agfa ePhoto CL30 Clik! digital camera has a built-in Iomega's PocketZip drive (courtesy of Iomega Corp.).

Figure 7–14
MVC-CD1000 2.1 from Sony has a built-in CD recorder for 156 MB 3" CD-R discs (courtesy of Sony Electronics Inc.).

from many other digital cameras is the built-in CD recorder for 156 MB 3" CD-R discs, which make capturing hundreds of images a very inexpensive business and costs literally pennies per shot, even at the highest image resolution. In addition, MVC-CD1000 2.1 features a USB connection for both IBM PC and Mac. The camera cost is approximately $1,300.

PERSONAL DIGITAL ASSISTANTS (PDA) . . . .

When people leave their desks (and desktop computers), they typically want to carry some information and applications with them: phone numbers, addresses, calendar, calculator, possibly an email program and web browser. To meet those needs, personal digital assistants were invented.

The first successful PDA was, perhaps, Apple Computer's Newton Message Pad. Of course, by today's standards the Newton was oversized and expensive, and its handwriting recognition wasn't too good, but it was a very popular high-tech device at the time. But the real success came to the PDAs in 1996, when the first Palm Pilot was introduced. It was simpler than the Newton, small and light, easy to operate, and could run for weeks on a couple of batteries.

One possible way (not the only one) to categorize PDA devices is by dividing them into *palm-sized* computers and *handheld* computers. They differ in size, data entry method, and logistics of software.

Handheld computers are meant to be a *replacement* to the larger computer but with somewhat limited capabilities (processing power, memory, software applications, etc.), while the palm-sized computers are there to just *complement* fully-functional computers.

Handheld computers are bigger and heavier, with large color liquid-crystal displays (LCD) and an integrated keyboard, but are slower and have less RAM. The operating system is a simplified version of Windows OS, called *PocketPC* (formerly known as Windows CE). The software includes simplified but fully functional versions of the same Windows applications such as Word, Excel, Outlook, and so on. These computers are, in general, more expensive than palm-sized PDAs.

Palm-sized computers are smaller and lighter, often come with a monochromatic touch-screen LCD, and have their operating system, which is the Palm OS from Palm, Inc. The Palm OS occupies less than 100 KB of memory. Again, palm-sized PDAs do not compete in functionality with the larger PCs, but attempt to complement them. Also, palm-sized PDAs are, in general, much cheaper.

In spite of focusing on apparently different goals, these two platforms are competing fiercely. So far, in spite of growing competition from the PocketPC family of handheld computers, the Pilot-like PDAs dominate the market.

There are plenty of Palm OS licensees nowadays, including such companies as IBM, HP, Compaq, and Sony, and there is a considerable choice of different features. While absorbing new technology and trying to stay ahead of the PocketPC devices, Pilot-like PDAs have gradually added more functionality (Internet connectivity and email, MP3, GPS, digital photo, etc.) and memory, improved handwriting recognition, and updated their design.

Palm Pilot VIIx

Palm Pilot VIIx (Figure 7–15) is the palm-sized PDA with the largest RAM available. A typical amount of RAM in today's palm-sized PDA is about 2 to 4 MB. In some PDA models, memory can be upgraded. Palm-sized PDAs come with their basic software stored in a small nonvolatile Flash memory (ROM), and with some larger amounts of RAM, which is constantly powered by a battery. The RAM is typically a solid-state static RAM (or SRAM), which reaches 8 MB in, for example, the Palm Pilot VIIx.

When the battery is depleted or removed, the entire content of the RAM is lost. This is why it is so important to use the enclosed synchronization software and have a copy of the data on your desktop computer. But, when the new battery is inserted, the Pilot comes online and restarts its OS kept in the ROM.

One of the latest PDAs from Palm, Inc. (*www.palm.com*), the Palm Pilot VIIx, comes Internet-ready with TCP/IP software to support Internet-based Web clipping applications and email, and costs about $450. Its large (8 MB) RAM allows for thousands of addresses, years of appointments, hundreds of to-do items, notes and memos, email messages, and still has about 2.5 MB of RAM left for add-on applications.

Figure 7–15
Palm Pilot VIIx (courtesy of Palm, Inc.).

The Flash memory design allows for future OS software upgrades, but the amount of storage provided with the Palm Pilot VIIx is still quite limited. The PDA can run for two to four weeks on two AAA batteries, but if the pilot is powered down, the entire content in RAM is lost and there is not sufficient ROM to store this data. This is why some other manufacturers of palm-sized PDAs try to find different storage solutions for their products.

Sony CLIÉ with a Memory Stick

CLIÉ™ from Sony (Figure 7–16) stands for communication, link, information and entertainment. The CLIÉ Handheld PDA runs Palm OS® version 3.5 and comes with 8 MB of internal memory and a slot for the removable Memory Stick allowing for virtually unlimited memory expansion. Additional Memory Sticks are available in capacities of 8 MB, 16 MB, 32 MB, and 64 MB. An 8 MB Memory Stick removable memory is supplied with the device. Sony estimates that 8 MB of internal memory is good for storing approximately 10,000 addresses, 3,000 to-do items, 3,000 memos, 400 email messages, and 5 years of appointments. An unlimited number of information can be stored when using the removable Memory Stick media. The device connects to the PC via a USB interface. CLIÉ costs about $350.

Figure 7–16
CLIÉ PDA from Sony stands for Communication, Link, Information, and Entertainment (courtesy of Sony Electronics Inc.).

TRGpro with the CompactFlash Expansion Slot

The TRGpro™ handheld computer (see *www.superpilot.com*) combines the application environment of the Palm OS platform with a CompactFlash expansion slot to enable access to large-scale information and databases typically confined to a desktop PC only (Figure 7–17).

It comes with 8 MB RAM and 2 MB Flash memory, but the expansion slot allows for almost unlimited memory supply, including such high-capacity devices as the 1 GB IBM Microdrive. In fact, any CF+ compatible device can be used with TRGpro. Clearly, this moves the TRGpro into another league in terms of storage capabilities. The TRGpro is priced around $330.

HP Jornada 548: Powered by PocketPC OS

Hewlett Packard produces both palm-sized and the hand-held computers running PocketPC OS. Its Jornada 548 computer (Figure 7–18) is equipped with 32 MB of RAM.

Figure 7–17
TRGpro™ handheld computer from TRG (courtesy of TRG).

Figure 7–18
Jornada 548 hand-held computer running PocketPC OS (courtesy of Hewlett Packard).

The user can view and edit Word and Excel documents on the road, enjoy a relatively fast 133 MHz 32-bit Hitachi processor, and transfer files to and from the desktop computer via USB connection.

Jornada 548 comes with 16 MB ROM and with the CompactFlash Type I card slot, which makes it possible to increase its storage capacity by an additional 94 MB (or even more) by just inserting an additional Flash memory card. A built-in lithium-ion rechargeable battery provides about 8 hours of operation time.

The cost of the Jornada 548 is about $500 to $550.

HP Jornada 720: Handheld PocketPC

This handheld PDA works faster than its earlier versions with its high-performance 206 MHz processor, 32MB SDRAM, high-speed 51 MHz memory data bus, and 2D graphics accelerator.

The Jornada 720 (Figure 7–19) has 32 MB of SDRAM, and allows for ROM expansion with one PC Card Type II card slot, one CompactFlash Type I card slot, and a Smart Card reader card slot. The result is that this PDA can expand its storage to up to 440 MB (with SanDisk 48 MB, 96 MB, and 440 MB memory) or to 340 MB with the IBM Microdrive (1 GB Microdrive is now available with even larger capacity models coming soon).

The Jornada 720's rechargeable lithium-ion battery provides up to 9 hours of battery life. This fully functional handheld PC costs about $1,000.

Figure 7–19
Jornada 720 can expand its ROM to 340 MB with IBM Microdrive (courtesy of Hewlett Packard).

PERSONAL VIDEO RECORDER . . . .

TiVo is the Personal Video Recorder (PVR) or Digital Video Recorder (DVR) that can perform simultaneous recording and playback of a TV signal. TiVo allows the user to "pause" a live TV program, rewind, fast/slow forward, and store hours of TV programs without the use of a VCR. The most impressive features are the ability to skip commercials and to record and playback at the same time. A similar technology is offered by ReplayTV.

The list below is a brief summary of what TiVo can do:

- Pause, slow-motion (including frame by frame), and instant replay of live TV.
- Fast forward to choose which program to watch or skip.
- Simultaneous playback and record.
- Skip commercials (!)
- Directly access all prerecorded programs (unlike video tape)
- Provide menu, automated recording of programs, program ratings, suggestions, tips, and so on (comes with subscription to TiVo service)

Basic Design

The TiVo system consists of the Philips Personal TV Receiver powered by the TiVo Service, which gives the user significant control over the viewing experience.

At the PVR input, an analog TV signal gets split into video and audio components (see Figure 7–20), which are converted into digital form and compressed using an MPEG-2 video encoder and audio compressor. The signal is then stored on the hard disk drive after passing the write buffer. During reading, compressed signals are decompressed and then combined into an analog signal.

There are other data carried with video and audio signals, such as second audio program (SAP), extended data services (EDS), closed captions (CC), and so on. They all should be properly processed by the PVR system. The most important component of the PVR is the hard disk drive. With the cost of MPEG-2 chips moving below $50, the hard drive is also the most expensive part.

The PVR of today saves TV programs to the internal hard drive that can hold from 14 to 30 hours of programming. There is a choice of trading video recording quality for recording capacity.

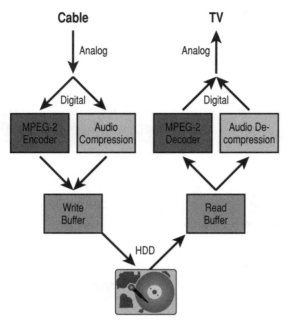

Figure 7–20
Signal processing within TiVo personal video recorder.

HDD drives used in today's systems should satisfy the following requirements:

- Have a low worst-case seek latency
- Be quiet (disk motor and the voice-coil actuator are the main sources of noise in the HDD)
- Work at high temperatures
- Be inexpensive

The first requirement explains why recordable DVD technology can't be used here: seek time of DVD drives is usually about 10 times longer. Plus, transfer rates of DVD drives are lower and writing takes much longer than reading.

The noise associated with HDD is a serious problem. Special seek cycle optimization and acoustic enclosure are used to reduce the noise level. The drives in the current TiVo receivers are typically Quantum Quickview drives, which have been optimized for TiVo needs.

When HDD is used inside a TiVo unit, it is very difficult to cool the drive, and the failure rate due to overheating may increase, making the drive's resistance to heat a priority.

Basic specifications of the TiVo PVR are summarized below:

- Available only in the US (for now).
- Compression: Supports MPEG-2-MP/ML for high quality digital television
- Uses Power PC processor running Linux
- Storage: 14 or 30 hours of programs (13.6 GB and 27.2 GB HDD); upgradeable!
- Inputs: cable-ready tuner, S-Video, Composite Video. Supports all US standards
- Outputs: RF, S-Video, two Composite Video
- Remote control: 30 buttons
- Telephone: RJ-11 connector
- Dimensions: $17\frac{1}{8}$" width $\times$ $12\frac{5}{8}$" depth $\times$ $4\frac{1}{8}$" height
- Compatible with all cable, satellite (DBS), and terrestrial Broadcast TV systems in the US
- Privacy: Latest encryption technology

The TiVo service is about $10 per month. There are currently two Philips PTV receiver models available: for 14-hour recording (~$400) and for 30-hour recording (~$700). The upgrade from one to another or to future models is possible.

8   Storage on the Web

In this chapter...

INTRODUCTION ·

The idea of Web-based storage is simple:

Instead of going to the trouble of buying, connecting, and supporting (and some-times, repairing) your personal back-up system (Zip, Jaz, CD-RW, tape, DVD-RAM, etc.), just download simple software from the Web, subscribe to an inexpensive service, and upload the most critical data you wish to keep safe. A specially trained team, with the best possible data back-up equipment, will guarantee data integrity and safety, and you will have easy access to your data from virtually anywhere in the Internet-capable world.

Another derivative of this idea is an Internet-shared office: rented on-line space elsewhere that is password-protected and shared by a select group of people, which allows the group to store and exchange documents, track projects, create discussion groups, and, of course, exchange emails. It also supports calendaring, to-do lists, con-ferencing, business information resources, and so on. Isn't it attractive? It surely is, but … there's a catch.

First, with the present variety, low cost, high reliability, and high level of stan-dardization of removable storage products (both magnetic and optical), it is not a prob-lem to keep several hundred megabytes of your most critical data on a few Zip disks or one CD-R or CD-RW. It is neither expensive nor difficult anymore (USB versions of these products are available and easy to install and operate). You can be almost sure that wherever you go, there will be a 100 MB Zip drive to read your data. And there is about 100% probability that one will find a CD-ROM drive anywhere, capable of read-ing your prerecorded data on a CD-R or CD-RW disc.

But this is not the main argument against Web storage. Actually, many people still may prefer to back up their data on a remote server via the Internet. Unfortunately, to transfer, say, 10 MB of data over a 28.8 Kbps line would take (at a maximum data transfer rate, which is rarely the reality) about 45 minutes. And what is 10 MB of data by today's standards? Not much. Table 8–1 summarizes rough estimates of the trans-fer times for 10 MB and 100 MB of data. Anything below 30 minutes is, probably, acceptable.

Of course, there are some ways around the transfer time issue.

Automatic data compression is one of them. But, even assuming that one uses an extremely effective 5:1 compression (possible only for a few file formats), transmitting 100 MB of compressed data (now equal to "only" 20 MB) via a 56 Kbps line will still take more than 45 minutes. And, if you lose the connection, you have to start over.

Automatic back-up during the night is another option. But this requires an on-line connection through the night; which is OK for the office, but undesirable at home.

Table 8–1   Estimates of Transfer Times for 10 MB and 100 MB of Data

Maximum connection speed (Kbps)	Time to transfer 10 MB of data (minutes)	Time to transfer 100 MB of data (minutes)
28.8	46	460
56	23	230
128	11.5	115
144	9	90
1,500	~1	~10
8,000	0.16	1.6

Intelligent back-up software will back up only changes in your files, thus reducing the amount of data to be transferred. Still, the very first back-up may take hours of your on-line time.

I would like to suggest the following:

- If you cannot afford to have fast Internet connection or if you have lots of data to back-up, then on-line storage is not for you yet.
- If you have a fast Internet connection or have a small amount of data to back up, then on-line storage may be just what you need!

Check below to find out what I mean by a fast Internet connection.

INTERNET SPEED AND CONNECTIONS . . . .

Modems

Let's start with the most popular method of connecting to the Internet: analog modem. The word "modem" itself is a combination of two words: modulate and demodulate. A modem is basically a device that takes a digital signal and converts or modulates it into an analog signal that another modem can later convert back, or demodulate, into digital form again. An analog connection suffers from busy signals, dropped connections, and the need to dial up each time, but it is the cheapest type of Internet connection available. The main factor affecting a modem's speed and dependability is electromagnetic interference (also called "static"), caused by various sources of electromagnetic waves intercepting the phone lines used to transmit the signal to and from a modem. These waves could be radio waves or a burst in the sun's activity, but they cause electrical current fluctuation, thus forcing the electronics to slow down ("fall back") to lower connection speeds.

Figure 8–1 illustrates data transmission over the Internet using a modem. Since the telephone lines are analog, the digital signal from the computers is first converted into an analog signal (this was discussed in the first chapter). The analog signal is then sent to the End Office (or Central Office) where it is converted back into its digital form and transmitted to another End Office (closest to the destination computer) over the extremely fast high-bandwidth digital line.

Then the digital signal is again converted into its analog form and sent to the destination address, where it is received by the modem. Finally, the modem converts this signal into digital form and makes it available for the computer.

The main reason for having a dial-up connection is that an analog transmission (and analog line) still dominates communication technology. The telephone system we use to connect to the Internet is mostly based on analog signaling and will remain analog in the near future. At the same time, the long-distance trunks are now largely digital (in many countries). The data transmission speed in this case is limited by the speed of the slowest analog line.

Unless something is done to improve the way we access the Internet, user traffic will ultimately burden the public switched telephone network (PSTN) beyond its original design means, and generate traffic congestion beyond anything we have seen so far. Internet users are already often frustrated by slow access and downloads, especial-

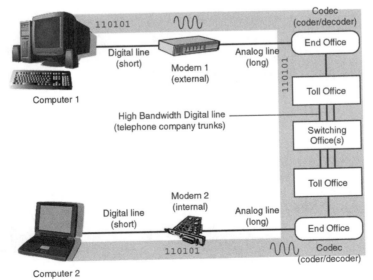

Figure 8–1
The illustration of data transmission over the Internet using a modem.

ly from 8 a.m. to 6 p.m. on business days, when congestion and bottlenecks are most prevalent. This is one limiting factor for the designers of graphically rich web sites, or the sites relying on newer multimedia technologies such as audio and video, interactive gaming, video-on-demand, and so on. But, the same applies to on-line data backup and storage technology—it is extremely bandwidth-sensitive and will not gain enough popularity in the narrowband environment.

Today's analog modem and telephone switch technology is hardly adequate for high-speed Internet access.

Broadband Internet: xDSL

DSL, which stands for *digital subscriber line*, is one of the most discussed elements of modern telecommunication technology. With all the advances in analog modem technology, the best current analog modems are capable of 56 Kbps. Standard analog modems operate in the *voiceband* spectrum, from 0 Hz to 4 kHz, and the 4 kHz limitation is near exhaustion. Unlike analog modems, DSL modems utilize bandwidth well up to 1.1 MHz. This, of course, requires some new equipment to allow the subscriber faster communications. With this done, speeds of up to 10 Mbps are not unrealistic anymore.

Other high-bandwidth technologies competing with DSL are *cable modems* and *satellite-based wireless Internet access*. The later provides fast download but slow upload and is hardly suitable for data back-up.

When compared to a cable modem, DSL offers several advantages:

- DSL is a private (meaning more secure) communication channel between you and your Internet service provider. Cable modems use shared cable.
- DSL technology is a dedicated service, which means that its performance is independent of other user's activity. Performance of cable modems depends on the number of users.
- DSL eliminates a busy signal to callers and your fax machine when you are on-line.

DSL operates over conventional existing POTS (Plain Old Telephone Service) but achieves higher data rates using different electronics and coding schemes. Telephone lines carrying analog and DSL signals share the same physical cables but use a different frequency range to transmit the digital signal. In reality, both analog signals and DSL data signals can be transmitted simultaneously so that your Internet connection doesn't make your telephone line busy.

There is an interesting confusion associated with the DSL acronym: it refers to the line while the technology itself comes from the modems (see Figure 8–2). A pair of DSL

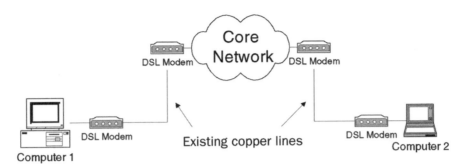

Figure 8–2
The illustration of DSL technology.

modems in conjunction with a traditional telephone line creates a digital subscriber line. When you get DSL, you get a modem for the already existing line. Therefore, DSL is a modem, not a line. In order to operate, a DSL requires two DSL modems.

DSL comes in different flavors: asymmetrical DSL (ADSL), high-bit-rate DSL (HDSL), symmetric DSL (SDSL), or very high speed DSL (VDSL). These flavors of DSL technology are sometimes simply referred to as "xDSL." Each flavor has its own unique requirements and limitations. Being much faster than the traditional dial-up Internet access, DSL technology opens up new opportunities for future on-line data storage.

The wide acceptance of xDSL in the near future depends on many factors, such as cost, ease of installation and use, security, reliability, service, and performance. In terms of cost, DSL charges in the range of $30-$100 per month (depending on speed, specific service options, etc.), which doesn't sound unreasonable with the cost of dial-up services being in the range of $10-$25. With its slightly higher cost, DSL can quickly capture a majority of the dial-up market.

Ease of installation, quality of customer support, reliable performance, and security are other big concerns. According to the most recent publications, installation can be a frustrating experience for many users, even those with experience in computer upgrades and repairs. Also, some DSL users complain about a lower than expected data transfer rate (DTR) or unexpected service interruptions. Finally, security becomes a bigger issue for the users of DSL lines, since they often have a static IP address and become the target for hacker attack.

There are also some technological factors limiting expansion of the DSL:

- The telephone company should have special equipment installed in its End Office near your home. Unless it is done, you have no way to get DSL.
- The next factor is the distance: to have DSL, the distance between your home and the End Office should not exceed approximately 13,000 to

18,500 feet. The closer you are to the End Office, the greater is the available transfer speed.

- The wiring at your home should be of good quality to support DSL. Otherwise, new wiring has to be installed.

Now let's look at some flavors of xDSL technology.

ADSL (Asymmetrical DSL)

ADSL is one of the most popular DSL technologies of today. Usually the "A" is dropped, so when we talk about DSL for home use, we're talking about ADSL.

ADSL is one of the new high-speed digital switching/routing and signal processing technology for broadband Internet. Started in 1994, ADSL promises enough user bandwidth for the high-bandwidth Internet. ADSL can transfer data over ordinary telephone lines nearly 200 times faster than contemporary modems and 90 times faster than ISDN. ADSL provides dedicated service between you and your service provider over an existing telephone line.

ADSL is designed to take advantage of the natural unevenness in bandwidth requirements. It provides for rates in excess of 1 MB/s from the network to the subscriber (download), and up to 0.2 MB/s from the subscriber to the network (upload). An ADSL is not a dial-up connection and is more expensive, but it is also a dedicated connection, is available for business, and is always on. ADSL relies on complex digital signal processing (DSP) techniques to transfer much more digital data over the same copper wires. In addition to increasing the bandwidth, ADSL preserves the voice channel allowing for Internet access and telephone conversation at the same time.

The benefits of ADSL are summarized next:

- ADSL is fast. A 10 MB-large file that takes 90 minutes to download using a conventional 14.4 Kbps modem would be downloaded in just about 10 seconds using an ADSL modem operating at 8 Mbps download speed.
- ADSL hardware is easy to install and fully compatible with existing telephone line technology. Little or no rewiring is necessary. Unlike other high-speed data transmission technologies, ADSL doesn't require changes to the "last mile" of the network, which is, typically, a twisted-pair copper telephone wire.

ADSL has a range of downstream speeds depending on distance (Table 8–2).

Table 8–2   ADSL Downstream Speeds

Distance from the End Office	DTR, Mbps/s
Up to 18,000 feet	1,544
16,000 feet	2,048
12,000 feet	6,312
9,000 feet	8,448

Data backup more often requires upstream data transfers (from your PC to the backup location) than the downstream transfers. Storage of and exchange with the large amount of data over the Internet may also require high-speed data transfer in both directions. Therefore, the asymmetry in DTR is the disadvantage of ADSL when it is considered for on-line storage and backup. Nevertheless, the overall performance of ADSL is quite acceptable for online data storage.

Other DSL Technologies

HDSL (High bit-rate DSL) allows for a very high speed connection over the basic copper line instead of the fiber line. The maximum allowed distance from the End Office is 12,000 feet and it requires four wires versus two wires needed for other DSL.

SDSL (Symmetric Digital Subscriber Line) is another derivative of DSL and provides the same fast download and upload of data. SDSL is simply a single line version of HDSL and requires one twisted pair only. SDSL will be the best for any application needing symmetric access.

RADSL (Rate adaptive ADSL) is supposed to carry data at different rates for different prices while adjusting to different conditions and lengths of the copper wire.

IDSL (ISDN DSL) provides ISDN-like speed over copper line, is moderately fast and moderately expensive, and allows business or home users otherwise far away from faster lines to benefit from the DSL links. ISDN (Integrated Services Digital Network) is a digital telephone line used for voice, fax, and data communications like a regular telephone line, but is five times faster (or more) than a 28.8 Kbps modem. It also allows you to talk on the phone while also sending data to another.

Table 8–3 compares the available technologies.

Table 8–3   Available Connection Technologies

Type of connection	Maximum download speed (Kbps)	Maximum upload speed (Kbps)	Best application
Analog 28 Kbps modem	20–24	20–24	Personal Web surfing
Analog 56 Kbps modem	53	53	Personal Web surfing
IDSL	144	144	Remote locations and offices
HDSL (High-bit-rate DSL)	1,500	1,500	Business
SDSL (Symmetric DSL)	1,500	1,500	Business
ADSL (Asymmetric DSL)	8,000	1,500	Personal Web surfing (available for business) and small business
RADSL (Rate adaptive ADSL)	8,000	1,500	Personal Web surfing (available for business) and small business
Cable modem	10,000–30,000	128–10,000	Personal Web surfing (in general, not available for business)

What is Your Connection Speed?

The speed of the Internet connection is one important parameter limiting the possibilities of Web backup and it's important to know your real speed of connection.

Fortunately, there is a way you can test the speed of your Internet connection. To perform this test, the MSN site (http://msn.zdnet.com/partners/msn/bandwidth/speedtest.htm) will transfer a group of data to your computer and display the result on the "Speed Test Thermometer."

DATA STORAGE ON THE WEB: CASE STUDIES . . . . .

Today, one can find almost anything on the Web.

Here I will provide a few examples of the Internet companies specializing in online storage. This is clearly not the full list, and the data presented next will certainly change with time.

On-Line Backup

Below are some examples of Internet backup services available today. Some of these services do not even need special software, thus increasing data accessibility and allowing access to your data from anywhere in the world using just a web browser.

The @**Backup** from SkyDesk (*www.backup.com*) provides an online backup option for 100 MB ($99/year) to 500 MB ($300/year) of data. @Backup performs automatic (user sets the time) and on-demand backups. The data files are encrypted and stored off site in two security vaults, and one can back up and restore files from any location using Internet connection. A download of the special software is required. This software will compress the data and transmit only the changes in data. In spite of this, the company admits that the first back-up session may take a few hours of online time.

Another example is **SafeGuard** (*www.sgii.com*), which charges $10/month with the restriction of no more than 10 GB of data transfer per day. You have an option of a partial or complete restore for your files.

The **i-drive** (*www.idrive.com*) is a free (for 50 MB) and secure place to keep the data that you want to store and access remotely. One can even play MP3 music from the i-drive using a feature called "Playlist." The i-drive has a drag-and-drop feature for the files in your Windows Explorer. One can drag and drop files from the desktop to the i-drive and back.

FreeDrive (*www.freedrive.com*) is a free service that gives you up to 50 MB of secured space to back up and share your data. There is no need to download any software: one can access this data from any browser. Security is limited to password protection, but for a price one can add secure encryption.

Driveway (*www.driveway.com*) provides for free 25 MB of password-protected space that one can access from any computer using a Web browser. The data is compressed, encrypted, and stored off site on what the company says is a disasterproof server.

On-Line Backup, Exchange, and Virtual Offices

AppsOnline (*www.appsonline.com*) service offers business applications you can use online, including collaboration, sales automation, e-commerce, and legal programs. There's no software to download. You can join the QuickPlace 2.0 program, share files and information, capture discussions, create and store related documents, and track progress from start to finish. The files are password-protected and Instant! QuickPlace 2.0 supports SSL (Secure Sockets Layer) for network security. Then, when you're done, you can end QuickPlace 2.0. Pricing for QuickPlace 2.0 is $14.95 per user/per month and includes 150 MB of total storage space for your QuickPlace needs.

HotOffice (*www.hotoffice.com*) offers a full spectrum of utilities needed for collaborative work, including email, calendaring, to-do lists, conferencing, business information resources, and more. Besides this, the package has online document publishing, viewing, and sharing capabilities. The package includes 20 MB of online storage space per user and costs $12.95/month per user for a group of up to 20 users. The price drops slightly for larger groups of users.

MagicalDesk (*www.magicaldesk.com*) provides business on-line applications (email, calendar, to-do list, etc.) and 5 MB of file storage. Published documents can be shared online. No special software is required.

Involv (*www.involv.com*) offers Team Space Environment, which includes a wide range of utilities needed for team and project management, including Group Discussion, Shared Group Calendar, Chat and Paging, and more. In addition, the package offers document management capabilities and provides centralized posting and managing for files and documents of all types.

9

SAN, NAS, and RAID Fundamentals

In this chapter...

This chapter discusses the basics of such modern technologies of mass data storage as network attached storage (NAS) and storage area network (SAN), as well as RAID technology, which is the key to high data availability in both NAS and SAN.

NAS and SAN technologies became increasingly popular because of the increasing demand for storage, and more and more companies are getting involved in the manufacturing of those systems. At the moment, the following companies are major manufacturers of high-end SAN and NAS systems (in alphabetical order):

SAN

- Compaq
- EMC
- Hewlett Packard
- IBM

NAS

- Auspex
- EMC
- Network Appliances
- Procom

STORAGE NETWORKING . . . .

Introduction

With a continuously increasing demand for data storage, the following key issues have to be addressed to have a successful storage solution:

- Scalability, or ability to increase storage capacity, performance, and so on, without increasing complexity of the system
- Heterogeneous connectivity, or an ability to operate in the mixed environment of different operating systems, such as Unix, Windows NT, and so on
- High performance
- High data availability, which is achieved via data redundancy
- Information sharing, or data transparency throughout the entire network

- Ease of use (out-of-the-box operation, plug-and-play, hot-swapping, etc.)
- Ease of management, including operation, maintenance, backup, monitoring, and so on
- Low total cost of ownership (TCO)

A traditional method of data storage for a simple computer network is based on multiple computers (users, clients) connected to the server, which is, in turn, connected to the directly attached storage device (disks, tapes, etc.) via one of the storage interfaces (IDE, SCSI, etc.) (see Figure 9–1).

In this system, the server manages both storage and applications. This means that the server stores and retrieves user's data and application programs to and from the disk or disk array. It also runs the application programs.

The efficiency of this network depends on the processing speed of the server, and the speed of its connection to the network (on one side) and to the storage (on the other side).

When the number of users or network bandwidth increases, a much larger number of data to store and retrieve may eventually create a bottleneck in between the server and storage or at the storage device, thus slowing the network down significantly. To deal with this, some new technologies and network architectures are used to improve performance of both the storage device itself and the server-to-storage connection.

The simplest solution to deal with the storage capacity bottleneck is to add more storage. But, if it is added in the form of individual drives, some problems such as

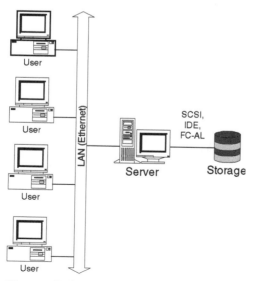

Figure 9–1
A traditional method of data storage for a simple computer network.

overall reliability and load leveling appear immediately. One way to address both reliability and load leveling is to use the RAID (redundant array of independent drives; see later in the chapter). RAID has its own controller that manages the load leveling, and provides data redundancy (of different levels) to allow for rebuilding the data if one or a few drives fail. Therefore, RAID solves the storage device bottleneck issue as well as some other problems. Some RAID schemes (RAID-0, 1, and 5) also increase the DTR between the server and storage by striping data across multiple drives and thus reducing latency.

The server-to-storage connection bottleneck has to be solved by switching to a higher-speed interface: faster IDE, SCSI, or FC-AL.

If the number of users and the network bandwidth will increase further, the server itself may become the next performance bottleneck. To address this, more servers are added with each of them having an individually attached storage (disks or RAID) (see Figure 9–2). This creates the problems of unnecessary data duplication, load balancing between the storage devices, data management, and, of course, system scalability.

So, what happens if one needs to increase performance and storage capacity of the network even further? Doing this by increasing the number of servers with directly attached storage will just aggravate the problems of load balancing, unnecessary data duplication, and data management, as well as effectively increase the cost.

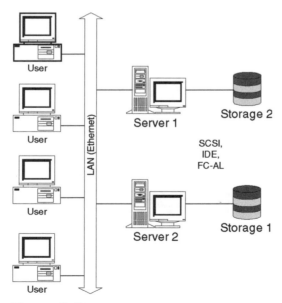

Figure 9–2
A computer network with multiple servers and each of them having an individually attached storage (disks or RAID).

To address these issues, two alternatives to the directly attached storage emerged eventually to become two competing and complementing technologies of mass data storage: network attached storage (NAS) and storage area network (SAN). One common thing for both NAS and SAN is storage networking. The concept of storage networking is illustrated in Figure 9–3 with multiple servers connected to the shared storage via the storage network.

The main goal of storage networking is to separate the *storage (or file) server* from the *application server*, which will provide the following benefits:

- Consolidation of storage resources and lower TCO
- Centralizes data management
- Solution to scalability problems
- Improved reliability

The two realizations of the storage networking concept—NAS and SAN—are optimized for different application environments.

This chapter discusses the basics of these technologies as well as the RAID technology currently used to provide high data availability.

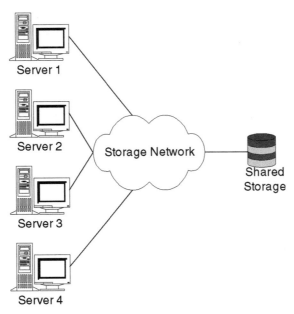

Figure 9–3
The illustration of a concept of Storage Networking, where multiple servers are connected to a shared storage via the storage network.

Fundamentals of NAS (Network Attached Storage)

A Network Attached Storage device is a *specialized file server* that connects directly to the network and uses specialized file-serving protocols such as NFS (for Unix) and CIFS (for NT).

A concept of NAS is based on assigning to storage some server functions to allow its direct connection to the network (see Figure 9–4). This can be called removing storage from behind the server.

The storage system has to support a LAN (local area network) interface, protocol, and has the logic optimized for file access. The server, in turn, does not need to support traditional storage interfaces (SCSI, IDE) anymore, but uses a LAN adapter to communicate with both storage and users.

NAS eliminates direct attachment of storage to any specific computer on the network: any user or server with any operating system can access NAS via the network. This

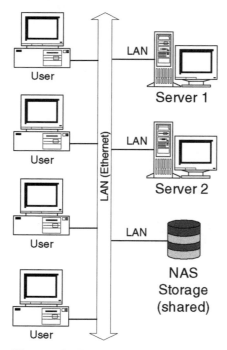

Figure 9–4
The illustration of a concept of NAS with the storage moved from behind the server to the front, and with assigning to storage some server functions to allow its direct connection to the network.

is the main benefit of NAS architecture. Since the file server manages all files on storage devices, the same exact file can be accessed by any users or servers simultaneously.

Also, since the storage device is not directly connected to the server, one can perform data backup without using server resources.

Finally, NAS simplifies the physical connection of devices by eliminating problems associated with connection of, for example, multiple SCSI devices with wide and short parallel cables, requirements for termination, and complex system configuration. Still, interfacing between the LAN adapter and the drives can be done via the same SCSI interface or even using the FC-AL interface for RAID implementations.

Unfortunately, the NAS implementation has some disadvantages too. The major one is the lack of a dedicated connection between the computers and storage, which compromises the performance. The reason for this is that the DTR between servers and storage becomes a function of the *network productivity* and a specific required bandwidth cannot be guaranteed anymore. For example, the network bottleneck created (unrelated to storage reasons) will slow down access to the files stored on NAS for all the network users. Also, the NAS itself contributes to the network traffic because the network has to accommodate now both the traditional user-to-server traffic and additional server-to-storage traffic.

In addition to that, the overhead of the network-to-storage transactions can be increased because the NAS adapter needs to packetize the data from a storage device before it will become suitable for LAN or WAN (wide area network) transactions. Ethernet, with its maximum packet size of about 1.5 KB, will require making more then 3,500 packets of data—which results in a significant time penalty—for a 5 MB file to be transmitted over the network.

Due to the above reason, NAS is not considered a solution for bandwidth-sensitive problems. Rather, it is used to solve issues of cross-platform storage networking with direct access to the data for all users of the network. In addition, NAS removes scalability problems and allows simple data backup of the centralized data.

When the bandwidth is an important issue, such technology as SAN is used.

Fundamentals of SAN (Storage Area Network)

A storage area network (SAN) is a high-speed network dedicated to shared storage and connecting different kinds of data storage devices to the network users. SAN can support thousands of storage devices and computers that are part of the same network. A storage area network is usually clustered in close proximity to other computing resources, such as IBM S/390, but may also extend to remote locations for data backup and archival storage using wide area network carrier technologies such as ATM or

SONET. The majority of storage area networks rely mostly on FC-AL technology (see Chapter 2) for data transport and on SCSI for data exchange between servers and drives.

FC-AL storage area networks have high bandwidth (100 MB/s now and higher in the future) over long distances (up to 10 km). SAN usually supports data mirroring, backup and restore procedures, data migration from one storage device to another, archival/retrieval of data, and data sharing among multiple servers of a network.

SAN is a type of network that is isolated from the messaging network and is optimized for high-speed data transfer between the multiple servers and multiple storage devices. While using network principles to transport the data, SAN doesn't rely on LAN protocols. Instead, most SAN systems use FC-AL to connect the network with the drives or drive arrays. With all that said, SAN allows for the server to "see" the storage as a "directly attached device" via a conventional interface, such as SCSI, which is 'encapsulated' into the Fibre Channel.

Figure 9–5 is a derivative of Figure 9–2 and illustrates the concept of a storage area network. By adding a FC-AL switch in between the servers and storage, one may build a SAN system. For this SAN, each server can access each storage device via the switch. Also, each user can use the data on any storage device, which is also managed by the switch. The connection to SAN, unlike to NAS, is a high-speed connection since

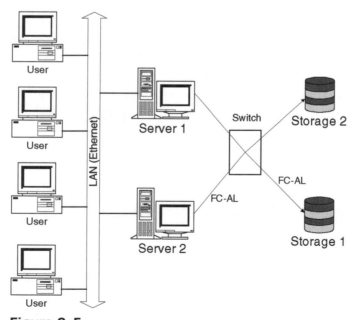

Figure 9–5
This figure is a derivative of the Figure 9.2 and illustrates the concept of storage area network (SAN).

the data exchange between the servers and storage isn't restricted by the network traffic anymore.

This architecture allows for almost unlimited scalability with all new servers and storage devices connected via FC switches.

Scalability is addressed in SAN via an increase in the number of storage devices attached to the switches (or directors or hubs). When the number of switch ports becomes insufficient, more switches can be added easily. The switches manage load balancing between the storage devices, which are typically the RAID systems used for high data availability.

Fibre Channel SAN also has such useful features as "zoning" support, where some part (or zone) of the managed storage network can be restricted to some groups of users only. This helps to protect sensitive data while still having the rest of it easily available for a large group of network users.

The major disadvantages of SAN are, perhaps, its high cost (all elements of FC-AL hardware are expensive) and the lack of standardization among hardware manufacturers. This often results in incompatibility of hardware from different makers.

Since both SAN and NAS rely on the storage networking concept, there is a lot of confusion regarding their place in today's storage architecture, and regarding their similarities and differences. The next part of this chapter will address these issues.

SAN versus NAS

Table 9–1 compares both technologies head-to-head.

Table 9–1   NAS versus SAN

NAS	SAN
Bandwidth isn't guaranteed at all	Low latency and high bandwidth
More LAN users slow the speed Performance is LAN-bandwidth dependent	The bandwidth increases with number of devices connected
Best for small data segments	Best for large and small data segments
Optimized for file-oriented applications	Optimized for block-oriented applications
Heterogeneous environment	Homogeneous environment, proprietary configurations (same maker for used hardware, i.e., switches, etc.)
More limited in scalability than SAN	Virtually no limit to scalability

The differences in the features of SAN and NAS define the differences in the target applications, as summarized in Table 9–2.

Table 9–2   Differences in the Applications of NAS and SAN

NAS	SAN
Email servers, search engines, Web hosting (simultaneous file sharing)	Performance-critical client/server applications (high bandwidth)
Libraries (shared access to files)	Databases (DB2, Oracle, SQL, etc.) and transaction-processing systems (fast access to a specific record or small set of records)
CAD (computer-aided design) environment	
Graphics and imaging	Data warehousing (data management, availability, cost of ownership)
	Graphics and real-time video editing (high speed, dedicated access, guaranteed bandwidth)

The future of SAN and NAS looks bright at the moment, with both being multi-billion dollar markets. This future is, most likely, in their close *integration* with NAS systems integrated with large SAN systems. For example, within the same enterprise, the network-shared resources and Web serving is best implemented with NAS, while the client/server and database applications are best suited for SAN. Therefore, instead of arguing on the future winner being either SAN or NAS, it is better to think of the best application for these technologies as complementing each other.

The next part of this chapter reviews RAID technology which is an important element of both SAN and NAS systems as well as some off-line workstation and desktop computer systems with high requirements for data availability.

RAID (REDUNDANT ARRAY OF INDEPENDENT [OR INEXPENSIVE] DRIVES) . . . .

If used correctly, disk (tape, CD-ROM, etc.) drive arrays may provide several advantages over the single drive: higher reliability and higher data transfer rate.

A simple replacement of one drive by a group of drives will not increase reliability since the life of the entire system will depend upon any one of these drives. In fact, reliability (mean time before failure or MTBF) will decrease with the increasing number of drives since the probability for one of them to fail is increased. This is why a certain level of redundancy is needed in the design of a drive array to increase the reliability of the entire storage system.

RAID is an assembly of disk drives, known as disk array, *that operates as one storage unit*. In general, the drives could be any storage system, such as magnetic hard disk drives, optical storage devices, magnetic tape drives, and so on. When the speed (data transfer rate) is an issue, the fastest SCSI and FC hard disk drives are typically used.

RAID Functions

Redundant Array of Independent Drives (RAID) technology serves the following functions:

- Immediate availability of data and, depending on the RAID level, recovery of lost data
- Redundancy of data at a chosen level

Depending on the level of RAID that you are using, this method of data storage provides data redundancy needed for a highly secure system, with the additional benefit of faster retrieval of data through multiple channel access. If one or a few disk drives fail, they can be normally exchanged without interruption of normal system operation. Thus, disk arrays can ensure that no data is lost if one disk drive in the array fails.

The array includes drives, controllers, enclosure, power supplies, fans, cables, and software. Each array is addressed by the host computer as one drive. There are several types of RAID configuration, called levels, which control the ways of organizing data on the drives and organizing the flow of data to and from the host computer.

In 1993, the Raid Advisory Board (RAB; *www.raid-advisory.com*) established the RAID Level Conformance program, which closely followed initial classification found in early UC Berkley work.

RAID Levels

There are six RAID levels defined. Please note that the numbers used to describe the RAID levels do not imply improved performance, complexity, or reliability.

RAID-0 is *striping* RAID (Figure 9–6). It does not, by itself, contribute to EDAP (Extended Data Availability and Protection) and provides NO redundancy, thus if one drive fails, all the data in the array will be lost. At the same time, RAID-0 improves data rates, since all drives are accessed in parallel.

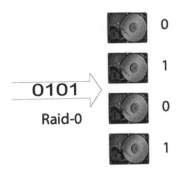

Figure 9–6
RAID-0 provides no data redundancy.

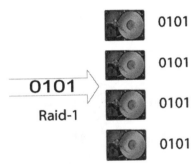

Figure 9–7
RAID-1 provides high data redundancy and is a mirroring RAID.

Two types of RAID provide EDAP for the drives: mirroring RAID and parity RAID.

Mirroring appeared earlier (in the UC Berkeley Papers) and was originally designated as RAID Level 1 (Figure 9–7). Its main problem was that it required 100% redundancy or twice as much capacity as was originally needed. On the other hand, its read performance was improved and the higher percentage of drives in a RAID-1 system are allowed to fail simultaneously as compared to a parity RAID system.

RAID Level 2 requires the use of nonstandard disk drives and is therefore not commercially viable.

Parity RAID was identified in the UC Berkeley Papers as RAID Levels 3, 4, 5, and 6.

This type of RAID significantly reduces redundancy overhead to a range of 10% to 33% (compared to 100% for Mirroring RAID-1). RAID Levels 3–5 (Figures 9–8, 9–9) provide EDAP in the event of a single disk failure, and RAID-6 tolerates the failure of two disks simultaneously or if the second disk fails later, during the reconstruction period.

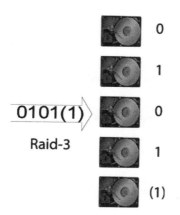

Figure 9–8
RAID-3 is a *parity* RAID with reduced redundancy overhead.

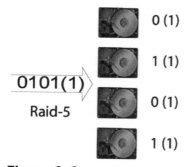

Figure 9–9
RAID-5 is a *parity* RAID with reduced redundancy overhead and data and parity information striping across all drives.

Levels 1, 3, and 5 are the most commonly used RAID levels and are discussed in Table 9–4.

Table 9–4   Most Commonly Used RAID Formats

RAID level	Key facts
RAID-0	• Provides no redundancy, since the data are written across multiple drives (so-called striping). If one drive fails, all the data in the array will be lost. • Provides higher data rates, since all drives are accessed in parallel.
RAID-1	• Data mirroring; high reliability; the same data is written or read on two (or more) drives • Faster reading, since the first drive to respond to a request will provide data, thus reducing latency • The cost is at least double for a given storage capacity
RAID-3	• One extra drive is added to store the parity data (error correction data). If one drive fails, the data can be recovered and the other drives will keep working until the failed one is replaced (of course, performance will suffer) • High reliability (cheaper than mirroring in RAID-1) • Very high data rates; data writing and reading occurs in parallel • For a given capacity, fewer drives are needed than for RAID-1 • Controller may be more complex and expensive
RAID-5	• Data and parity information striping across all drives • High reliability, high performance

Data Availability

RAID-0 is inappropriate when data availability (reliability) is an issue, since it provides no data redundancy and failure tolerance. Data mirroring (RAID-1) or parity check (RAID-3 to RAID-5) are needed in this case. RAID-5 is recommended because of its combination of high data availability and good performance. But, in the case of a drive failure, even if the data is still physically available, it may be inaccessible within the needed period due to a drastic drop in the system's performance. A performance drop of, say, 50% is not totally unusual during the reconstruction of the system.

RAID Performance Characteristics

With the falling price of hard disk drives, RAID systems have also become affordable for home use. RAID-0 and RAID-1 are the simplest to integrate than the other, more complex systems. Table 9–5 compares the characteristics of RAID systems.

Table 9–5   Characteristics of RAID Systems

RAID level	Capacity	Large data transfers	High I/O rate	Data availability
Single Disk	Fixed (100%)	Good	Good	10,000 to 1,000,000 hours
RAID-0	Excellent	Very Good	Very Good	Poor*
RAID-1	Moderate (50%)	Good	Good	Good
RAID-2	Very Good	Good	Poor	Good
RAID-3	Very Good	Very Good	Poor	Good
RAID-4	Very Good	Very Good	Poor	Good
RAID-5	Very Good	Very Good	Good	Good

Availability is equal to MTBF of one disk divided by the number of disks in the array.

Hot-Spare Drives

A hot-spare drive is a special drive that is designated for automatic use if any drive within an array fails.

The hot-spare has a storage capacity greater than or equal to that of the largest drive in an array. It is possible to define as many hot spares as you want. If a drive within an array fails, the adapter will automatically engage a hot spare instead of the failed disk drive, and rebuild the data that was on the failed disk onto the hot spare.

Extended Data Availability and Protection (EDAP)

EDAP is the ability of a disk system to provide timely, continuous, online access to reliable data under certain specified abnormal conditions. These conditions, as described by RAB, include (this is the RAB's exact description):

- Internal failures
  - Failures within the disk system
- External failures
  - Failures of equipment attached to the disk system, including host I/O buses and host computers

- Environmental failures
  - Failures resulting from abnormal environmental conditions, including: external power source out of operating range; temperature out of operating range; natural disasters such as floods and earthquakes; accidental disasters such as fires; and unlawful acts such as sabotage, arson, terrorism, and so on.

- Replacement periods
  - Replacement periods are the intervals required for replacement of a failed component. If "hot swap" is not supported by the disk system, then the component replacement period is tantamount to disk system downtime. If "hot swap" is supported, then downtime due to a replacement period is eliminated; however, until the failed component is replaced, the disk system is in a vulnerable period.

- Vulnerable periods
  - Vulnerable periods occur when the disk system has invoked its ability to circumvent a failure, rendering the system vulnerable to additional failures and causing the system to operate at something less than optimum performance until the fault is corrected.

New RAID Classification

In 1996, RAB introduced an improved classification of the RAID systems. It divides RAID into three types:

- Failure-resistant disk systems (protect against data loss due to disk failure)
- Failure-tolerant disk systems (protect against loss of data access due to failure of any single component)
- Disaster-tolerant disk systems (consist of two or more independent zones, either of which provides access to stored data)

The original "Berkley" RAID classification is still kept as an important historical reference point and it also recognizes that RAID Levels 0–6 successfully define all known data mapping and protection schemes for disks.

Unfortunately, the original classification has caused some confusion due to the assumption that higher RAID levels imply higher redundancy and performance. This point has been exploited by some RAID system manufacturers, which have given birth to the products with such names as RAID-7, RAID-10, RAID-30, RAID-S, and so on.

The new system describes the data availability characteristics of the RAID system rather then the details of its implementation.

The next list provides criteria for all three classes of RAID (according to RAB):

Failure-resistant disk systems (meets criteria 1 to 6 minimum):

1. Protection against data loss and loss of access to data due to disk drive failure
2. Reconstruction of failed drive content to a replacement drive
3. Protection against data loss due to a "write hole"
4. Protection against data loss due to host and host I/O bus failure
5. Protection against data loss due to replaceable unit failure
6. Replaceable unit monitoring and failure indication

Failure-tolerant disk systems (meets criteria 1 to 15 minimum):

7. Disk automatic swap and hot swap
8. Protection against data loss due to cache failure
9. Protection against data loss due to external power failure
10. Protection against data loss due to a temperature out of operating range
11. Replaceable unit and environmental failure warning
12. Protection against loss of access to data due to device channel failure
13. Protection against loss of access to data due to controller module failure
14. Protection against loss of access to data due to cache failure
15. Protection against loss of access to data due to power supply failure

Disaster-tolerant disk systems (meets criteria 1 to 21):

16. Protection against loss of access to data due to host and host I/O bus failure
17. Protection against loss of access to data due to external power failure
18. Protection against loss of access to data due to component replacement
19. Protection against loss of data and loss of access to data due to multiple disk failure
20. Protection against loss of access to data due to zone failure
21. Long-distance protection against loss of data due to zone failure

10 Data Loss and Recovery

In this chapter...

INTRODUCTION: WHY IT HAPPENS . . . .

Storage devices exist to hold information. In spite of how much you have paid for the hardware, the data itself is the most valuable asset. This is why the worst thing possible is the loss of this data.

There are many ways to lose the stored data, for example:

- The drive or storage media can fail or be damaged
- An accidental data deletion may occur
- The data can be (erroneously) deleted intentionally
- Your computer can be hit by a virus

And, if the damage to your data is irreversible, then a permanent data loss occurs.

The reasons for drive failure vary from a simple bad connection (which is easily recoverable) to damage to the media itself, which could still be recoverable, but much less frequently. If the damage occurred to the drive's electronics, the problem can be most likely fixed. If the damage occurred to the system areas of the disk, leaving the data zone intact, the data could be theoretically (and in many cases practically) recovered by a professional. But, if the data zone itself is damaged, one can only rely on the backup.

There are two *major* reasons for early and sudden failure of your data storage device: poor handling and manufacturing defects.

Poor Handling

Even if today's hard drives, for example, are capable of handling operational shock up to 150 G, their electronics or mechanical components still could be damaged by a vibration or by an impact.

Liquid spilled on the drive may short electric connections or even penetrate inside the drive, especially inside the drives with removable media (Zip, CD-everything, tape drives, etc.). Contamination of the drive's insides by dirty media or the environment could speed up mechanical wear or result in immediate failure.

One more reason for damage to the drive's electronics is an electrostatic discharge, the so-called ESD, which often takes place between your fingers and the drive's body. During this discharge, a large potential can be generated at the very small gaps and over small areas causing heat dissipation, melting, and disintegration of the IC elements. This is why most electronic and storage devices are shipped inside special ESD-protecting plastic bags. When handling the drives, try to keep your other hand on a metal part of your PC such as the frame, which will serve as a "ground." Also, touch the metal part of your PC with both hands before handling any ESD-sensitive device.

Manufacturing Defects

Unfortunately, even those of us who handle things with great care are not immune from disaster. All media, drives, and storage system components undergo thorough testing, but in spite of this, statistics guarantee a few bad drives among hundreds of good ones. You may be unlucky and buy one of these. But even in this case, data backup and a good manufacturer's warranty can make losses partially or completely recoverable.

But, even if your storage device functions perfectly fine, there is still a risk of losing the data due to a variety of *human errors*, accidental data deletion being the major one and much more dangerous than computer viruses (see Figure 10–1).

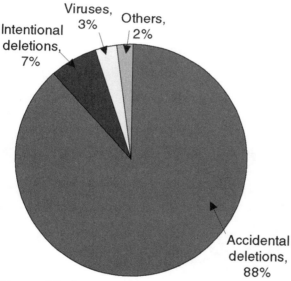

Figure 10–1
Besides the mechanical reasons, human error is a major cause of data loss. This graph shows that accidental deletion is the major reason of data loss caused by human error. (Source: American Business Research Corp.)

HOW TO PREVENT DATA LOSS . . . .

The best prevention is to always remember to backup your data!

Accidents may happen: you spill coffee on your CD or Zip drive, or a CD falls on the floor where it gets scratched, or the hard drive suddenly won't spin after being unused for two humid summer months. Anything may happen, but you should not worry if your most valuable data is stored separately in a safe place. Figure 10–2 shows how Windows NT managers protect the data from unexpected surprises. Apparently, most of them still rely on a traditional backup procedure.

Another thing to remember is to *use antivirus software routinely*, especially if you download from the Internet! Your data could be as easily corrupted by a computer virus as by any natural disaster. To protect your data from the newest viruses, update your antiviral program as often as possible.

Prevent impacts on your storage device, especially when it is running! For example, don't move your desktop when the power is on! All commercial storage systems are designed to withstand significant shock and vibration, but there is always a chance that your drive may be damaged by an impact.

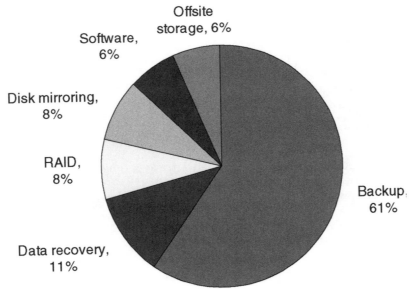

Figure 10–2
The statistics of how the Windows NT managers protect the data from unexpected surprises. Apparently, most of them still rely on a traditional backup procedure. (Source: American Business Research Corp.)

Try to prevent drops of removable storage media (Zip, Jaz, tape cartridge, CD, DVD, etc.), since it may damage them.

Avoid electrostatic discharge (ESD) during installation of the drives and later handling. Do not touch electric contacts on the controller board with your bare hands. Before handling the drive touch the metal parts of your PC with your hands. This will reduce the charge on your hands.

Keep your storage systems clean! Particulate contamination is a clear and present danger for all types of storage media, since it causes mechanical damage that is rarely recoverable and can crash the entire storage device!

For tape storage, don't use pencil, grease pen, or other debris-generating writing tools to mark tape cartridge labels since debris can penetrate inside the cartridge or even inside the drive.

Store all your disks and tape cartridges in protective cases. Don't touch the tape with your fingers: the oil from your hands can cause various problems such as hard read/write errors or "Failure to calibrate" reports.

Keep your data cool! Storage systems, especially magnetic media, may suffer from so-called "thermal decay" of magnetic information. In other words, your magnetic domains will lose their magnetization much faster at higher temperatures, and your bits of information will disappear. Magnetic drives are designed to operate in conditions comfortable for humans. Therefore, there is no danger in keeping your drives at 40°C (104°F) and even 50°C (122°F). But, exceeding this temperature by much can be harmful.

Keep away your magnetic storage *from magnetic fields* surrounding such things as the magnets, loudspeakers, electric motors, and other magnetic sources.

SOFTWARE FOR DATA PROTECTION AND RECOVERY ·

AntiVirus Software

McAfee Virus Scan™ (McAfee.com). List Price: $30.

McAfee's Macro Hunter and ViruLogic technology protects the PC from most virus types. The software works with:

- floppy disks
- email attachments

- shared files
- online services
- Internet downloads
- networks
- CD-ROM

This software can analyze Microsoft Word and Excel macros, seeks and destroys unidentified macro viruses, and repairs files automatically!

Norton Antivirus™ (Symantec). List Price: $36 (download); $40 (mail).

The software ensures that you are protected while surfing the Internet and scans incoming email attachments automatically for the most popular email products, hopefully preventing viruses from entering your system. Email products include:

- MS Outlook
- MS Outlook Express
- Eudora Pro
- Eudora Lite
- Netscape Messenger
- Netscape Mail

The software detects and repairs viruses in compressed files—including those within multiple compressed layers. Compressed file formats include:

- MIME/UU
- LHA/LZH
- ARJ
- CAB
- PKLite
- LZEXE
- ZIP

Backup Software

DriveCopy™ (Powerquest). List Price: $30 (Upgrade: $10).

With a few simple steps, everything from your old hard drive is automatically copied to your new drive without losing a single preference, setting, or byte of data.

DriveCopy™ supports all of the popular operating systems and the file systems used. Trial version is available.

DataKeeper™ (Powerquest). List Price: $63.

The first "real-time" backup solution that allows you to continuously back up your Windows 95 or 98 system with little or no intervention. Trial version is available. Here is a list of some features:

- Works with any removable disk drive, network drive, hard disk, or floppy drive.
- Provides protection against data loss using continuous monitoring and backup.
- Backup data is compressed using the highest compression rate available.
- Provides full registry protection.
- Will segment large files across multiple disks.
- Ability to store multiple backup sets
- Selective File Restore

Drive Image Pro™ (Powerquest). List Price: $220–600.

Drive Image Pro is professional software that allows you to create a compressed hard disk drive image file, and use that image file to quickly and easily deploy Windows workstations or upgrade existing workstations. Using PowerCasting™ (SmartSector® technology combined with TCP/IP multi-casting), IS professionals can deploy Windows across an enterprise, distribute applications, and manage changing desktop environments. Drive Image Pro's SmartSector™ imaging speeds up the entire process and ensures that you'll preserve your Windows optimizations. Drive Image Pro™ also includes the technology of PartitionMagic® Professional for added flexibility.

Diagnostics, Analysis, and Recovery

Norton Zip Rescue™ (Symantec) is a free system recovery utility for Windows® 95 or 98 on a single 100 MB or 250 MB Zip disk. (Not for use with Zip USB drives.)

With Norton Zip Rescue you can fight problems like Windows registry corruption, partition table damage, virus contamination, missing or damaged system files, or boot record damage.

Your custom-created Zip Rescue disk is unique to your system, and contains a condensed version of Windows, the Norton Zip Rescue software, and a record of your desktop settings. (Your desktop settings indicate how your icons and toolbars are organized, as well as other things such as your background and screen saver.) So, if your

OS stops working and you need to recover it, you get your Windows back instead of reverting back to the original Windows defaults. Here's what you need to do to create a Zip Rescue Disk:

- Download Norton Zip Rescue.
- Install the software.
- Create and test your customized Zip Rescue Disk.
- Store your Zip Rescue Disk in a safe place.

Norton Utilities 2000™ (Symantec). List Price: $50.

Norton Utilities provides comprehensive solutions to fix and prevent even the most complicated PC problems quickly and easily.

Norton System Works 2000™ (Symantec). List Price: $60.

NSW 2000 gives you five easy-to-use utilities in one fully integrated suite. Norton Utilities is good for detecting, repairing, and preventing hardware and software problems.

- Norton AntiVirus offers powerful antivirus capabilities.
- Norton CleanSweep safely and completely removes unneeded programs and files.
- Norton CrashGuard protects your work against system crashes and screen freezes.

GoBack™ (Wild File) is a $70 utility, which keeps track of all changes to your system and allows you to access the log and "go back in time" and restore some deleted files and directories. You can download and install software, exchange email and delete files without fear—most of it could be reversed later. The program uses about 100 MB of space and just a few percents of system resources. About 10% of the hard disk drive is set aside for GoBack, which will keep at least one week's worth of history. One thing to mention: You cannot run GoBack on the system with compressed drives or with more than one OS installed. Next is a list of some features:

- Immediate recovery from system crashes, virus attacks, failed software installations, and file deletion/overwriting
- Ongoing data protection
- Security
- Ability for you to "fix" your own PC
- Don't need to know what went wrong to get your PC operating again

Hard Drive Mechanics™ (Encore Software). List Price: $50.

Encore Software claims that Hard Drive Mechanics recovers from over 98% of hard drive crashes. Next is a list of some features:

- It automatically repairs:
  - All file allocation tables (FAT)
  - Partitions (any number or size)
  - Root directory
  - Boot sector on a single PC
  - Windows® 98, 95, 3.x, and DOS systems
  - FAT 16, 32 compatible
  - Supports multiple hard drives
- Prevents loss of valuable data by predicting hardware failure (for SMART drives)
- Avoids reformatting the drive or reinstalling applications

Norton Ghost 2000™ (Symantec). List Price: $63.

Norton Ghost 2000 Personal Edition is the software for cloning and imaging your hard disk drive. Technically savvy home computer users can use it to:

- Migrate data files, applications, and system settings when replacing an old PC with a new one
- Clone an entire hard drive when upgrading your hardware
- Create compressed hard disk backups and restore disk images during disaster recovery
- Copy disk images to removable media, then restore entire images or individual files and directories as needed
- Clone directly to another PC via parallel ports or NetBIOS interfaces

WHAT TO DO IF THE DISASTER ALREADY HAPPENED . . . .

The main rule is simple: if the data you are about to lose are really important to you, do not experiment with the damaged media for too long (or at all)! You may further damage it beyond recovering (for an updatable list of professional data recovery services go to *www.usbyte.com*).

Floppy Disks

Floppy diskettes are designed to be robust and to operate in an unfriendly environment filled with dirt, abrasive particles, moisture, and so on. But, still, the environment and the way we handle floppy disks may cause the damage.

If you cannot read from a new floppy disk, it just may need formatting! But, make sure there is no data on the floppy disk—formatting will definitely erase all the data forever! Nowadays most floppy disks are sold preformatted for IBM-type PCs or for the Macintosh. Check if the operating system marked on the floppy is the same as the operating system you are using.

If you cannot write to the floppy, check if the switch on the back of the floppy is in write-protect mode. If it is, switch it to another position. Also, try to read this floppy using another floppy drive (ask a friend or colleague), maybe the problem is in the drive, not in the floppy.

Slide the metal window on the floppy aside and visually check the surface for damage. Usually, the surface will appear as a dark mirror, and you can see if there is a circumferential scratch on the surface (see Figure 10–3). If there is a scratch, you have mechanical damage to your magnetic media. One can rarely recover data from mechanically damaged areas since the magnetic bits may not exist there anymore. But, there is still a chance to recover data from other parts of the disk. If these data are valuable to you, do not try anything else on your own. Contact professional data recovery services (for an updatable list of services, go to *www.usbyte.com*).

If there is no visible scratch, there could be some particle or dirt stuck to the disk surface. It is sometimes helpful to blow air on the disk surface through the open metal window. You may simultaneously gently rotate the disk to treat the entire surface. Be

Figure 10–3
Low magnification (X25) image of the scratch on the floppy disk surface. This scratch prevented read and write operations from the floppy.

careful, don't spit on the disk accidentally! After you are done, try reading from this floppy again. If it does not work, contact professionals in data recovery.

If your floppy drive won't work, check the cables. Check the power cable for a bad connection, and check the twisted cable for the correct configuration: drive A: should be connected to the end-most connector (after the cable twist) and drive B: to the middle connector (before the twist). If this does not help, replace the twisted cable. Finally, to make sure that the problem is in the drive, check to see if a different floppy drive will work in the same place.

If the above measures didn't solve your problem, it is time to contact data recovery specialists.

Removable Media Magnetic Storage

Zip, Jaz, and similar products are also designed to be robust and operate in an environment filled with dirt, abrasive particles, moisture, and so on. I personally have never experienced Zip disk failures. The enclosure of Zip and Zip-like disks is less open than that of the floppy and keeps the dirt away.

Therefore, there is not much that can be done if it suddenly stops reading or writing. Just remember a couple of things:

- Try to read this Zip or Zip-like disk using another drive (ask a friend or colleague). Maybe the problem is in the drive, not in the disk.
- Blowing air through the opening of the disk cartridge may not be a good idea, since the slider/disk interface of the Zip-like drives is more delicate than that for floppy drives (especially for high-density Jaz and Orb disks). If the data on the disk is valuable to you, do not try anything else and contact a professional data recovery service.

Magnetic Hard Disk Drive

The rule is: do not try this at home. The hard disk drive (HDD) is, perhaps, the most complex data storage system available.

Typically, drives are assembled in clean room conditions to prevent its internal components from being exposed to particulate contamination. Since in a typical room environment there are zillions of particles much larger than the spacing between the flying slider and the disk, opening the disk outside the clean room may significantly shorten the drive's life. Plus, there is hardly anything you can do yourself. It is also important to not open the drive since, if it is opened, the warranty will be voided, and you will lose the drive along with the data.

Warning!

Repeated attempts to restart the drive after it has failed to start may cause irreparable damage!

The first indicator of an approaching HDD problem is an increasing frequency of drive-related computer failures, when your PC dies suddenly (which can also be due to bad RAM, a bad IDE connector/cable, or other reasons), or shows diagnostic messages with one of the many drive error codes. Running the Scandisk utility (Windows) or any similar program may cure the problem if the bad bits, which the program will mark, do not grow in size or migrate with time. If the use of disk utilities doesn't solve your problems, you may start thinking about backing up your data and contacting the drive manufacturer to ask for a replacement drive.

Sound can be used to evaluate the drive's condition. Unless your drive is in sleep mode (power-saving mode), you can hear the spindle sound. Press the "Save" button in any application program and you will hear the sound of the voice-coil actuator (VCA) moving the head above the disk surface. If your drive makes no sound at all, this may indicate several things: bad connection of your power cable; problem with the drive's electronics (mostly reparable by the expert); or high stiction, when the motor cannot overcome static friction between the disks and the heads in the drive. The stiction problem may occur if you have not used your drive for a while, and this problem is exacerbated by high humidity.

Finally, no sound or a strange rubbing sound may indicate a head crash, which is usually associated with damage to the magnetic media and with partial (at least) data loss.

Dealing with the hard disk drive problems beyond software fixes and checking connections is simple: Don't! Go to a professional or risk losing the data.

Before sending your final SOS signal, check all cables on both sides for bad connections. Sometimes it helps.

One more thing. Experts from the largest hard drive manufacturer, Seagate Technologies, estimate that a significant percent of the drives returned by the customers for warranty replacement ends up with a "No Problem Found" diagnosis. Therefore, before you send it in for replacement, it is to your benefit to know if a replacement drive will solve your problem. This is a list of typical reasons for a "No Problem Found" drive diagnosis:

- File system corruption
- Driver corruption
- Damaged master boot record
- Virus attack
- Hardware conflicts

Seagate provides an easy troubleshooting procedure (*www.seagate.com/support/ npf/index.html*). I recommend you use it before you spend money and send your drive in for replacement. Select your drive type, go to the above address, and follow the procedure.

If nothing else works, or if you do not have the warranty, we recommend you contact the drive's manufacturer or a data recovery expert. It is what we do in case of a serious problem with the hard drive.

The last portion of this chapter discusses professional data recovery services. They have experience and equipment. If it is possible to save your drive, they will do so.

CD, CD-R, CD-RW, and DVD

If you have problems with reading the CD or DVD, its mirror surface(s) could be contaminated with particles, fingerprints, various stains, or, unfortunately, scratches.

To clean your CD or DVD use a soft lint-free cloth and apply light strokes in a radial direction only! The data on a CD and DVD is stored and read in a circumferential direction and the drive's optic is less sensitive to radial scratches you may generate yourself!

Data on the optical discs is protected by a layer of lacquer on one side (mirror side) and by another layer of polycarbonate (PC) plastic on the other side (label side). The data is stored in the form of shallow bits in the PC matrix covered with a thin reflective layer of aluminum. If you scratch the disc and this scratch is deep enough to damage (remove) the bits, your data is lost locally. Fortunately, CDs and DVDs are robust and not all scratches cause irreversible damage. If you have scratches on the mirror side of a CD or DVD and you really want to try recovering the data yourself (instead of looking for professional help), then there are a few things you may try.

- Try polishing shallow scratches away with mild abrasives (i.e., toothpaste or furniture polish). Clean away the residue. Use radial strokes only!
- Try to use fillers for deeper scratches (furniture wax, car wax, etc.). Cover the entire surface and buff out using a clean cloth. Again, use radial strokes only!
- Try to copy or duplicate the damaged disc as soon as possible.

Warning!

Damage to the label side of the CD or DVD can sometimes be even more dangerous than to the mirror side!

DATA RECOVERY SERVICES . . . .

In the case of data loss or damage to your storage media or drive, do not panic and do not try to fix the problem immediately—you may destroy your last hope with your own hands (by, for example, repeatedly restarting your hard drive hoping that it will finally boot up in spite of that squeaky sound coming from the inside).

Visit *www.usbyte.com* and check an updatable list of companies who specialize in data recovery. They have experience and equipment. If it is possible to save your drive, they will do so.

11

How to Choose or Upgrade Your DVD, HDD, or CD-ROM

In this chapter…

This chapter summarizes the most important material of the previous chapters. For more information on the subjects below please refer to the previous chapters of the book.

INTERFACE . . . .

What is Interface?

A hardware and/or software data transmission regulator that controls data exchange between the PC and other devices, including such data storage devices as hard disk drives, floppy drives, tape drives, CD drives, and DVD drives. The interface is provided by the electronics of the data transfer controller and the drive electronics. There are several standards adopted for the interface protocols allowing connection of any standard peripheral device.

What Kind of Interfaces are There?

The most common types of interfaces used are parallel, serial, USB, ATA (IDE, EIDE, UDMA, ATAPI), SCSI, IEEE 1394 FireWire, and PC Card (formerly known as PCMCIA). Fibre Channel and SSA are used in high-end storage applications. For details on interfaces, see Chapter 2.

What is My Interface of Choice?

You need to choose which interface best suits your specific needs. As a general rule, you have to give up either convenience, performance, or higher cost. The short descriptions below may help you to make your choice.

- Serial: Set up is easy; external; slowest.
- Parallel: Set up is easy; external; slow; faster than serial.
- IDE (ATA). Set up is moderately difficult. For internal devices and short cables. Requires opening PC and connecting some cables inside. Performance is much better than parallel or serial interface, or USB-devices and FireWire devices. Supports two devices per channel only.
- PC Card: Set up is easy. Good performance. Typically used for laptop computers and other mobile devices.

- USB: Set up is very easy. Good performer. Hot swappable. Requires Windows 98 and higher. Supports multiple devices (up to 127).
- IEEE 1394 FireWire: Set up is easy. Excellent performer. Costly. Requires Windows 98 and higher. May require a plug-in card. For external devices mostly. Supports multiple devices (up to 63).
- SCSI: Set up is even more difficult than that for IDE. Best performer. Best when multiple devices are used. Generally needs a separate SCSI card. Multiple devices (up to 16).
- FC-AL: High-end interface for enterprise environment. Setup is difficult. Expensive. Best performer over long distances (up to 10 km). Multiple devices (up to 127).

HARD DISK DRIVE . . . .

What is the Hard Disk Drive?

The magnetic hard disk drive (HDD) is a direct access data storage device that, like all magnetic storage devices, uses small magnetized areas (called bits) on the rigid magnetic disks to store information. For details on the basic design and operating principles of the HDD, see Chapter 3.

Who are the Main Manufacturers of Hard Disk Drives?

Not very many companies survived years of the fierce technological competition and ruthless price wars. Today, there are only eight companies left: Seagate, IBM, Quantum/Maxtor (merged recently), Western Digital, Samsung, Hitachi, Toshiba, and Fujitsu.

What is the Price Range I Should be Looking For?

The price of HDD storage is falling rapidly thanks to tough competition among manufacturers and continuous technological advances. The price is still changing on a monthly basis, making an HDD of many GBs in capacity relatively inexpensive and easily affordable for almost anyone.

As a rule, you pay less (about $100 less) for the IDE drive than for the SCSI drive, for lower drive RPM (revolutions per minute) than for higher RPM, and for an internal drive than for an external drive. For example, for a good-performance UDMA 7,200 RPM drive with 46 GB of storage and 9 ms of the average seek time (Maxtor DiamondMax Plus 45 46GB), you pay just around $180. A similar drive with a smaller capacity of 15.4 GB may cost about $100. This translates into $3.9–$6.5 per GB of storage for this high-performance drive, with larger capacity drives being cheaper per gigabyte.

You also pay more for a just-released drive. Since there are various available online sites comparing prices (i.e., *www.cnet.com*), I advise you to shop around for the best deal.

What HDD Interface Should I Choose: IDE, EIDE, ATA, UDMA, ATA-33, ATA-66, ATA-100, SCSI, USB, Parallel, etc.?

First of all, there are two major (meaning most popular) types of interfaces: IDE and SCSI. IDE stands for Integrated Drive Electronics; SCSI stands for Small Computer System Interface. IDE is also known as EIDE, ATA, UDMA (direct memory access), ATA-3, 33, 66, or 100 (for a data transfer rate of up to 16 MB/sec, 33 MB/sec, 66 MB/s, and 100 MB/s). There are two major differences from the user's point of view: data transfer rate and possible number of drives attached.

If your requirements for data transfer rate are *low to moderate*, which is common for a typical user of word processors, spreadsheets, graphic applications, small- to medium-size databases, email programs, and for Internet surfing, the IDE drive is the most satisfactory choice. Low-end (low-throughput) ATA-3 enhanced IDE drives are very inexpensive nowadays (thanks to IDE technology and the price wars) and provide up to 16 MB/sec data transfer rates. More advanced IDE drives, called ultra DMA or ATA-33/66/100 drives, provide from up to 33 MB/sec to 100 MB/sec data transfer rates, which rivals more expensive SCSI drives.

If you are a multimedia professional, graphic designer, network administrator, or software developer, or just want to get the maximum performance out of multiple hard drives, you may need to buy a SCSI hard disk drive. Another possible reason for using SCSI is the need for a fast external hard disk drive. External drives are also available with parallel port, USB, and FireWire interfaces, which are simpler to use. I would recommend USB or FireWire type interfaces for the external HDD, since they combine acceptable performance with ease of use.

Table 11–1 summarizes your choices and possible recommendations.

Table 11–1   **HDD Interface Choices**

HDD interface	Data rate (MB/s)	Applications	Price (relative)	Pros/Cons
IDE (ATA, ultra DMA, or enhanced DMA)	up to 16 (EDMA) up to 100 (UDMA)	Text processing, spreadsheets, medium intensity graphic editing, medium size databases, email, and Internet access	Low to medium	Low cost, simplicity of installation, relatively high performance/limited expandability, poor multitasking
SCSI	40 to 320	Multimedia, graphic design, network administration, software development, large databases, multiple hard drives (more than 4), external hard drives	Medium to high (extra $100 to $400 for a comparable drive)	Extremely high data rates, excellent expandability (up to 7 to 15 drives), maximum performance out of multiple drives/ higher cost, need for special card, more complex installation, and configuration
Parallel port, USB, FireWire	Up to 2 (parallel EPP); up to 1.5 (USB); up to 12 (FireWire)	External HDD	Higher than that for internal drives. Lowest (parallel)—highest (FireWire)	External, removable/expensive, slower.

USB, FireWire, and parallel-port interfaces are used for external drives, which are, in general, slower and also more expensive than internal drives. Choose USB and FireWire over parallel port interface, when possible.

What are the Main Performance Parameters to Look for?

The main performance parameters to look for depend on what your applications are. For example, for high-end servers or for real-time applications (video, audio, etc.), the data transfer rate (DTR) may be the most important parameter. The DTR is, in general, a function of the drive's RPM (i.e., 3,600, 4,200, 5,400, 7,200, 10,000, or 15,000 RPM) for a given type of drive interface. Look for higher RPM values or read data rate values directly from the drive's cover or from the provided datasheet. A faster interface type and a larger on-board memory buffer will improve performance too.

Quite often, people pay too much attention to the *average seek time* or *access time*. But, these parameters are the measures of the drive's internal data transfer rate rather than the external (between the drive and the host PC). In fact, these parameters represent the time needed for the magnetic head to be positioned over the needed bit of data or make this data available for the system. I will encourage you to pay more attention to the DTR values in the drive's specification, since they correspond to the real drive throughput and not to the internal data transfer rate.

Another important parameter is the total drive storage capacity. For laptop (mobile) computers, for example, the data rate could be much less important than capacity, since laptops are rarely used for speed-hungry applications such as video-editing, heavy graphics, large databases, and so on, but frequently need to store large quantities of data.

A head-to-head comparison of the drives' performance is also a good way to select your favorite drive. This information is not provided with the drive but still can be found elsewhere on the Internet or in some more traditional publications (*PC World*, for example).

What Other Parameters Should I Consider before Buying a Drive?

Nowadays, the manufacturer's warranty is usually the same for all drive manufacturers, that is, 3 years for a desktop drive. A different question is—will this company exist to honor this warranty 2 or 3 years later. I may risk to predict that IBM and Seagate, for example, will still be around, while the future of some other smaller companies is less certain.

High reliability figures, such as MTBF (mean time before failure), is also something to look for, but this also doesn't differ too much from one drive to another.

Customer support and ease of drive installation could also vary significantly from one manufacturer to another.

How Many Drives Can I Install on My Computer?

IDE controllers are limited to two devices per channel (typically, with two channels per motherboard).

SCSI controllers are designed for multitasking and can support from 7 to 15 devices. In particular, SCSI-1, Fast SCSI-2, Ultra SCSI-3 (8-bit), and Ultra-2 SCSI support seven devices on a chain, while SCSI-2, Wide SCSI-2, Fast Wide SCSI-2, Ultra SCSI-3 (16-bit), and Wide Ultra-2 SCSI support up to 15 devices.

Therefore, if you have an IDE controller and need more HDD storage, you may go with fewer but larger drives. Or, you may buy an IDE plug-in card and increase the number of drives by connecting them to the card.

A SCSI controller will allow you to use multiple smaller drives, thus increasing system reliability (and complexity) by mirroring some data.

Is There Any Capacity Limitation for the Drive?

Unfortunately, yes. Earlier computers used much smaller hard disk drives and the BIOS designers did not anticipate future multigigabyte drives.

If your computer was built in 1997 or earlier, there is a good chance that it's BIOS (Basic Input/Output System) does not support hard disk drives larger than 8.4 GB (or even less than that). When the system accesses the disk (reads or writes data), the BIOS uses a software interrupt 13h (unlucky number!). This interrupt was initially assigned 24 bits of addressing, which only allows the system to access 8.4 GB on a disk drive. Since then, the extensions for interrupt 13h were defined allowing for 64 bits of addressing, which is equal to an upper limit of 9.4 Tera (or $\times 10^{12}$) Gigabytes, which effectively eliminates the problem. Most systems newer than 1998 should properly address interrupt 13h. Systems without this support can be modified to use drives greater than 8.4 GB.

If your current system has this problem, it could be addressed as following:

- Contact your PC or BIOS manufacturer to obtain a newer version of BIOS that supports the interrupt 13h extensions.
- A majority of modern PCs have a so-called Flash BIOS with all information recorded on an updatable Flash memory chip (see Chapter 6). Using a software utility one can modify the BIOS. For example, for IBM-made drives, download Disk Manager from the IBM web site (*www.storage.ibm.com*).

Another limitation is related to the file system and could be solved by upgrading your operating system. If you have Windows 98, you will have no problem with your file system limitations since it is FAT32 (file allocation table for 32-bits OS). If you have Windows 95, you may check if it supports the FAT32 file system in the following way:

Go to START → SETTINGS → CONTROL PANEL → SYSTEM icon → GENERAL

If SYSTEMS PROPERTIES shows:

- *4.00.950b*—This version supports the extended file system (FAT32.) and you have no problem with the file system.
- *4.00.950* or *4.00.950a*—This version only supports FAT16 and you have a 2.1 GB limitation. This means that if you use a larger drive, you will be forced to partition it with the FDISK program to many logical disks of not larger than 2.1 GB.

Can I Use the Same Drive for Desktop and for Laptop Computers?

If your laptop has parallel, SCSI, FireWire, or USB port, you may always connect it to the external drive with the same interface type.

Usually, mobile computers use the small form-factor internal hard drives similar to those used in the desktops but mounted inside a custom holder that slips into the laptop's case and locks in place. Therefore, when buying the drive for the laptop, make sure to check its compatibility with your type of computer.

The IDE drives used in laptop computers can be used in desktop computers with the help of a cable adapter but there could be some problem with physically fixing a smaller drive inside the larger bay of the desktop.

REMOVABLE MAGNETIC STORAGE . . . .

What is the Removable Magnetic Storage?

Removable magnetic storage consists of a device that uses media magnetization to store and retrieve information and can be moved around (like external hard disk drives) or use the media that can be removed (floppy, Zip, etc.). For more information, see Chapter 3.

Who are the Main Manufacturers of Removable Magnetic Storage Devices?

There are plenty of manufacturers. The limiting factor here is standardization: everyone wants removable storage that can be used everywhere.

So far, Iomega seems to be the most successful in this arena. Sony, Imation, Castlewood, and a few others are trying to compete with Iomega to become the next preinstalled removable magnetic storage standard inside every sold computer, but the outcome of this battle is hard to predict. It is possible that the companies that will win in the near future will dominate the market for many years to come.

What Type of Removable Magnetic Storage Should I Buy?

The choice of removable magnetic media can be quite straightforward and defined by the number 10. You should try to fit all the data you are going to move on not more than 10 disks of your choice. More disks means more volume and more hassle, and it also means you should probably choose a system with a higher storage capacity.

If the amount of data you are planning to move around could fit on 10 storage units of your choice, you don't need larger, and generally speaking more expensive, storage. For example, if you are planning to move MS Word documents, MS Excel spreadsheets, or other similar documents, a few 40 MB Clik! disks, 100 MB Zip disks, or 120 MB Superdisks (by Imation) will meet your needs. Increasing demand for storage will force you to migrate to the 250 MB Zip drive (which, by the way, can read 100 MB disks as well), and later, to the 1 GB or 2 GB Jaz drive.

Note

The 2 GB Jaz drive does not read 1 GB disks and could be damaged by them.

To better understand your choices, read Chapter 3.

What is the Price Range I Should be Looking For?

The price for the removable magnetic storage products may vary from about $100 for a 100 MB Zip with parallel interface to over $300 for a Jaz 2 GB SCSI drive. Removable and external hard disk drives are priced depending on their capacity, performance, and interface type. It is advisable to shop around for the best deal.

What Interface Type Should I Select: ATAPI, SCSI, Parallel, USB, or FireWire?

Most systems have a full range of options from parallel port to USB (universal serial bus). If you have Windows 98 and higher, I would advise you use the USB, which combines a sufficiently high data transfer rate with convenience of installation and use. FireWire devices are another good choice, but they are still much less popular among computer users than the USB. The PC card interface is specifically meant for the laptop computers.

What are the Main Performance Parameters to Look For?

I believe that the main performance parameter for removable storage is its storage *capacity*. It is always better to fit all your data on one or two disks. Isn't it why the floppies have lost their popularity?

What Other Parameters Should I Consider?

Other important parameters are speed (data transfer rate), size, and convenience of use. Depending on your preferences, one can choose an appropriate system: from relatively slow and low on capacity, but convenient and portable 40 MB Clik! drives to much larger, SCSI-based, and extremely fast Jaz 2 GB or Orb 2.2 GB drives or, even larger, heavier, and somewhat cumbersome, but ultimately fastest removable hard disk drives.

Can I Use the Same Drive for Desktop and for Laptop Computers?

Yes, as long as you have an appropriate interface connector: parallel, USB, FireWire, PC card, or SCSI.

CD, CD-R, AND CD-RW . . . .

What is CD, CD-R, and CD-RW?

All CD-type storage systems use slight changes in the light reflected from the pits and lands on the surface of the disc to store the information. Some of them are just capable of reading and are called CD-ROM (read only memory), others can write (burn) on the disc (CD-R) or even write and rewrite data, like CD-RW. All of them are capable of storing up to 650 MB of data per disc. For more information, go to Chapter 4.

Who are the Main Manufacturers of CD Drives?

There are plenty—Plextor, Mitsumi, MicroSolutions, Hi-Val, Sony, HP, Panasonic, AOpen, Kenwood, ASUS, and more.

What Type of CD Storage Should I Buy?

CD-ROM drives are very inexpensive nowadays (some are less than $40) and are a must-have for any PC user. They are good for quick software installation, for playing games, for multimedia applications, and other applications requiring a high data transfer rate and large storage capacity.

Recordable and rewritable CDs serve a different purpose—they are relatively inexpensive storage media for data backup, exchange, distribution, and so on.

What is Spin Rate?

The spin rate is a measure of the drive's data transfer rate (DTR) relative to the very first CD-ROM drive, with a data rate of about 0.15 MB/s.

Nowadays, CD drives spin at a very high speed (some are faster than 8,500 RPM) and provide much faster data rates. Unfortunately, unlike older drives, which had a constant linear velocity (CLV) and data transfer rate being independent on the data track radius, today's drives often have a higher data rate at the outer diameter and a lower one at the inner diameter. This means that the reported spin rate for the CD drive corresponds to its maximum possible DTR, which is achieved only while reading the very outermost tracks. An average data transfer rate is, therefore, lower than the "promised" spin rate.

Since the data on a CD is written starting from the inner diameter and not every CD is filled with data completely, one cannot always realize the maximum potential of the drive.

Nevertheless, the spin rate is, probably, the most important measure of a drive's performance and higher spin rates are always desirable.

There are some newer CD drive designs (i.e., from Kenwood) that use a multi-beam technology that decreases RPM significantly and, therefore, reduces vibrations and noise associated with high RPM. For more information, go to Chapter 4.

How to Understand the Markings of CD-ROM, CD-R, and CD-RW

CD-ROM marking "number X" (i.e., 12X, 32X, 50X, etc.) corresponds to the spin rate as compared to the first CD drive with a data rate of about 0.15 MB/sec. The "X" rating usually corresponds to the *maximum* spin rate, with the average spin rate being lower. In general, a higher "X"-rating corresponds to a higher drive reading rate.

CD-R marking, such as 8X/2X, corresponds to the reading rate/recording rate, again compared to the same first CD drive with a 0.15 MB/sec data transfer rate.

CD-RW marking, such as 24X/4X/2X, corresponds to the reading rate/recording rate/rewriting rate values.

What is the Price Range I Should be Looking For?

CD-ROM drives are the cheapest and the CD-RW drives are the most expensive.

The rule is: the prices for all drives may significantly vary depending on the spin rate (higher, more expensive), brand name, support of different CD formats, interface type (with internal ATAPI/ IDE being the cheapest and SCSI and external drives being more expensive), existence of the audio output, and so on. The advice is to shop around for the best deals and the most recent prices.

What Interface Should I Choose: ATAPI, SCSI, Parallel, or USB?

In general, SCSI is faster than ATAPI/IDE, which is much faster than parallel interface or USB. Also, SCSI seems to be the only option making possible real-time CD duplication. The degree of interface complexity is almost inversely proportional to the data rate, with SCSI being the most complex and parallel and USB the easiest to deal with. Also, SCSI drives may require a separate adapter card, which is not always sold with the drive. The FireWire drive is a good option too but may also require a plug-in card and is on the expensive side.

If you are looking for an internal drive, pick ATAPI or SCSI. For external drives your choice is between SCSI, parallel port, USB, and FireWire drives and should be based on a balance of requirements of high performance and low cost.

Should I Buy Internal, External, Single-Disc, or Jukebox?

There is basically no reason to buy an external CD drive for the desktop PC. CD-ROMs are very inexpensive, and CD-R and CD-RW are rarely required on all the computers you have, unless you want to have very high system flexibility.

If you have a number of discs you need to access frequently, then consider the jukebox, which allows you to select discs directly from your Windows Explorer. Jukeboxes are typically more expensive then single-disc drives and are behind in performance when compared to the latest single-disc drives.

What are the Main Performance Parameters to Look For?

In short you are looking for speed, which can be determined from the spin rate factor ("number X") and average access time (in milliseconds).

In the case of a CD-ROM, I advise you to look for at least a 32X spin rate and average access time of less than 100 ms. For CD-R and CD-RW, look for an average access time of less than 150 milliseconds.

What Other Parameters Should I Consider before Buying the Drive?

Consider the type of the drive: internal or external.

Consider the type of interface: IDE/ATAPI, SCSI, parallel, or USB.

Consider the data formats: your drive should read at least CD-ROM, CD-R, CD-RW, audio CD, and Photo-CD formats.

Consider the warranty: at least 1 year on parts and labor with 24 hour/7 day a week technical support.

How Many CD Drives Can I Install on My Computer?

IDE controllers are limited to two devices per channel. SCSI controllers are designed for multitasking and can support from 7 to 15 devices. In particular, SCSI-1, Fast SCSI-2, Ultra SCSI-3 (8-bit), and Ultra-2 SCSI support seven devices on a chain, while SCSI-2, Wide SCSI-2, Fast Wide SCSI-2, Ultra SCSI-3 (16-bit), and Wide Ultra-2 SCSI support up to 15 devices.

Can I Use the Same CD Drive for Desktop and for Laptop Computers?

If your laptop has a parallel, SCSI, FireWire, or USB port, you may always connect it to the external CD drive with the same interface type.

DVD . . . .

What is a DVD?

It looks like a CD, but it has a much higher density of recording.

DVD still uses the optical recording technology (like a CD), but it has smaller pit length, closer tracks, larger data area of the disc, and other features that result in significantly larger storage capacities. Single-sided, single-layered DVD-ROM can store 4.7 GB of data versus about 670 MB for a CD-ROM. But instead of just playing music, it delivers more than two hours of high-quality video. A single-sided, single-layer DVD can contain up to 133 minutes of video, enough to handle 95% of all movies, without the interruption for flipping the disc over or changing discs. Because DVD can deliver more than 500 lines of horizontal resolution, the picture detail is more than twice as good as a VCR.

DVDs aren't just for the eyes, they are also good to your ears. They feature a Dolby Digital™ multichannel surround sound audio system. Unlike Dolby Pro Logic's sound, the new system is all-digital. Separate Left and Right sound channels deliver accurate sound effects. What's more, a special bass effects channel brings added realism to movie soundtracks and music videos.

There are several modern DVD-ROM formats available with some extra DVD-RAM under consideration. For details, go to Chapter 4.

Who are the Main Manufacturers of DVD?

Again, there are plenty—Hitachi, Sony, Maxell, JVC, Mitsubishi, Pioneer, TDK—and will be more, with this format becoming the dominant optical storage format.

What Type of DVD Storage Should I Buy?

Unlike CDs and CD-ROMs, all DVD discs have both identical physical and logical formats, and also an identical file system. This means that all modern DVD players are capable of playing back all DVD-ROM, audio, and video, and also, CD, CD-ROM, CD-R, and CD-RW.

You may choose to buy a DVD drive if your future use of it is computer-related, such as multimedia applications, games, and so on. You will be also able to play movies on the same drive.

An MPEG-2 decoder is needed to play DVD-Video on DVD-ROM. Software decoders are generally cheaper, but require a fast CPU plus a suitable graphic card. Hardware decoders allow for required video quality on slower processors, have outputs to the TV instead of the PC monitor, and are generally recommended.

If you are mostly planning to watch movies, you should buy a DVD-Video player, which is better customized for this specific purpose. Also, all DVD-Video players should be capable of playing all types of DVD-Video, CD audio, and Video CDs.

What is the Price Range I Should be Looking For?

DVD-ROM drives are getting cheaper, but are still quite expensive.

The rule is: the drives using software MPEG-2 decoders are cheaper but lack performance of the more expensive drives with hardware-based data decoding. If you are interested in watching movies on your DVD drive, I advise you to buy a drive with hardware-based data compression.

DVD-RAM can easily cost over $500, but this price is expected to fall quickly. Since the prices for all drives vary significantly, shop around for the best deal and the most recent prices.

What Interface Should I Choose: EIDE, SCSI, or FireWire?

Unless you are specifically thinking of using many devices simultaneously, or you ran out of IDE connectors or drive bays, the IDE is the interface of choice. SCSI will put less load on your PC's processor, has somewhat better performance, and is a good solution if you need an external DVD drive, but is also much more expensive and is harder to set up. FireWire is a good option for the external drive but may require, like SCSI, a plug-in card.

What are the Main Performance Parameters to Look For?

The drive's speed will be one. Even a 4x-speed DVD drive can match a 32x CD-ROM in terms of data transfer rate, which is fast enough already. 10x DVD drives are already available today and much faster DVD drives will be available in the future.

What Other Parameters Should I Consider before Buying a DVD Drive?

Watch out for compatibility issues. Some earlier DVD drives were not compatible with CD-R and CD-RW, but this was corrected in the newest drives.

Also, choose a hardware MPEG-2 decoder over a software decoder.

How Many DVD Drives Can I Install on My Computer?

IDE controllers are limited to two devices per channel. SCSI controllers are designed for multitasking and can support from 7 to 15 devices. In particular, SCSI-1, Fast SCSI-2, Ultra SCSI-3 (8-bit), and Ultra-2 SCSI support seven devices on a chain, while SCSI-2, Wide SCSI-2, Fast Wide SCSI-2, Ultra SCSI-3 (16-bit), and Wide Ultra-2 SCSI support up to 15 devices.

Can I Use the Same DVD Drive for Desktop and for Laptop Computers?

Yes, if you are using a SCSI or FireWire drive and have a SCSI or FireWire connector on your laptop.

MAGNETIC TAPE DRIVE . . . .

What is Magnetic Tape Storage?

Magnetic tape storage uses a flexible tape to store information magnetically, like a hard disk drive or a Zip drive do. In fact, modern Zip disks use technology similar to that used in some modern magnetic tapes (DLT tape IV, DDS-3, 4 tapes): ATOMM, or Advanced super Thin layer and high-Output Metal Media.

The main difference between the tape storage and other popular types of storage devices is its *lack of direct access to data*: to read and write data, a tape drive moves along the tape in a linear way, passing by all the data physically stored before the data requested. There is a difference with direct-access storage devices (DASD), which skips unnecessary data and goes directly to the requested file.

Unlike magnetic hard disk drives, which follow specific standards in interface design and drive form-factors, a large variety of different tape storage systems is available. These include 4 and 8 mm, 0.5"-wide helical drives, as well as 1/4-inch and 1/2-inch linear tape drives in different form-factors.

The main applications of tape storage are data backup, data transport, offline and near-line storage, and archiving, since it has the lowest cost per unit of storage and allows for inexpensive storage of large quantities of information.

What Type of Tape Storage Should I Look For?

Depending on your application and work environment, one can choose anything between the low-end QIC tape format and the high-end SuperDLT tape or LTO formats. Table 11–2 summarizes the formats and major performance characteristics.

Table 11–2   Formats and Major Performance Characteristics of MTDs

Tape format	Capacity (native/ compressed), GB	Sustained data transfer rate (burst), MB/s	Storage market segment
QIC (Travan, etc.)	10/20	1/2	low-end
4-mm DAT (DDS-4)	20/40	3/6	low-end/mid-range
Mammoth	20/40	3/6	low-end/mid-range
Mammoth-2	60/150	12/30	mid-range/high-end
AIT-1	25/50	3/6	mid-range
AIT-2	50/100	6/12	mid-range/high-end
DLT	40/80	6/12	mid-range/high-end
Super DLT	110/220	11/22	high-end
LTO	100 (400 in the future)	20 (160 in the future)	mid-range/high-end
Automated library (i.e., Magstar 3590)	up to 748,000	14/42	high-end and beyond

In some cases, when the degree of automation of the backup procedure is required, one may look for tape *stackers* or even *autoloaders* (see Chapter 3).

If there is a need to support large-scale backups, near online access, user-initiated file recovery, and simultaneously support multiple users and hosts, this can be addressed by using tape *libraries*. Libraries are built around multiple tape drives and are much more flexible than stackers or autoloaders, but are also more complex and more expensive.

Who are the Main Manufacturers of Tape Storage?

The major tape storage manufacturers are summarized by tape format in Table 11–3.

Table 11–3   Major Tape Storage Manufacturers

Format	Major manufacturers
QIC (Travan, etc.)	Seagate, HP, Imation, Iomega, Tandberg, etc.
4-mm DAT (DDS-4)	Sony, HP, Seagate, IBM, Compaq, etc.
Mammoth	Exabyte
Mammoth-2	Exabyte
AIT-1	Sony, Seagate
AIT-2	Sony, Seagate
DLT	Quantum, Tandberg, ADIC, HP, Compaq, etc.
Super DLT	Quantum
LTO	IBM, Seagate, HP
Automated library (i.e., Magstar)	IBM, StorageTek, etc.

What is the Price Range I Should be Looking For?

The price can vary from $200–$350 for a low-end IDE tape drive (Travan) to about $3,000 for a mid-range Sony AIT drive, about $7,000 for a mid-range to high-end Quantum DLT 7000, to over $90,000 for a fully automated tape library (IBM Magstar).

In any case, the price you pay per unit of storage (i.e., GB) is the lowest *for any tape storage* product when compared to almost any other storage technologies.

What Interface Should I Choose: Parallel, Floppy, IDE/ATAPI, or SCSI

Unless you are specifically thinking of using many devices simultaneously, or you ran out of IDE connectors or drive bays, the IDE is the interface of choice. SCSI will put less load on your PC's processor, has slightly better performance, and is the high-end solution, but is also much more expensive and is harder to set up. Parallel port will be the easiest but slowest to use. FC is the solution for high-end drives and libraries.

What are the Main Performance Parameters to Look For?

Capacity, data transfer rate, and cost. The capacity of the tape drive (or a tape used in the drive) should exceed the capacity of your hard disk drive or any of several drives you use. This will enable for a periodical complete system backup, which is a good idea for those whose data is important to them. Low cost is an important parameter of any backup system.

What are Other Parameters Should I Consider before Buying a Drive?

Reliability is an important drive parameter that depends on a duty cycle. Since different tape drives are designed for different applications, some of them require a 100% duty cycle (always "on") while a 20% duty cycle is typical for others (desktop drives).

Tape drive reliability is measured in MTBF (mean time before failure), which is provided in the drive specification and is measured in hours (see Table 11–4). Longer MTBF translates (on average, of course) into higher reliability of the drive.

If you already have tape storage and would like to buy more, watch out for compatibility (or backward compatibility) issues.

Table 11–4   Tape Drive Reliability

Format	MTBF (hours) (100% duty cycle)
QIC (Hornet 20 Travan) (*20% duty cycle*)	330,000
4-mm DAT (Seagate Scorpion 40 DAT) (*20% duty cycle*)	412,000
Mammoth	>250,000
Mammoth-2	>250,000
AIT-1	200,000
AIT-2	200,000
DLT-7000/8000	300,000/250,000
Super DLT	250,000
LTO	N/A
Automated library (i.e., Magstar)	N/A

How Many Tape Drives Can I Install on My Computer?

IDE controllers are limited to two devices per channel. SCSI controllers are designed for multitasking and can support from 7 to 15 devices. In particular, SCSI-1, Fast SCSI-2, Ultra SCSI-3 (8-bit), and Ultra-2 SCSI support seven devices on a chain, while SCSI-2, Wide SCSI-2, Fast Wide SCSI-2, Ultra SCSI-3 (16-bit), and Wide Ultra-2 SCSI support up to 15 devices.

WEB STORAGE ALTERNATIVES . . . .

What is Web Storage?

Web storage is online data backup and storage technology with access to the data from any Web browser anywhere in the world.

Simply speaking, you transfer the data over the Internet to a remote and safe location, where this data is stored on a highly reliable storage system, that is, RAID. This process ensures safety of your data in case something happens at your main data location (fire, earthquake, etc.). In this case, you can always restore the damaged data.

For details, go to Chapter 8.

Who are the Main Providers of Web Storage?

There are plenty and the number is growing. Some names to mention are @Backup, idrive, FreeDrive, Driveway, and others.

How do I Choose the Right Service Provider?

Shop around! Most of them give you a free trial period. This is the only way to find out who is best for your needs.

What is the Price Range I Should be Looking For?

Some of these service providers are free! If you need to pay, then think again: maybe you better use your own backup or removable storage system. Something like Zip or recordable CD.

At present, the cost of online storage is relatively low and will hardly decrease dramatically in the future. What will definitely become cheaper is the cost per unit of online storage—it is impractically high today (if you have to pay, of course).

What are the Main Performance Parameters to Look For?

Speed of connection and download and convenience of the software are the major things to look for.

Also, look for those systems that do not require any special software to access your data. Otherwise, this will limit your flexibility when on the road.

Can I Access this Data from Another Computer or Another Location?

Yes, especially if your service does not require any special software. Typically, you will just need the URL address, the user name, and the password to access your data. If special software is required, you may need to install it first on the computer you are going to use.

Regarding the location: you can access your data from anywhere in the world using the Internet.

Glossary

Actuator

The internal part of the drive that moves the read/write element from one location to another. Today's hard disk drives are equipped with voice-coil actuators (VCA) that are much faster than the previously used step motor. A typical drive's VCA consists of a rotary voice coil and the element-mounting arm. As current is applied to the rotor, it rotates at frequencies of 50 Hz or more, positioning the heads over the desired cylinder on the media.

Access time

See average access time.

Adaptive Battery Life Extender

A technology used in mobile hard disk drives to reduce power consumption by approximately 20 percent. It is accomplished by adapting power mode transitions based on the access patterns of individual users, rather than relying on conventional timers. As a result the power consumption may be lowered and battery life increased.

ADC

Analog-to-digital conversion. A multistage process of converting analog signal into its digital equivalent.

ADSL

Asymmetric DSL. ADSL is one of the most popular DSL technologies of today. Usually, the "A" is dropped, so, when we talk about DSL for home use, we're talking about ADSL.

AFM

Atomic Force Microscope. Physical tool for measurements of nanoscale topography and forces. Basically, the AFM consists of a thin, short lever with a sharp tip at the end. The tip's radius is usually made on the order of a few nanometers. When this tip is brought in proximity to the surface, surface forces act on the tip and result in bending and torsion of the lever, which is measured (mostly optically).The bending and torsion provides for a measure of the topography and forces.

Air-bearing slider

A small ceramic slider with a self-pressurized air bearing and magnetic read-write element at the end. When a magnetic rigid disk starts spinning, the lift force is generated between the slider and disk, which makes the slider fly at a very small height of a few dozen nanometers. This slider design was first used in the IBM "Winchester"-type hard disk drives that revolutionized drive technology.

AIT
Advanced Intelligent Tape. Relatively new 8-mm magnetic tape format.

AME
Advanced Metal Evaporated (ME) tape. The newer generation of ME tapes.

AMP
Advanced Metal Particle (MP) tape. The newer generation of MP tapes.

ANSI
American National Standards Institute represents the United States in the International Organization for Standardization (ISO) and works on coding and signaling standards.

Arbitrated loop
When devices form a Fibre Channel Arbitrated Loop, the transmitters are connected to a receiver for all nodes involved. When a node port "wins" arbitration, it establishes a point-to-point connection with another node.

Areal density
Is an important indicator of the disk (and drive) performance. Corresponds to the number of magnetic bits per unit area, and is usually measured in Gb/in^2.

Asynchronous Data Transfer
The data transfer scheme that allows packets of data to be transferred only after receiving a response from the receiving device. The retries are mandated if errors occur. This method sacrifices transfer speed for reliability. *See also* synchronous data transfer and isochronous data transfer.

ATAPI
Advanced Technology Attachment Packet Interface. A type of interface used to connect additional hardware devices to a computer. This interface is commonly used to connect internal devices such as CD-ROMs, hard drives, tape drives, and Zip drives. The advantages of ATAPI are that it is economical and offers high performance. To install an ATAPI device you must open your computer case and be able to identify the IDE channel(s) on your computer's motherboard.

ATA/ATA-1
Advanced Technology Attachment. A type of interface used to connect additional internal hardware devices to a computer. ATA is the official name given by ANSI to the IDE interface.

ATA-2/Fast ATA-2
ATA-2 is also known as enhanced IDE. Fast ATA-2 includes upgrades in DMA and PIO modes and offers higher DTR and some new commands.

ATA-3
An update to the ATA-2 standard and includes SMART capability. ATA-3 doesn't offer higher speed but adds new commands and more precisely defined procedures.

ATA-4
ATA-4 is also known as Ultra ATA, UDMA, or ATA-33. An update to the ATA-3 standard, it includes Ultra DMA (direct memory access) capability. Supports the maximum DTR of 33 MB/sec (in burst mode) and provides for enhanced reliability and data integrity through the use of double-edge clocking and Cyclical Redundancy Checking (CRC).

ATA-5 (or ATA-66)
One of the newest and fastest IDE interfaces that doubles the maximum DTR of ATA-33

to 66 MB/sec (in burst mode). Provides for enhanced reliability and integrity through CRC and the use of newer 40-pin 80-conductor cable instead of the 40-pin 40-conductor cable. The ATA-5 drives are completely backward-compatible with the previous ATA drives and host systems.

ATA-6 (or ATA-100)

This is the newest and the fastest IDE interface at the moment. Supports the maximum DTR of 100 MB/sec (in burst mode). Provides for enhanced reliability and integrity through CRC. Uses a new 40-pin 80-conductor cable instead of the 40-pin 40-connector cable. IDE connectors and the ATA-6 drives are completely backward-compatible with the previous ATA drives and host systems.

ATOMM

Advanced super Thin layer and high-Output Metal Media. The latest advancement in the world of MP media.

ATM

Asynchronous Transfer Mode. A high-speed switching technique used to transmit voice, data, and video.

Average access time

The average delay within the drive between receiving a write or read command and the instance when the head begins reading or writing. The access time includes seek time, settling time, and latency.

Backup (of data)

Important procedure of saving data on a separate data storage device to prevent complete data loss in case of unexpected failure of main storage system. A daily backup is highly recommended for active computer users.

Bad block

A block of data (usually the size of a sector)

that cannot reliably hold data because of a media flaw or damaged format markings.

Bandwidth

The amount of data that can be transmitted in a given amount of time. Bandwidth is also the difference between the highest and lowest frequencies of the signal used. Usually expressed in bits per second (bps) or in Hz (MHz, GHz).

Benchmark

A specialized set of programs used to evaluate the performance of a computer or one of its elements, such as a drive or memory.

Bezel

A decorative cover for the drive and is also known as the faceplate.

Block

A group of bytes stored and accessed as a logical data unit. One block of data is typically stored on the hard disk as one physical sector of data.

BIOS

Basic Input/Output System. The BIOS is built-in software that defines what a PC does without accessing programs from a disk. It makes it possible for a computer to boot itself. On PCs, the BIOS contains all the code required to control the disk drives, keyboard, display, serial communications, and some other functions. The BIOS is typically found on a ROM chip that comes with the computer. Since RAM is faster than ROM, many computer manufacturers make systems that copy BIOS from ROM to RAM every time the computer is restarted. This process is called shadowing.

BIOS Flash/Upgrade

BIOS Flash or BIOS Upgrade is the replacement of a current BIOS with a newer version having increased capabilities. Usually done to make the BIOS compatible with a newly installed hard disk drive or another storage device of greater capacity.

Bit

Abbreviation for a binary digit—the smallest unit of information in the digital world. A bit is represented by the numbers, 1 and 0, which correspond to the states "on" and "off," "true" and "false," or "yes" and "no." Bits are the building blocks for all information processing that goes on in digital electronics and computers. The term was introduced by John Tukey, an American statistician and early computer scientist. He first used the term in 1946, as a shortened form of the term "binary digit." Bits are usually combined into larger units called bytes.

BPI

Acronym for bits per inch. A measure of linear density of magnetic recording. *See also* TPI and FCI.

Bus

A set of hardware lines—wires—used for data transfer among the components of a computer system. A bus is a "highway" that connects different parts of the system— including the microprocessor, disk-drive controller, memory, and input/output ports— and enables them to transfer information. Bus is characterized by the number of bits they can transfer at a single time. A computer with an 8-bit data bus, for example, transfers 8 bits of data at a time, and one with a 16-bit data bus transfers 16 bits at a time.

Bus enumeration

The process of detecting and identifying devices on the bus (e.g., USB).

Buffer

See cache memory.

Byte

The basic unit of computer memory made of 8 bits and large enough to hold one character of alphanumeric data.

Cache memory

Specialized RAM used to optimize data transfers between system elements with different performance characteristics, for example, disk to main memory or main memory to CPU. Having certain data stored in cache speeds up the operation of the computer. When an item is called for, the computer first checks the internal cache, then the external cache, and finally the slower main storage.

CAV

Constant Angular Velocity

CD

Compact Disc

CD-DA

Compact Disc-Digital Audio

CD-I

Compact Disc-Interactive

CD-ROM

Compact Disc-Read Only Memory

CD-ROM/XA

CD-ROM/Extended Architecture

CD-R

Compact Disc-Recordable

CD-RW

Compact Disc-Rewritable

CD-WORM

Compact Disc-Write Once Read Many times

Cluster

A group of sectors on a hard disk drive that is addressed as one logical unit by the operating system. It is also the smallest contiguous area that can be allocated for the storage of data even if the actual data require less storage.

CLV
Constant Linear Velocity

CMOS
Complementary Metal Oxide Semiconductor. A memory chip that keeps a data record of the components installed in a computer. The CMOS uses power of a small battery and retains data even when the computer is turned off. CMOS is used by a computer to store a PC's configuration settings, such as date, time, boot sequence, drive(s) parameters, and so on.

Controller
Printed on a drive or plugged-in circuit board, which deals with all drive operations (read, write, access, load–unload, etc.) and communicates with the operating system.

Coercivity (H_c)
A measure of the magnetic field that is needed to reduce magnetization in a material to zero. The measure for coercivity is an Oersted (Oe).

CPU
Central processing unit. CPU (or just processor) is on a single chip that performs arithmetic and logical operations, decodes, and executes instructions.

Control Transfer
A transfer of data from the host computer to a USB device to provide it with configuration and control information.

Control Redundancy Check (CRC)
Procedure used to detect errors during transmission of data. The CRC data is transmitted along with the data packets for comparison with a CRC calculated by the receiving device.

CSS
Contact Start–Stop technology. The idea of

CSS is that when the hard disk drive is turned "off" and the slider is not flying, it lands on a specially prepared landing zone where it rests until the next "power-on" cycle. Durability of CSS drives is usually measured in CSS cycles. Newest mobile and server drives use different technology called Load–Unload (L/U), where the slider is parked on a special ramp when the drive is turned "off."

Cylinder
A group of tracks with the same radius in an assembly of hard disks.

DAD
Digital Audio Disk (optical)

Daisy chain
A way of connecting multiple drives (and other devices) to one PC controller. All drives have different numbers, which are set using jumpers, switches, or assigned automatically. In a daisy chain, any signal from the controller goes through the devices until the device whose number matches receives it.

DAT
Digital Audio Tape

Data compression
A process of data encoding based on locating and cutting out repeating data strings. When the data is read back, the cut-out string is restored. Depending on the file format, some 80% of compression could be achieved. Other "denser" file formats may not benefit from compression at all.

Data loss/recovery
No technology is fail-safe to various unfortunate accidents that may happen at any time, and disabling your storage system or damaging your storage media. If the data are not physically destroyed (i.e., magnetic or optical bits are not physically damaged), then there is a

chance to recover the loss. Periodic data back-up is the best protection against data loss.

Data Transfer Rate (DTR)

The speed at which bits of data are sent. For example, this could describe the rate at which the bits of information are read from the disk and sent to the drive's controller (internal rate), or characterize data exchange between the drive's controller and PC's CPU (external rate).

DDS

Digital Data Storage. A name used for DAT tape format.

Dedicated Servo System

Older drive designs utilized servo system that used entirely one side of one disk and also one head. Modern drives usually use an Embedded Servo System.

Defragmentation

Different parts of the same file could be scattered all over the hard disk drive, which increases access time to this data. Running Disk Defragmenter (comes with Windows OS) will help to keep file fragmentation to its minimum.

Desktop drive

Modern desktop drives usually come in a 3.5" form-factor, with one or several disk platters and twice as many MR (or GMR) magnetic heads. Drives have integrated drive electronics (IDE drives) or a separate controller card (SCSI drives), spin at 3,600 to 7,200 RPM, and use CSS technology.

Device endpoint

A uniquely identifiable portion of a USB device that is the source or sink of information in a communication flow between the host and device.

Diskette

Floppy disk or floppy diskette. Nowadays, diskettes usually come in a 3.5-inch form-factor and with 1.44 MB of storage capacity. Some newer high-density diskettes offered by different manufacturers have two modes of operation: low-density, with 1.44 MB, and high-density, with 120 MB of storage and more.

Digital tape

Magnetic tape optimized and used for storing data in a binary (digital) format.

Disk array

A linked group of independent drives used to replace larger, single disk drive systems and addressed by a computer as one unit. *See also* RAID.

Downstream

A direction of data flow away from the host.

DLT

Digital Linear Tape

DMA

Direct Memory Access. A technology designed to speed up data exchange between the computer peripherals and the RAM by avoiding CPU-imposed delays.

DOW

Direct OverWrite technology used in magneto-optical storage systems for faster data overwrite.

DRAM

Dynamic RAM.

Drive utilities

A set of programs used to optimize drive performance (i.e., Disk Defragmenter, Speed Disk, etc.) to increase drive capacity (Compression Agent, etc.), recover errors or media damage (Disk Scan, CHKDSK, etc.), and simplify or make possible drive installation (EZ-DRIVE, etc.).

Driver

A small program responsible for interfacing to a hardware device.

DSL

Digital Subscriber Line. One of the most popular elements of modern telecommunication technology. Unlike analog modems, DSL modems utilize bandwidth well up to 1.1 MHz.

DSP

Digital Signal Processing. A discipline dealing with processing the digital signal, its amplification, noise reduction, elimination of nonlinearity, separation of different signals in the same data stream, data compression, and many other useful things.

DTR

Data Transfer Rate

DVD

DVD initially stood for Digital Video Disk but now stands for Digital Versatile Disc. Is a "read-only" (ROM) technology.

ASMO

One of the rewritable DVD standards using magneto-optical recording principles.

DVD-R

Write-once DVD standard, which uses dye-polymer recording technology.

DVD-RAM

Digital Versatile Disc-Random Access Memory. One of the rewritable DVD standards using phase-changing recording principles.

DVD-R/W

One of the rewritable DVD standards using phase-changing recording principles.

DVD+RW

One of the rewritable DVD standards using phase-changing recording principles.

ECC

Error Correction Code. A procedure embedded into the drive controller's hardware, which allows for correction of read errors. It can typically correct a single burst error of 11 bits long or less. This maximum correction length is a function of the controller.

EDAP

Extended Data Availability and Protection.

EFM

Eight-to-Fourteen Modulation. A popular data encoding method used in CD-ROM, which represents 8 user-bits with the (minimally required) 14 channel-bits.

Embedded Servo System

Drive design in which the data used by its servo system along with the system data and user's data are stored on the same disk, unlike the earlier designs utilizing Dedicated Servo technology.

Encoding

Element of the ADC process.

Endpoint

See Device Endpoint.

Endpoint address

The combination of a device address and an endpoint number on a USB device.

Enhanced IDE (EIDE)

An interface that allows the attachment of up to 2 devices per connector. *See also* ATA-2.

Erasing data from the disk

There are a few different levels of data erasure from the disk. At first, when the file is erased, it just means that the system will not consider this data as the file, will not provide access to it, and will not prevent it from being overwritten by other data. Therefore, when the file has just been erased, there is still a good chance of recovering it before it is overwritten. Later, the data that belong to this file will be replaced with other data, making file recovery impossible. This process poses a security risk, when some of the previously erased data could be accessed and recovered by a stranger. To prevent this, there are special software programs that physically erase the file data from the media, making their recovery impossible.

Error Correction Code

See ECC.

ESD

Electro-Static Discharge. A phenomenon that is damaging to the electronic components of the PC and drives.

ESDI

Enhanced Small Device Interface.
Obsolete interface standard mostly used in older hard drives. Had a data transfer rate up to 3 MB/s.

Fabric

The web of connections using Fiber Channel (FC) switches or routers.

FAT

File Allocation Table. Area of the disk or diskette containing information about files on the disk, clusters making these files, and free area on the disk. FAT keeps track of all information on the disks and all relations between different pieces of information. A loss of FAT translates into loss of data, since the system will not be able to attribute data to specific files even if the data themselves are intact.

Fast SCSI

A variation of SCSI that doubles the data transfer rate by increasing the speed at which data is transferred, as opposed to Wide SCSI, which increases the volume of data transferred. Most SCSI hard disk drives now offer a combination of both variables, called fast/wide, for an even faster data transfer rate.

FCI

Flux Changes per Inch. A measure of linear storage density in magnetic recording. *See also* BPI.

FC-AL

Fibre Channel-Arbitrated Loop. A high-performance serial interface that provides for extremely high data transfer rates and allows data to be quickly transmitted over long distances.

FC-LE

Fibre Channel—Link Encapsulation

FC-SBCCS

Fibre Channel—Single Byte Command Code Set mapping

Formatting

A procedure needed to make the drive ready for data storage and retrieval. At first, the drive is physically divided into tracks and sectors. Low-level formatting stays unchanged through the entire life of the drive unless the drive is reformatted. The next level of formatting—partitioning—means dividing the drive into logical drives (C:, D:, E:, etc.). Every drive has at least one "primary partition" (C:) and may have many extended partitions. Finally, high level formatting creates a root directory, from which all other subdirectories could be created, and creates a File Allocation Table (FAT), which keeps track of all information on the disks and all relations between different pieces of information.

Form factor

Term used to describe the drive's external size. Industry-standard form factors are typically 1.8", 2.5", 3.0", 3.5", and 5.25". Some other form factors can be found in newer products like the 1" form factor recently introduced for palm-size computers and digital cameras (i.e., IBM Microdrive).

Formatted capacity
Storage capacity of a disk after formatting.

FireWire
A nickname used for IEEE 1394 computer interface.

Firmware
Permanent set of instructions and data programmed directly into the circuitry of read-only memory for controlling the operation of the computer or disk drive. Distinct from software, which is stored in read/write memory and can be altered.

Flash memory
Semiconductor memory that is called so because the entire sections of the microchip are always erased at once (or flashed). Flash memory card loses power when they are disconnected (removed) from the PC, yet the data stored in it is retained for an indefinitely long period of time or until it is rewritten.

Floppy disk
See Diskette.

Flying height
The smallest distance separating the slider in a Winchester-type storage device (all modern hard drives, some of the removable storage systems) and the disk. Flying height equals zero in contact recording systems (floppy, Zip, etc.).

Frame
A term frequently used in different technologies. For example, the frame is a basic unit of information stored on a CD. Also, the frame is a discrete data packet used to move data from one Fibre Channel (FC) device to another.

Frequency Modulation (FM)
A data-encoding scheme. This technology uses up to half of the disk space with timing information for the encoding process and was replaced with a better standard called Modified Frequency Modulation (MFM).

Full duplex
Computer data transmission in both directions simultaneously.

G
Giga-, equals to 10^9.

G
Equals 9.8 kg/cm^2. The measure of a drive's shock resistance. Drive's specification usually includes values for operational and nonoperational shock (i.e., operating shock: 30 G @ 2 ms duration and nonoperating shock 250 G @ 2 ms duration).

GB
~10^9 bytes, one billion bytes, or 1,000 MB. In reality (binary capacity), 1 GB equals two to the thirtieth power or 1,073,741,824 bytes in decimal notation.

Gimbal
Part of the slider suspension (in the hard disk drive) with low roll and pitch stiffness, but high lateral and vertical stiffness. Used as a link between the slider and the suspension.

GMR element (head)
Giant MR element (head). Newer generation of the magnetoresistive (MR) heads with better read performance.

Half-height
One of the standard drive sizes equivalent to half the vertical dimension of a 5.25-inch drive.

Hard disk
Storage medium that stores data in the form of magnetic patterns on a rigid disk. Modern

hard disks are usually made of several thin films deposited on both sides of the aluminum, glass, etc., substrate. Hard disks are much more rigid than floppy disks, spin much faster than floppy disks, and can transfer data faster and store more in the same volume.

Hard error

A data error that does not go away with time (unlike a soft error), and is usually caused by defects in the physical structure of the disk.

Head (magnetic, optical, read/write)

A component of the storage system (hard drives, tapes, CDs, floppy drives, etc.) used for data reading (read head) and/or writing (write head). Can operate on magnetic, magneto-optical, optical, or other principles.

Head crash

General term used to describe a catastrophic phenomenon that causes mechanical damage to the disks and/or head, and may lead to the permanent damage and unrecoverable loss of data. *See also* Data loss/recovery.

Head material

Nowadays, magnetic heads consist of multiple layers of metal alloys and insulating materials. An inductive thin-film head has the "simplest" design, while GMR (giant magneto-resistive) head has the most complex design.

Head parking

Since the disk and the slider in a magnetic hard disk drive are extremely smooth, strong adhesive forces may prevent disks from rotating (during the "power-on" cycle) if the slider is landed on the disk surface. To prevent this from happening, many modern hard disks have special landing zones—a narrow band close to the disk center, which is textured using a laser. A spiral of tiny laser bumps is created, which increases the disk's roughness, decreases adhesion, and allows for slider landing and take-off from the landing zone. Another method of head parking is based on using a load–unload ramp fixed at the outer edge of the disk. When the suspension is moved beyond the disk area, it slides onto the ramp, thus parking the head. Both landing on the landing zone and parking on the ramp increase the drive's nonoperational shock resistance and prevent accidental damage during transportation.

Head landing/takeoff

A procedure performed during powering-down and powering-up CSS-type drives (most of today's desktop hard drives, many hard drives for servers and laptops).

Head suspension

An elastic beam-like element of the magnetic drive with the slider (and magnetic element) at one end and attached to the VCA (*see* Actuator) arm at the other end. Elastic deformation of the suspension creates preload force needed for successful performance of the system.

Head-disk interface

The zone of contact between a fast-spinning disk and flying or sliding slider. A source of many durability problems for magnetic drives; head crash is one example.

HDD

Hard disk drive

HDSL

High bit-rate DSL. Allows for a high-speed connection over the basic copper line instead of the fiber line.

High-level formatting

Formatting is performed by the operating system's format program (for example, the DOS FORMAT program) that creates the root directory, file allocation tables, and other basic configurations. *See also* low-level formatting.

HIPPI
High Performance Parallel Interface framing protocol

Host adapter
A plug-in board or circuitry on the motherboard acting as the interface between a computer system bus and the drive.

Hot Plug (Hot Swap)
Procedure involving plugging in or removal of a drive into/from the system with the power turned "on."

HVD
High Voltage Differential. Refers to SCSI differential signals with a maximum logic voltage of 5V. *See also* LVD.

IC
Integrated Circuit.

IDE
Integrated Drive Electronics. The most popular drive interface on the market. Also known as ATA (Advanced Technology Attachment).

IDSL
ISDN DSL. Provides ISDN-like speed over copper line, is moderately fast and moderately expensive, and allows business or home users otherwise far away from faster lines to benefit from the DSL links.

ISDN
Integrated Services Digital Network. Is a digital telephone line used for voice, fax, and data communications like a regular telephone line, but five times faster (or more) than a 28.8 Kbps modem. It allows you to talk on the phone while also sending data.

Index pulse
A pulse that defines the starting point for each data sequence and provides for initial synchronization.

Interleaving
Distributing access order in another fashion than straight access. Electronics of the older drives were not fast enough to read sectors one after another. Therefore, sector renumbering was introduced creating artificial delays in the stream of incoming data. Interleaving factor 3:1 meant that two sectors would be skipped before reading the next one. Modern drives have electronics capable of handling data stream generated by the drive, thus making interleaving obsolete.

Inductive heads
A type of magnetic head that relies on principles of magnetic inductance to sense magnetization of the media and to also magnetize the media.

Internet storage
A new type of online data storage where the data is stored on a remote host to free local storage and is accessed via the Internet.

Interface
A hardware and/or software data transmission regulator that controls data exchange between the PC and other devices, including such data storage devices as hard disk drives, floppy drives, tape drives, CD drives, DVD drives, and so on. The interface is provided by the electronics of the data transfer controller and the drive electronics. There are standards adopted for the interface protocols, allowing for connection of any standard peripheral device.

IP
Internet Protocol

IPI
Intelligent Peripheral Interface

ISA
Industry Standard Architecture

Isochronous Data Transfer
This mode implies uniform in time data transfer and provides for the guaranteed bandwidth by transferring the same amount of data every second. This method is used for video cameras, for example, where if the error has occurred, it's too late to resend the data again. *See also* synchronous data transfer and asynchronous data transfer.

Jumper
A special connector box that slips over two pins on a circuit board. The jumpers are moved to change electrical connections and device configuration.

Kilobyte (KB)
A unit of storage capacity equal to 1,024 bytes.

LAN
Local Area Network. A network within the organization that connects computers, printers, scanners, and so on, and allows them to communicate with each other.

Landing zone
Special part of the magnetic hard disk in the shape of a narrow circular band used for landing a slider after powering the drive down. This part of the disk is usually specially textured. The rest of the disk is typically referred to as the data zone.

Latency
Average time it takes for a bit of data to rotate under the read element after it was positioned over the needed track.

Lands
Areas in between the pits, which are the holes on the surface of the optical storage media. *See also* Pits.

Linear bit density
Bit density in the circumferential direction (around the track) on the disk. Typically measured in BPI (bits per inch).

Loading/Unloading the slider
See Load/Unload and Head parking.

Load/Unload
The idea of Load/Unload technology is that when the drive is turned off and the slider is not flying, the slider lands on a specially prepared ramp outside the disk where it rests until the next power-on cycle. The newest mobile and server drives use this technology. *See also* CSS.

Logogram
Signs used in logographic writing system.

Low-level formatting
A process of creating tracks and sectors on the disk surface so that the operating system can access the required areas.

LTO
Linear Tape-Open. New tape technology with scalable, open tape architecture for the midrange to enterprise-class servers. Open format is meant to enable compatibility between products from different vendors.

LVD
Low Voltage Differential. The newer generation of SCSI devices. LVD combines the lower power and cost of a single-ended SCSI with the long cable lengths and data integrity of high voltage differential (HVD) SCSI. It also doubles the data transfer rate of Ultra SCSI. The advantage of this technology is in greater cable length (up to 12 meters for 15 devices) and faster data transfer rate.

L/U
See Load/Unload.

Magnetoresistive effect

A change in the material's electrical resistance in the presence of an external magnetic field.

Master Boot Record (MBR)

An important record located on the first sector of a hard disk. MBR contains a table of all of the hard disk drive's partitions, the location of the operating system, and a program that loads the operating system into the RAM. Loss of MBR leads to unrecoverable loss of data on the disk drive.

MB/sec or MByte/sec

Megabytes per second. A unit of the data transfer rate.

ME

Metal Evaporated tape. Unlike MP tape, the films on the ME tape are produced in a vacuum chamber where a flexible tape substrate is exposed to a "vapor" of metal (i.e., nickel alloy).

Megabyte (MB)

Equals 10^6 bytes, but an accurate definition is 2^{16} bytes, 1,024 kilobytes, or 1,048,576 bytes.

Media (magnetic)

A film on magnetic disks used to store magnetic data in the form of small magnetized areas.

Media data rate

An internal drive's data rate between the media and the buffer as opposite to the external data rate between the buffer and the PC.

Micro-

Equals 10^{-6}.

Micrometer

Equals 10^{-6} meter, 10^{-3} mm, 1,000 nm.

Micron

Micrometer

Micro-inch

Equals 10^{-3} inch or 2.54×10^{-3} cm.

MFM code

Modified Frequency Modulation code. A method of encoding analog signals into magnetic bits or optical pits. MFM uses a fixed length encoding scheme that eliminates the need for space-consuming timing information used in FM. Bits are evenly spaced in time on the disk surface. This type of encoding scheme allows for even single bit errors to be detected and corrected by the controller electronics. MFM was eventually replaced by the RLL method in the hard disk drives, but is still used in floppy drives.

MO

Magneto-optical (storage technology)

MOSFET

Metal-Oxide-Semiconductor Field-Effect Transistor. A four-terminal semiconductor device, which is the basis for a large variety of digital-integrated circuits (IC), including memory devices.

MP

Metal Particles tape. Most of the magnetic tapes are MP tapes, mixture of metal oxide particles with a glue-like binder on a flexible polymer base film made of polyethylene terephthalate (PET).

MP3

A compression system for music. This format helps to reduce the size of a song while keeping its quality close to that of the original.

MPEG

An acronym for Moving Picture Experts Group. DVD may use such video compression standards as MPEG-1 and MPEG-2, but only MPEG-2 video data can be copy-protected and region-coded.

MR
Magnetoresistive (effect, material, read element, head).

MSR
Magnetically induced Super Resolution. A technology used in MO storage systems. MSR allows for increases in storage density.

MTBF
Mean Time Before Failure. An average reliability characteristics measured in hours.

nano
Equals 10^{-9}.

nanometer
Equal to 10^{-9} meter, 10^{-6} mm, 10^{-3} micrometers or 10 angstrom.

NAS
Network Attached Storage

Native capacity
Noncompressed storage capacity.

Nonvolatile memory
See volatile memory.

OEM
Original Equipment Manufacturer. A manufacturer that provides a product or component for use in another company's own name brand product.

Overhead
Extra processing time required prior to the execution of a command or extra space required for nondata information such as location and timing. Disk overhead may occupy up to 10 percent of its capacity.

Overwrite
Writing new data on top of the old, thus completely erasing old data.

Overclocking
Means running a CPU or other devices at a higher frequency than it intended. Overclocking increases performance, but may damage the components.

Parity
A data-checking technique, which uses one or more extra bits added to the original data and analyzed by the receiving device.

Partition
A procedure of dividing the physical hard disk drive into one or many logical volumes.

Parallel port
Also called a printer port. A 25-pin port that sends 8 bits of data in parallel.

Particulate media
Magnetic media design consisting of a mixture of iron oxide magnetic particles and a polymer matrix. Nowadays, used in the floppy disks, magnetic tapes, and other magnetic storage systems that do not require extremely high recording density. *See also* Thin film disk.

PC Card
A small form-factor memory card used with mobile, handheld, subnotebook, and desktop personal computers, industrial controllers, laser printers, and other devices. Formerly known as a PCMCIA card.

PC
Personal computer

PC
Polycarbonate. A polymeric material for substrates of CD and DVD.

PCI
Peripheral Component Interconnect

PCMCIA card
Personal Computer Memory Card International Association. *See* PC Card.

PDA

Personal Digital Assistant

PFA

Predictive Failure Analysis. Technology meant to increase drive reliability by automatically warning a user of approaching drive failures. It monitors key device performance indicators, including head-to-disk spacing, and reports when specific levels and thresholds are exceeded. *See also* SMART.

Physical Vapor Deposition (PVD)

A process of thin film formation by transporting atoms evaporated from one surface onto another surface. Evaporation occurs during surface heating or bombardment by high-energy ions in a vacuum. The film composition replicates the target composition, unless it is additionally doped with other materials.

Pits

Holes on the surface of the optical storage media. Pits are the coded data and carry the information. *See also* Lands.

Photodetector

A solid-state electronic device converting light intensity into electric current.

Platter

Rigid disk in a hard disk drive. Most drives use more than one platter. Each platter typically requires two magnetic read/write elements, one for each side.

PIO (Processor Input/Output)

A means of data transfer requiring the use of a CPU.

Point-to-point connection

The simplest Fibre Channel (FC) topology, with two nodes (e.g., a computer and a hard disk drive) connected directly.

PRML

Partial Response Maximum Likelihood. A type of digital read channel designed for higher recording density and data transfer rates. Partial Response is a sampling procedure used to detect signals so that intersymbol interference is reduced and the signal-to-noise ratio is enhanced. Maximum Likelihood technique analyzes the read signal and constructs the data stream with the statistically smallest error.

PVR

Personal Video Recorder (i.e., TiVo, ReplayTV, etc.).

Quantization

A step in an analog-to-digital conversion (ADC) process.

QIC

The ¼-inch cartridge tape format that is the dominant tape format for the low-end segment of the market with such well-known products as Travan.

RAMAC

Random Access Method of Accounting and Control. Introduced in 1956, IBM-made RAMAC was the first hard disk drive. It consisted of 50 magnetic disks 24 inches in diameter, rotating at 1,200 RPM. Two air-bearing-supported magnetic heads accessed all 50 disks. The storage capacity of this system was 5 MB with the data rate of 12.5 kB/s, and the system was rented to the end user for $130 a month. The system used aluminum sliders, metal heads, had 20 tracks per inch and 0.002 Mb/in^2, and the slider/disk spacing was about 20 µm (micrometers, or 20,000 nm).

RAM

Random Access Memory. A memory chip that allows for data to be stored and retrieved by a microprocessor or controller. The data can be stored and accessed in any order, and all storage locations are equally accessible.

RAID

Redundant Arrays of Independent Drives. RAID is an assembly of disk drives, known as a disk array, that operates as one storage unit. In general, the drives could be any storage system with random data access, such as magnetic hard disk drives, optical storage, magnetic tapes, and so on. When the speed (data transfer rate) is an issue, the fastest SCSI or FC drives are typically used.

Removable storage

A type of storage with removable media, such as magnetic removable storage, optical storage, magneto-optical storage, and so on. Removable hard disk drives can be also qualified as removable storage.

Remnant magnetization (Mr)

The magnetization that remains in a material after the magnetic field is removed. *See also* Coercivity.

Read/write element

See Head.

RADSL

Rate-adaptive ADSL. Is supposed to carry data at different rates for different prices while adjusting to different conditions and lengths of the copper wire.

ROM

Read Only Memory. Memory unit containing programs and data that can be read but cannot be modified. CD-ROM is one example of read only memory.

Random Access

An access method when the data can be stored and accessed in any order, and all storage locations are equally accessible.

Rigid disk

See Hard disk.

RISK

Type of CPU that sacrifices completeness of instructions in return for very high speed.

RLL

Run Length Limited code. An encoding scheme used in CD drives to encode data into magnetic pulses or pits. RLL requires more processing, but stores almost 50 percent more data per disc than the older MFM (modified frequency modulation) method.

RPM

Revolutions Per Minute. Rotational speed. Related to linear velocity in the following way: $V = \pi RN/30$, where V is linear velocity [m/s], R is the radius [m], $\pi = 3.14...$, and N is rotation speed measured in RPM.

S.M.A.R.T.

Self-Monitoring, Analysis, and Reporting Technology. Nowadays, most ATA and SCSI drives use S.M.A.R.T. to predict failure and to protect data. Not all failure (even the graduate ones) can be predicted, but S.M.A.R.T. keeps evolving and reaches its third generation already. S.M.A.R.T.-III, which not only monitors the drive activity (for failure prediction), adds failure prevention by attempting to detect and repair sector errors.

Sampling

A step in the analog-to-digital conversion (ADC) process.

SAN

Storage Area Network

SCSI

Small Computer System Interface (pronounced "scuzzy"). A high performance peripheral interface that can independently distribute data among multiple peripherals on the PC. Unlike ATA, SCSI incorporates those instructions needed for communication with the host PC, thus freeing the host computer from this job. This makes PCs more efficient in performing its user-oriented activities. SCSI is a specification for a peripheral bus and command set defined in an ANSI standard X3.131-1986.

SDSL

Symmetric Digital Subscriber Line. A derivative of DSL that provides similarly fast download and upload of data.

Sector

A part of each track defined with magnetic marking and an ID number. Sector has a sector header and error correction code (ECC). In modern drives, sectors are numbered sequentially.

Self-loading slider

See Air-bearing slider.

Seek time

Average time required for the magnetic or optical head to move to a new track.

Server

Specialized shared computer on the network.

Servo (mark, mechanism)

Feedback positioning system embedded in the platters in order to help the magnetic head evaluate its current position.

Settling time

The time required for the servo system to lock onto the new track.

Shock resistance

Ability of the drive to withstand impact-like acceleration. Measured in G units.

Signal-to-noise ratio (SNR)

The ratio of the signal power to the noise power in the data channel, measured in dB.

Sleep mode

Power-saving option when the hard drive is powered down (spindle rotation is stopped and the heads are parked on the landing zone or on the ramp) after a preset period of time. Most often used in mobile computers.

Slider

A microfabricated part of the magnetic disk drive that carries read/write elements. *See also* Air-bearing slider.

SONET

Synchronous Optical Network. A standard for multiplexing high-speed digital data onto fiber optic cabling. SONET converts electric pulses into optical pulses and vice versa.

SRAM

Static RAM

Start of Frame (SOF)

The first transaction in each frame. SOF allows endpoints to identify the start of frame and synchronize internal endpoint clocks to the host.

Stage

A part in the sequence of a control transfer, for example, the setup stage, data stage, and status stage.

Stepper motor actuator

An actuator using a stepper motor that moves one step at a time. Was used in older hard drives before being replaced by the Voice Coil Actuator.

Storage capacity

Formatted capacity of the drive.

Stiction

A phenomenon caused by the surface tension of liquids. The liquid in between two solid surfaces tends to retain the smallest surface area and pulls these solid surfaces together. This effect is noticeable for very smooth surfaces only. The forces generated could be extremely high and, like in the case of the magnetic hard disk drive, could prevent a disk from rotating when the slider sticks to a very smooth disk surface.

SSA
Serial Storage Architecture. A high performance serial interface that provides for extremely high data transfer rates and allows data to be quickly transmitted over long distances.

Super-paramagnetic limit
A limit of density of magnetic recording due to the fact that at the very high recording density, the magnetic bits become so small that they cannot keep residual magnetization for any practically useful amount of time. Predicted to occur at around 100 Gb/inch^2.

Super DLT
Newer generation of DLT tape products.

Suspension
See Head suspension

Synchronous data transfer
Data sent with the clock pulse defining the intervals between bits, as opposite to asynchronous data transfer. *See also* isochronous data transfer.

Termination
A procedure used to electrically end a SCSI cable and prevent signal reflections. Passive termination is provided by resistors at the end of the cable. Active termination controls the impedance of the cable to provide better signals. Both types absorb the signal at the end of the cable, preventing it from bouncing back and causing noise.

Thin film disk
A substrate coated on both sides with a thin magnetic film and other performance-enhancing films. Thin film technology replaced particulate media technology in magnetic hard disk drives.

Thin film head
A read/write element made of thin layers of different materials using (typically) a Physical Vapor Deposition process.

Thermal recalibration
A function used in older hard disk drives. During thermal recalibration, all operations of the drive are stopped, the drive spins down, adjusts and fine tunes the position of the read/write element, and then resumes operation. This technology was replaced by Dedicated servo, and then by Embedded servo.

TPI
Tracks Per Inch. A measure of density of magnetic recording. *See also* BPI.

Track
A concentric set of magnetic bits on the disk is called track. Each track is (typically) divided into 512-byte sectors.

Track pitch
The distance between the centers of two adjacent tracks.

Track density
The density of data tracks measured in tracks per inch (TPI).

Tribology
A multidisciplinary science about phenomena associated with the contact and relative motion of solids. Phenomena include wear, friction, chemical reaction, fatigue, and so on. Tribology improves reliability via lubrication, coating, material structure optimization, and so on. Tribological performance of the head/disk interface is a key issue in the hard disk drives, floppy drives, magnetic tape drives, removable magnetic storage, and so on.

TrueX Multibeam

Instead of illuminating a single track on the surface of the optical disc, this technology uses multiple track illumination in order to detect bits simultaneously and read them in parallel.

Ultra-SCSI

Ultra SCSI doubles the data transfer rate of fast SCSI.

Ultra DMA

Advanced capability provided by ATA-4 interface. *See also* ATA, DMA.

Universal Serial Bus (USB)

A serial bus designed for easy, hassle-free, and relatively inexpensive low- and medium-speed applications. At the low end, USB can sustain a transfer rate of less then 0.2 MB/s; in its fastest mode USB is capable of about 1.5 MB/s. Allows for connection of up to 127 USB devices.

VCA

Voice-Coil Actuator. *See* Actuator.

Volatile memory

When the power is turned off, the nonvolatile memory (hard disk drive, tapes, CD, etc.) retains all the information stored while the volatile memory (DRAM, SRAM, etc.) loses all the information.

WAN

Wide Area Network. A network connecting computers in different organizations, cities, and countries.

Winchester drive

An old IBM drive named "30–30," after 30 MB of fixed storage and 30 MB of removable storage. The name itself is reminiscent of the Winchester "30–30" rifle.

WORM

Write Once Read Many times. A class of recording systems (mostly optical) that allow recording but not altering the data. Additional data could be written on the WORM media, but already written data cannot be altered.

Write current

Current passed through the write element in order to generate magnetic field strong enough to cause local magnetization of the media.

Zone texturing

See landing zone.

References

Anderson, Don, *Firewire System Architecture,* MindShare, Inc., 1999.

Anderson, Douglas T., Dawson, Pat, and Honomichl, Sandra, *The Hard Disk Technical Guide,* Boulder, CO: Micro House International, Inc., 1996.

Anderson, Don, *Universal Serial Bus System Architecture,* MindShare, Inc., 1997.

Ashar, Kanu G., *Magnetic Disk Drive Technology: Heads, Media, Channel, Interfaces, and Integration.* New York: IEEE Press, 1997.

Baert, Luc, Theunissen, Luc, and Vergult, Guido, *Digital Audio and Compact Disc Technology,* Oxford: Heinemann Newnes, 1988.

Brown, William D., and Brewer, Joe E., *Nonvolatile Semiconductor Memory Technology,* New York: IEEE Press, 1998.

Clark, Tom, *Designing Storage Area Networks,* Reading, MA: Addison-Wesley, 1999.

Daniel, Eric D., Mee, C. Denis and Clark, Mark H., *Magnetic Recording: The First 100 Years,* New York: IEEE Press, 1999.

Gambino, Richard J., and Suzuki, Takao, *Magneto-optical Recording Materials,* New York: IEEE Press, 1999.

Mansuripur, Masud, *The Physical Principles of Magneto-optical Recording,* Cambridge: Cambridge University Press, 1995.

McDowell, Steven, and Seyer, Martin D., *USB Explained,* Upper Saddle River, NJ: Prentice Hall PTR, 1999.

Mee, Denis C., and Daniel, Eric D., *Magnetic Recording Handbook: Technology & Applications,* New York: McGraw Hill, 1988.

Norton, Peter, and Goodman, John, *Peter Norton's Inside the PC,* Sams Publishing, Indianapolis, 1997.

Ifeachor, Emmanuel C. and Jervis, Barrie W., *Digital Signal Processing,* Suffolk, Great Britain: Addison-Wesley Publishing Company, 1993.

Purcell, Lee, *CD-R/DVD: Disc Recording Demystified,* New York: McGraw Hill, 2000

Schmidt, Friedhelm, *The SCSI Bus and IDE Interface,* Reading, MA: Addison-Wesley, Longman Limited, 1998.

Steinmetz, Ralf and Nahrstedt, Klara, *Multimedia: Computing, Communications and Applications,* Upper Saddle River, NJ: Prentice Hall PTR, 1995.

Thornburgh, Ralph H., *Fibre Channel for Mass Storage,* Upper Saddle River, NJ: Prentice Hall PTR, 1999.

Watkinson, John, *The Art of Digital Audio,* Oxford: Focal Press, 1991.

Williams, Michael R., *A History of Computer Technology,* Los Alamitos, CA: IEEE Computer Society Press, 1997.

Index